Praise for *Successful AI Product Creation*

"Shub's book is a much-needed resource in the space where AI product creation remains elusive. It provides a comprehensive step-by-step framework and insightful case studies, addressing both generative AI and traditional AI. This guide is invaluable for experienced and aspiring AI product managers and product creators, offering practical strategies to bring AI products to life."

—Pascal Bornet, best-selling author on AI;
formerly with McKinsey & Company

"In Successful AI Product Creation: A 9-Step Framework, *Shub A. brings his two decades of experience as an AI practitioner and researcher to bear on a user-friendly, step-by-step guide for anyone seeking to better operate at the intersection of product management and AI. A major pain point for business leaders in the wake of the AI/ ML explosion has been figuring out how to make AI core to their company's strategy and products. Through detailed models, rich case studies, and helpful comparisons to more traditional software product management, Shub delivers a practical 'how to' that should help alleviate that pain."*

—Noah Askin, Professor at UC Irvine and
INSEAD's Product Leadership Programme

"If you want to create successful AI products, Shub's book is a must-read. He shares incredible insights drawn from his many years of doing this. His book makes these easily accessible to help you navigate the complexities and challenges."

—Jim Berardone, Professor of the Practice of Product Management,
Carnegie Mellon University School of Computer Science

"Shub, a visionary leader with a proven track record in AI, shares his battlefield-tested strategies in his new book. This seminal guide equips product leaders and entrepreneurs with the tools to build innovative AI products, streamline team interactions, and foster a culture of AI-driven product development. This book is poised to become the definitive resource for navigating the AI product landscape."

—Mac Gainor, Founder and CTO, TipHaus;
former Director of Engineering at a Silicon Valley-based Generative AI startup

Shub Agarwal

Successful AI Product Creation

A 9-Step Framework

*To Kiran, my wife and foundation.
Your endless patience, understanding,
and support made this book possible.
Through countless late nights and long
discussions, your grace and wisdom
kept me grounded and inspired.*

*To my father, whose legacy as an
educator and author lives on.
You taught me that knowledge
shared is knowledge multiplied.
Your passion for teaching, your joy in
watching others grow, and your
dedication to writing planted the seeds
for this book.*

*To my mother, who taught me that
my father's path—of giving, learning,
and touching lives—is the truest measure
of success.*

Contents

Preface

Today's businesses are caught in a paradox. The rapid democratization of AI tools and technologies has made AI development more accessible than ever. Yet creating successful AI products remains a complex challenge that eludes even the most experienced teams. The gap lies not in the availability of technology but in the absence of a systematic approach to AI product creation.

AI development fundamentally differs from traditional software development. Its probabilistic nature, its hunger for data, and its ability to learn and adapt demand new frameworks and methodologies. This is not about replacing existing product development wisdom, but about building specialized knowledge for the AI age.

Our goal is simple: to transform AI product creation from an art of chance into a discipline of methodology.

The future of product creation is being rewritten by AI—and we need AI product creators. Our success in this new era depends not just on mastering the technology, but on following a disciplined approach to bringing AI products to life.

Foreword by Jia Li

As someone who has been at the forefront of AI innovation—from serving as Head of R&D at Google Cloud AI, to leading AI research at Stanford, to founding/leading successful AI companies—I have witnessed firsthand both the tremendous potential and the significant challenges in bringing AI products to life. When asked to write the foreword for this book, I was struck by how timely and necessary this contribution is to our field.

The release of *Successful AI Product Creation: A 9-Step Framework* arrives at a pivotal moment in the evolution of artificial intelligence. This is both the most promising and the most challenging time to create AI products. AI technology is scaling at an unprecedented rate, fueled by AI Agents and tools that offer unmatched efficiency and innovation. Yet this rapid progress demands a steep learning curve—one that businesses and individuals must master to translate potential into meaningful impact.

Bridging the Gap: From Demos to Impactful Products

Throughout my career in AI, I've observed that although millions of AI demos showcase remarkable capabilities, only a small fraction evolve into fully realized products that generate real-world value. The gap between prototype and successful productization is where many efforts falter. Shub Agarwal's book provides a clear, actionable roadmap for overcoming these challenges, guiding readers through the essential steps to build AI products that succeed in the marketplace.

A Unique Perspective

Shub brings an unparalleled perspective to this subject. As an early pioneer in AI, he has over two decades of experience driving innovation across industries including technology, retail, and financial services. His work has led to multiple U.S. and international patents, and his leadership has reshaped how Fortune 50 companies and startups approach AI adoption.

In today's AI-driven world, interdisciplinary expertise is more critical than ever. Building successful AI products requires a blend of technical knowledge, business strategy, and user-focused design. Shub embodies this approach. As a senior product executive and faculty member at the University of Southern California's graduate program in Product Management and AI, he bridges the gap between industry and academia, equipping future leaders to thrive in this fast-evolving field.

Why This Book Matters

This book goes beyond abstract theories and buzzwords. It delivers a structured, actionable framework for AI product creation that addresses both the opportunities and challenges of the current landscape. By focusing on practical implementation, *Successful AI Product Creation* empowers readers to move from innovative ideas to impactful outcomes.

As I turned the pages of this book, I found myself learning and reflecting at every step. Shub's insights felt not only deeply relevant but also inspiring. The blend of technical expertise and strategic vision shared here made me reconsider what it truly takes to succeed in building AI products today. This book doesn't just teach—it motivates and equips you to take action.

Whether you are an entrepreneur, product manager, engineer, academic, or business leader, this book provides the tools and strategies needed to navigate the complexities of this era and seize its extraordinary opportunities. Shub Agarwal's insights and expertise make this guide an indispensable resource for anyone looking to succeed in the transformative world of AI.

Jia Li, Ph.D.
Co-Founder, Chief AI Officer & President, LiveX AI
IEEE Fellow
Founding Head of R&D, Google Cloud AI

Foreword by Ted Shelton

We are living through a profound shift in how we organize, work, and unlock human potential. Unlike past technological revolutions, this one doesn't just change how we do things—it changes who we are capable of becoming. The emergence of AI and automation doesn't need to replace human ingenuity; instead, it can amplify it—if we make the right choices. That's why this book matters.

When I first read this book, I knew it stood apart. There are many books on AI, automation, and the future of work, but few that take such a balanced, insightful, and deeply human approach. Rather than focusing only on disruption or utopian possibilities, this book offers something far more valuable: a guide to action. It reminds us that many of the challenges we face today—navigating transformation, aligning technology with human well-being, and structuring work and society for long-term success—are not new. History has given us lessons on how to adapt to change, and this book brings those lessons to life in a way that is both rigorous and accessible.

What makes this book truly exciting is how it explores what is different this time. AI is not just another industrial innovation; it is a new kind of intelligence, one that requires us to rethink fundamental questions about human potential, decision-making, and collaboration. This book doesn't just describe these shifts—it equips readers with the frameworks to navigate them.

What's particularly impressive is how it bridges audiences. Some readers will be drawn to its technical depth, using it as a resource to stay ahead in this rapidly evolving space. Others will focus on its insights into leadership, human creativity, and organizational transformation. Wherever you fall on this spectrum, you will walk away more informed, more prepared, and—perhaps most importantly—more optimistic about what is possible.

Working as a consultant for some of the largest companies in the world and currently in my role at Inflection AI, I've had the opportunity to witness technology's enduring power to reshape industries and redefine human potential. We are living at a time of a historic opportunity when we will shape the future and define how technology and humanity flourish together.

This book is a crucial guide for anyone who wants to understand and shape the future. We are not just witnessing change; we are responsible for steering it in the right direction. And with the insights in these pages, we have a much better chance of getting it right.

Ted Shelton
Chief Operating Officer, Inflection AI
Former Expert Partner, Bain & Company

Introduction: Creating Successful AI Products— A Nine-Step Framework

The Evolution of AI Product Management

Creating successful AI products requires a new breed of product manager—one who combines a deep understanding of AI technologies with strategic leadership and user empathy. These roles span from AI product managers to AI engineering managers, both bearing responsibilities to develop AI products. As the field matures, these roles are being differentiated into two distinct groups: AI product creators and AI product operators.

Although AI's potential is vast, the systematic knowledge needed to consistently deliver successful AI products remains elusive. This book presents a battle-tested nine-step framework for successful AI product creation, distilled from two decades of hands-on experience, proven success across industries, academic research, and educational teaching.

From my early days as an AI researcher, fascinated by algorithms that mimic human intelligence, to my journey into product leadership and academia, I have witnessed firsthand the transformative power of AI. AI's impact is evident in its ability to improve efficiency, reduce human error, and increase productivity across various industries. For instance, in manufacturing, AI-powered robots perform tasks with unprecedented precision, and in customer service, chatbots handle routine inquiries, allowing human agents to focus on more complex issues. Yet despite these advancements, I've observed the persistent challenges product managers face in aligning AI's capabilities with business goals and executing AI capabilities in a way that is sustainable, builds breakthrough products, and pivots from software development thinking to AI-first thinking.

A Personal Journey Through AI

I stumbled into the AI world as a wide-eyed researcher, fascinated by algorithms that could cluster Google search results into meaningful patterns for human consumption. Working alongside colleagues, we dreamed of converting SQL into natural language and watched in amazement as robots learned through reinforcement in our labs. Little did I know that this early fascination would shape my entire career trajectory—from research labs to Fortune 50 companies, from Silicon Valley startups to university classrooms.

The real impact of AI crystallized during my time in industry. At a leading retail brand, I found myself in the president's office, facing hostile buyers who believed our AI-driven recommendations were "distracting" their customers. I still remember the tension in that room—being new to the company, surrounded by angry buyers, nervous about this pivotal moment. Armed with A/B testing data and revenue metrics—this was before "AI" even entered our corporate vocabulary—I watched skepticism transform into enthusiasm as the numbers revealed massive revenue impacts. That meeting shifted from hostility to excitement about scaling our recommendation engine, teaching me an invaluable lesson about the importance of measurable business impact alongside technical excellence.

Similar stories played out at Home Depot, where our "Frequently Bought Together" feature initially met strong resistance. But once launched, the ML-driven recommendations revealed insights human eyes had missed, diving deep into the catalog to uncover patterns nobody had spotted. The skeptics became our biggest champions, with business units practically begging for early access to our unfinished capabilities.

Amazon brought a different challenge entirely. Instead of chasing revenue, we leveraged computer vision to remove counterfeit products from the marketplace—a move that would deliberately reduce selection and impact short-term revenue. It was a powerful reminder that AI's value extends beyond immediate profits to building long-term trust and brand integrity.

Later, at a start-up, we were doing generative AI before it was cool, building AI assistants so convincing that users would try to ask them on dates. We grappled with AI management, ethics, and behavior control—issues that would later dominate global headlines. Each experience added new layers to my understanding of what it takes to create successful AI products.

Now, as I teach AI and business communications at USC, I'm struck by how the fundamental intuitions behind AI haven't changed, even as the technology has exploded. The frameworks I've developed through years in Silicon Valley start-ups, Fortune 50 companies, and academia still hold true. Although the landscape constantly evolves, it becomes much easier to grapple with this changing world if we can develop and maintain strong intuition about AI's capabilities and limitations.

The Nine-Step Framework

Let me walk you through our framework's journey, as illustrated in Figure I.1. This structured framework guides you through nine essential steps of successful AI product creation. Each step builds naturally on the previous ones, creating a comprehensive approach that you'll return to again and again as you develop AI products. This isn't just a high-level overview—we'll get into the weeds of day-to-day implementation and challenges, making this framework a practical companion for your daily development work.

The methodologies detailed within these pages have been rigorously tested and refined, ensuring their relevance and effectiveness across the diverse landscape of AI applications. From the precision-driven world of machine learning to the human-like understanding of natural language processing, and from the creative frontiers of generative AI to deep learning, the principles laid out here are robust and adaptable. Furthermore, the frameworks are detailed, not just high-level, and we get into the weeds of the day-to-day implementation and challenges. So I will expect readers to come back to these frameworks and details as they go through daily development. This is why not only AI product managers but also their counterparts, including engineering leaders and business leaders in this space, will find it useful.

We begin with mapping business problems to AI opportunities, developing the crucial skill of identifying where AI can create genuine value. You'll then build your understanding of AI use cases and essential machine learning concepts, creating a strong technical foundation. This pillar culminates in developing an experimentation mindset, teaching you to create space for innovation while maintaining practical constraints.

Moving forward, you'll master the critical integration of the model development life cycle (MDLC) with the traditional software development life cycle (SDLC)—a

AI Product Creation: 9-Step Framework

Business Value	Technical Excellence	User Impact

Strategic Foundation
"Value-First Focus with Strong Tech Innovation"

Step 1: Mapping Problems to Business Goals for AI Products
Defining Strategic AI Value

Step 2: Curiosity to Learn AI Use Cases and Emerging Technical ML Concepts
Building Technical Mastery

Step 3: Experimentation Mindset and Room in the Roadmap to Innovate
Embracing Learning Through Iteration

Implementation & Integration
"Bridging Research and Reality in AI Development"

Step 4: Integrating MDLC with SDLC
Harmonizing Development Lifecycles

Step 5: Scaling Research to Production
From Research to Real-World Impact

Step 6: Acceptance Criteria in the World of AI
Defining Success with Stakeholders

Sustainable Excellence & Innovation
"Achieving Breakthrough Performance with Responsible Innovation"

Step 7: Patience and Plan to Surpass Human-Level Performance
Strategic Excellence Through Patience

Step 8: Model Explainability, Interpretability, Ethics, and Bias
Building Trust Through Transparency

Step 9: Model Operations: Model Drift Management
Ensuring Sustainable Excellence

Transformative Outcome: AI Is the New UX
Redefining Human–AI Interaction Through Successful Framework Implementation

FIGURE I.1 A nine-step framework for AI product creation, organized into three strategic pillars: strategic foundation, implementation and integration, and sustainable excellence and innovation. These steps align across business value, technical excellence, and user impact dimensions, driving AI as the new user experience paradigm.

key challenge in AI product creation. You'll learn to scale AI projects from research environments to production systems and establish clear acceptance criteria that acknowledge AI's unique characteristics.

The journey continues through planning for surpassing human-level performance while maintaining responsibility and ethics. You'll tackle the complex challenges of model explainability and bias, ensuring that your AI solutions build trust through transparency. The framework culminates in mastering model operations, where you'll learn to manage model drift and ensure sustained excellence in production.

This systematic progression, visualized in Figure I.1, will be your constant companion throughout the book. Each step builds naturally on the previous ones, creating a comprehensive approach to AI product creation. The framework culminates Chapter 10, where we explore how this systematic approach enables AI to become the new user experience paradigm—fundamentally transforming how humans interact with technology. The final chapter then expands into the creative frontiers of generative AI, equipping you with essential intuition to harness this transformative technology that is reshaping the boundaries of what AI can achieve.

Who This Book Is For

This book is meticulously designed for a diverse yet specialized audience poised at the forefront of technological innovation in the AI space:

▶ **AI product managers/creators:** Those at the helm of crafting AI-driven products will find this framework indispensable for navigating the nuanced challenges specific to AI product development. For the purpose of this book, I use these terms interchangeably: AI product creators today encompass not just product managers but also engineering and data science executives and others responsible for creating AI products.

▶ **Entrepreneurs in the AI domain:** Visionary founders can leverage this book as a roadmap to transforming innovative ideas into tangible, market-ready products.

▶ **Senior leaders:** Executives and decision-makers will gain strategic insights into effectively integrating AI into their product ecosystem.

▶ **Engineering and data science executives:** Technical leaders will gain comprehensive understanding of both strategic vision and implementation challenges in AI product development.

▶ **Academics and students:** Educators and learners will find a structured curriculum enhancing their understanding of AI's practical applications.

▶ **Technology enthusiasts:** Anyone fascinated by the intersection of artificial intelligence and product innovation will appreciate the practical guidance on realizing AI's promise.

Our Journey Ahead

As we stand at the dawn of the AI era, we have an extraordinary opportunity—and responsibility—to shape this technology's trajectory. My goal is simple yet ambitious: to help you develop the intuition needed to build AI solutions that deliver real economic value, execute with predictability, and remain responsible and sustainable. These aren't just theoretical frameworks—they're proven, practical approaches forged in the crucible of real-world challenges and deep reflection.

As you navigate through these nine steps, you will not only build a foundational understanding of creating AI products and integrating AI into existing offerings but also develop the foresight to anticipate trends, the agility to adapt to the dynamic AI landscape, and the vision to lead with innovation. This book affirms that with the right approach, anyone involved in AI can help shape a future of success, discovery, and creation.

Let's begin this journey of creating AI products that don't just work—they transform.

Part I

Strategic Foundation

Value-First Focus with Strong Tech Innovation

Mapping Problems to Business Goals for AI Products

As product managers, our primary directive is to drive and fulfill business goals.[1] In the field of artificial intelligence (AI), this becomes even more crucial as we navigate the cutting-edge intersection of technology and strategic business outcomes. This chapter delves into why understanding and aligning AI capabilities with business objectives is beneficial and essential for product managers in steering their organizations toward success. We will explore the indispensable role of AI in resolving business challenges, underscore the importance of ensuring that AI solutions are in harmony with business goals, and introduce a strategic framework for implementing AI decisions effectively. Additionally, we illuminate these concepts with real-world examples of AI applications, demonstrating their transformative impact across different sectors. This foundation equips product managers with the insights needed to harness AI effectively, ensuring that it is a powerful lever to achieve business ambitions and drive organizational progress.

> The product manager's job is to clearly define the business problem and assess whether AI provides a unique advantage over existing solutions (human expertise or rule-based systems) while delivering tangible business value.

Understanding the Role of AI in Business Problem-Solving

People frequently associate AI with significant accomplishments, such as curing cancer or solving climate change. Everybody dreams up the biggest problems possible and attempts to solve them with AI. Or there's the flip side: not knowing what to do with AI and avoiding it accordingly. Hence, according to McKinsey, just 20 percent of surveyed executives use AI-related technologies in their businesses. Although emerging technologies are great, we can't realize their full potential and benefits until we utilize them to solve business problems or create new business opportunities.

When we talk about crafting the path for AI within the business sphere, it's essential to start with a fundamental premise: AI is not an end but a means to tackle complex business challenges. The role of an AI product manager begins with a crucial skill that may seem straightforward yet is profound in its implications—mapping problems to specific business goals. This process is less about the deep complexities of AI technology and more about leveraging this potent tool to drive strategic outcomes. The journey of mapping problems to business goals with AI starts with a comprehensive problem analysis. Understanding this premise allows AI product managers to sift through AI's myriad possibilities and anchor their focus on applications that align with their organization's strategic objectives. This alignment is crucial for several reasons. First, it ensures that applying AI technologies directly contributes to achieving key business outcomes, whether enhancing customer experience, streamlining operations, or unlocking new market opportunities. By starting with clear business goals, AI initiatives are more likely to receive the necessary support and resources from organizational stakeholders, from top management to frontline employees who will interact with AI systems daily.

Moreover, this focus on problem-solving and goal alignment fosters a culture of innovation and pragmatism. Instead of chasing AI for AI's sake, teams are encouraged to think critically about their challenges and the best tools for addressing them. This could mean deploying AI to automate mundane tasks and free up human creativity for more complex problems or using AI to analyze data in previously impossible ways, revealing insights that can drive more informed decision-making. In essence, AI becomes not just a technological investment but a catalyst for rethinking how business is done.

The Importance of Aligning AI Solutions with Business Goals

Aligning AI solutions with business goals is fundamental to the success of any AI initiative within an organization. As illustrated in Figure 1.1, aligning AI with business objectives drives substantial benefits across key business goals. In contrast, AI initiatives developed purely for the sake of technology, without a clear connection to business objectives, often fail to deliver meaningful impact. Throughout my journey across tech, fintech, banking, retail, and other industries—spanning both traditional companies and Silicon Valley start-ups—I've observed that one of the most significant challenges business executives face is effectively aligning AI initiatives with core business objectives. This strategic alignment is crucial because it ensures that investments in AI technology directly support the overarching objectives of the business. Ensuring that AI projects are tightly linked to business goals allows organizations to avoid the pitfalls of pursuing technology for technology's sake and instead leverage AI as a powerful tool to solve real-world business challenges. It is proven that businesses that effectively map problems to their strategic goals are better positioned to gain a competitive advantage because they can respond to challenges and opportunities in a more structured and purposeful manner.

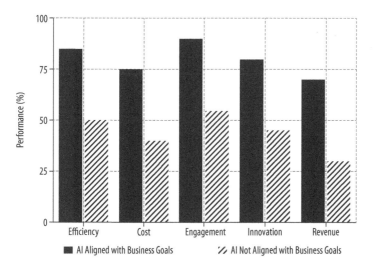

FIGURE 1.1 Aligning AI with business goals boosts performance across efficiency, cost, engagement, innovation, and revenue metrics

At the core of this alignment lies the critical role of AI product management, acting as the bridge between the potential of AI technologies and the strategic needs of the business. This starts with a deep understanding of the business's core objectives: market expansion, customer engagement improvement, or operational efficiency. It's about identifying the "why" behind each goal and mapping how AI can serve as a "how" to achieve these ends. For instance, if the goal is to enhance customer engagement, deploying AI-driven chatbots for 24/7 customer service might be identified as a strategic solution, directly linking AI capabilities with business aspirations. The rapid evolution of AI has revolutionized the way businesses approach problem-solving. Industries like healthcare, finance, and transportation have been transformed with the implementation of AI, solving problems that were once deemed too complex or time-consuming. For example, AI-powered diagnostic tools have improved the accuracy and speed of disease detection. Even though it is not a panacea for all business problems, the impact of this new technology also affects many other aspects.

The importance of aligning AI with business goals stems from the unique capability of AI to analyze data and generate insights at a scale and speed beyond human capacity. However, these technological capabilities risk underutilization or misdirection without a clear connection to business goals. When AI solutions are aligned with business objectives, they have the potential to transform business operations by automating routine tasks, uncovering new insights from data, and enabling more personalized customer experiences. This can lead to significant competitive advantages, such as increased efficiency, reduced costs, and improved customer engagement. AI enables businesses to make data-driven decisions by analyzing vast amounts of data quickly and accurately: this empowers organizations to base their strategies on real insights rather than intuition or incomplete information. In addition, AI-driven predictive analytics can forecast future trends, customer behavior, and market dynamics so that businesses can anticipate demand, identify potential issues, and make proactive decisions to stay ahead of the competition.

On top of that, this AI alignment is essential for securing the necessary support and resources from across the organization. It helps to ensure that AI projects are prioritized according to their potential to impact the business's bottom line. It also facilitates clearer communication about AI initiatives' purpose and expected outcomes, making it easier to rally cross-functional teams around these projects and foster a culture of innovation and collaboration. AI automates repetitive and time-consuming tasks, freeing employees to focus on more creative and strategic problem-solving, increasing overall productivity, and reducing operational costs. It also allows businesses to offer highly personalized experiences to their customers. Through customer data analysis, AI can suggest products or services tailored to individual preferences, enhancing customer satisfaction and engagement. Powered by AI, chatbots and virtual assistants offer 24/7 customer support, answer queries, address problems, assist customers efficiently, enhance customer service, and minimize response times.

AI can optimize supply chain management by predicting demand, managing inventory, improving logistics, reducing costs, minimizing waste, and ensuring that products are available when and where needed. The algorithms can detect fraudulent activities in real time by analyzing transaction data and identifying unusual patterns; this way, businesses can protect themselves from financial losses and maintain the trust of their customers. In manufacturing and production, AI-powered systems can inspect and identify defects in real time, ensuring product quality and reducing the number of defective items that reach the market. Regarding human resources, AI can streamline the hiring process by analyzing resumes, conducting initial screenings, and identifying the most qualified candidates. AI can also assist in talent management and employee engagement.

AI can predict demand fluctuations and optimize inventory management, preventing overstocking or understocking, reducing costs, and improving customer satisfaction. In addition, AI-driven content-generation tools can create written content, such as reports, articles, and product descriptions, saving time and resources for businesses. In the financial sector, AI assesses and manages risk by analyzing complex datasets and identifying potential threats or opportunities. It can assist in product development by analyzing market data and consumer preferences, helping businesses create products more likely to succeed in the market. AI can accelerate research and development efforts in various industries, from pharmaceuticals to materials science, by analyzing large datasets and simulating experiments.

We are standing at the intersection of human intuition and artificial intelligence—where do you draw the line? While AI promises revolutionary solutions, sometimes the most elegant answer lies in human expertise or well-crafted business rules. This is where skilled AI product creators shine. They're like conductors orchestrating a complex symphony, knowing precisely when to let AI take center stage and when to bring in the human element. Their deep understanding of AI's strengths and limitations helps them craft solutions that don't just replace human judgment but enhance it.

Picture a business landscape where AI and human insight dance in perfect harmony—that's the sweet spot these AI product managers aim for. They're not just implementing technology; they're architecting solutions that help organizations pivot swiftly as markets shift and customer demands evolve. These leaders act as bridges between cutting-edge AI capabilities and real-world business challenges, ensuring every AI implementation drives tangible value. Their expertise transforms AI from a buzzword into a powerful tool that gives organizations their competitive edge, turning technological potential into business reality.

Problem Analysis Framework

Before jumping into the complexities of AI implementation decisions, it's essential to establish a robust groundwork for problem analysis. This process is essential for product managers to ensure that the deployment of AI technologies is strategic and addresses the core challenges at hand. To this end, a problem analysis framework is introduced, serving as a crucial step prior to discussing AI implementation strategies.

The problem analysis framework encompasses three key components (see Figure 1.2):

1. **Identifying the problem:** This initial step requires articulating the business challenge clearly and concisely. It's about drilling down to the root cause of the issue, moving beyond symptoms to understand the entire problem. This involves asking critical questions to uncover the full scope of the challenge, ensuring that subsequent AI solutions are targeted and effective. Let's break it down:

Identify the   Identify the   Access Potential
Problem   Stakeholders   AI Impact

FIGURE 1.2 The problem analysis framework: a structured approach for AI challenges. Identify problems, engage stakeholders, and assess potential impact

▶ **Define the challenge:** Begin with a clear, concise statement of the business challenge. This involves separating symptoms from the root cause. For example, if sales are declining, the symptom is reduced revenue, but the root cause might be an outdated product offering or ineffective marketing.

▶ **Critical questioning:** Use a series of why, what, and how questions to drill deeper into the problem. For example, "Why have sales dropped in Q3?" "What has changed in our market positioning?" and "How are consumer behaviors affecting our sales?"

▶ **Scope clarity:** Ensure that you understand the breadth and depth of the issue. Is it a localized problem affecting a single department or a systemic issue impacting the entire organization?

▶ **Data collection:** Gather quantitative and qualitative data to support your understanding of the problem. This might include sales data, market research, customer feedback, and competitor analysis.

2. **Identifying stakeholders:** It is crucial to recognize all parties impacted by the problem. This includes not only those who are directly affected but also those who have a vested interest in the solution. Understanding stakeholders' perspectives, needs, and expectations ensures that the AI solution is designed with a comprehensive view of the problem landscape. Let's break it down:

▶ **Direct and indirect stakeholders:** Direct stakeholders could be the sales team in the case of declining sales, whereas indirect stakeholders might include marketing, product development, and customer service teams.

▶ **Needs and expectations:** Understand what each stakeholder group expects from a solution. This might involve conducting interviews, surveys, or focus groups to gather insights.

▶ **Impact analysis:** Evaluate how the problem (and its potential solution) impacts each stakeholder group. This helps prioritize needs and expectations in the solution design.

3. **Assessing potential AI impact:** With a clear understanding of the problem and stakeholders, the next step is to evaluate how AI can make a tangible difference. This involves considering the specific capabilities of AI technologies that can address the identified problem and understanding the potential benefits and limitations of applying AI in this context. Again, let's break it down:

   ▶ **AI suitability:** Identify areas where AI technologies can be effectively applied. This involves understanding the capabilities of AI, such as data analysis, pattern recognition, predictive analytics, and natural language processing.

   ▶ **Benefits and limitations:** For each identified AI application, assess the potential benefits (for example, increased efficiency, enhanced accuracy, predictive insights) and limitations (for example, data privacy concerns, implementation costs, required skill sets).

   ▶ **Feasibility and readiness:** Evaluate the organization's readiness for implementing AI solutions, including the availability of data, technological infrastructure, and skills.

   ▶ **Stakeholder alignment:** Ensure that the proposed AI solution aligns with the needs and expectations of all stakeholders. This might involve creating a feedback loop where stakeholders can express their concerns and expectations regarding the AI implementation.

Through systematic analysis of problems with this framework, product managers can ensure a strategic approach to AI implementation that is firmly rooted in addressing genuine business needs and capable of delivering measurable impact. This framework guides the initial stages of AI project planning. It sets the stage for a more detailed exploration of implementation decisions, ensuring that AI solutions are both purposeful and powerful tools for achieving business goals.

Developing a Framework for AI Implementation Decisions

Before fully embracing the transformative potential of AI, it's vital to approach the decision-making process with a strategic framework. This framework evaluates the optimal mix of artificial intelligence, human intuition, and intervention.

Acknowledging the complexity and variety of business challenges is key, as is aiming to implement AI solutions that are not just technologically advanced but also in perfect harmony with the unique requirements and dynamics of the organization. Although certain tasks may benefit significantly from AI's capabilities, others might necessitate the deep understanding and empathy that only human expertise can provide.

At the foundation of establishing this decision-making framework is the need to thoroughly understand each challenge the business encounters. It goes beyond merely identifying opportunities for AI application; it involves discerning the exact nature of each problem. Questions arise: Is the challenge one that is laden with data ready to be unraveled by AI's analytical might? Or does the situation call for the kind of empathy and adaptability that is inherently human? The approach starts with a detailed analysis, dissecting problems into their fundamental elements to weigh the potential benefits of AI-driven solutions against those led by human insight and intervention.

The next critical step in the framework is to assess the current operational processes and their efficacy. This involves a meticulous review of existing task execution methods, pinpointing both the strengths and limitations. Understanding the current state of affairs enables organizations to identify precise areas where AI can contribute significant value. This phase ensures that the integration of AI enhances and augments what is already in place, fostering greater efficiency and effectiveness without unnecessary overhaul.

A pivotal aspect of this strategic framework is evaluating the organization's readiness in terms of data. The power of AI largely depends on access to high-quality, relevant data. Thus, the framework mandates a thorough examination of the data landscape, posing essential questions regarding the volume, quality, and accessibility of the data. Are the available datasets robust and clean enough to train dependable AI models? Does the organization possess the infrastructure to support the seamless integration of AI technologies? Addressing these queries is fundamental in gauging the feasibility of embarking on AI projects and their likelihood of success.

A framework that can be employed for this evaluation includes the following steps (see Figure 1.3):

1. **Define the problem:** Clearly articulate the business problem that needs to be addressed.

2. **Evaluate existing solutions:** Assess the current solutions in place, if any, and their effectiveness.

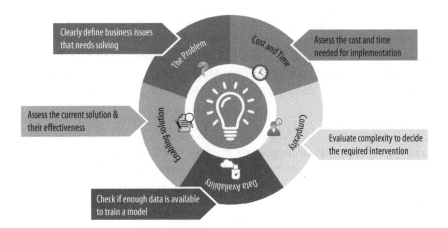

FIGURE 1.3 AI solution feasibility framework: a step-by-step guide to evaluate AI project viability by defining the problem, assessing existing solutions, ensuring data availability, and considering cost, time, and complexity

3. **Assess data availability:** Determine whether sufficient data is available to train an AI model.

4. **Determine complexity:** Evaluate the complexity of the problem to determine whether human intervention or business rules can provide a solution.

5. **Evaluate cost and time:** Assess the cost and time involved in implementing an AI solution versus human intervention or business rules.

Embedded within this comprehensive evaluation is the recognition that some tasks are inherently suited for AI due to their need for rapid processing, scalability, or continuous operation. AI can perform these tasks with a level of consistency and speed unattainable by humans. Conversely, complex challenges requiring subjective judgment, creativity, or deep insight often demand human intervention. Understanding when and where to deploy AI versus human capabilities is crucial for optimizing operational efficiency and ensuring that solutions are effective and sensitive to the unique demands of each task.

Moreover, it's essential to remember that AI systems must operate within ethical and legal boundaries, particularly when dealing with sensitive data or decisions that carry ethical implications. Ensuring compliance with regulations and maintaining ethical standards may necessitate human oversight. Additionally, humans possess the innate ability to adapt to unforeseen challenges and dynamic conditions—capabilities that AI systems, which operate within set parameters, might not fully replicate. Therefore, deciding between AI and human intervention becomes a strategic choice that balances efficiency, adaptability, and ethical considerations.

Recognizing the specific domains where AI excels is invaluable in navigating the complexities of implementing AI. Whether a business problem calls for an AI solution, human intervention, or a synergistic combination of both, it is the principal responsibility of an AI product manager. This discernment allows for strategically allocating human and AI resources, ensuring that each contributes strengths to the organization's objectives effectively.

Practical Examples of AI Solutions in Action

Integrating AI into various sectors has yielded transformative results, demonstrating its capability to address diverse and complex business challenges. Here are five real-world examples of AI solutions in action, showcasing the broad spectrum of AI's applicability:

Healthcare: AI-Driven Diagnostic Tools

AI has made significant strides in enhancing diagnostic accuracy and speed in the healthcare sector. For instance, AI algorithms can analyze medical imaging data, such as X-rays and MRIs, to detect diseases like cancer at earlier stages than previously possible. This improves patient outcomes by enabling early intervention and streamlines the diagnostic process, reducing the workload on radiologists. A notable example is Google's DeepMind AI, which has demonstrated the ability to outperform human doctors in diagnosing certain types of cancer, showcasing AI's potential to complement and augment the expertise of healthcare professionals.

▶ **Business problem:** Delayed diagnosis and human error in interpreting medical images.

▶ **Business goal:** Improve diagnostic accuracy and speed for diseases like cancer.

▶ **AI solution:** Utilize AI algorithms to analyze medical imaging data for early disease detection.

One notable company specializing in AI-driven diagnostic tools is Annalise.ai. Founded in 2019, Annalise.ai focuses on developing comprehensive decision-support solutions for medical imaging. Its flagship product, Annalise CXR, is designed to detect up to 124 findings from chest X-rays within seconds, assisting clinicians in interpreting images with greater accuracy and efficiency.

Finance: Fraud Detection Systems

The financial industry benefits from AI through advanced fraud detection systems. These systems leverage machine learning algorithms to analyze transaction patterns and flag anomalies that may indicate fraudulent activity. For example, Visa's AI-powered fraud detection tools assess risk in real time, evaluating thousands of transaction variables to identify potential fraud. This capability significantly reduces false positives, enhances customer trust, and saves millions of dollars by preventing fraud before it occurs.

▶ **Business problem:** High prevalence of transactional fraud and false positives in fraud detection.

▶ **Business goal:** Reduce fraudulent transactions and minimize false positives to enhance customer trust and reduce losses.

▶ **AI solution:** Implement machine learning algorithms to analyze transaction patterns and flag potential fraud in real time.

Stripe, a leading financial technology company, aims to reduce fraudulent transactions while minimizing false positives to enhance customer trust and cut financial losses. Its AI-driven solution, Radar, analyzes transaction patterns in real time to detect fraud with precision, keeping false positives low to avoid disrupting legitimate transactions. With Radar Assistant, Stripe enables businesses to create custom fraud rules using plain language, making fraud prevention accessible and adaptable without needing technical expertise. This approach strengthens Stripe's core goals of protecting revenue and boosting customer confidence.

Retail: Personalized Recommendations

AI has revolutionized the retail sector by enabling personalized shopping experiences. Amazon's recommendation engine is a prime example, utilizing AI to analyze customer browsing and purchasing history to suggest products that individual users are likely to buy. This personalization enhances the customer experience, driving sales and increasing customer loyalty by making relevant recommendations that reflect each shopper's unique preferences and behaviors.

▶ **Business problem:** Inability to engage customers with personalized shopping experiences at scale.

▶ **Business goal:** Increase sales and customer loyalty by providing personalized product recommendations.

▶ **AI solution:** Deploy AI to analyze customer browsing and purchasing history to suggest personalized products.

An innovative e-commerce company like Shopify leverages AI to elevate the retail experience through personalized shopping journeys. Shopify's AI-driven recommendation tools analyze individual browsing and purchase patterns to suggest products that align with each shopper's unique preferences.

▶ **Business problem:** Delivering personalized shopping at scale.

▶ **Business goal:** Drive sales and build customer loyalty by providing relevant product recommendations.

▶ **AI solution:** Use machine learning models that analyze customer interactions, enabling dynamic suggestions that enrich the shopping experience and increase engagement.

Transportation: Autonomous Vehicles

The transportation industry is undergoing a significant transformation with the development of autonomous vehicles. Companies like Tesla and Waymo leverage AI to process data from sensors and cameras to navigate safely. This technology promises to reduce traffic accidents caused by human error, improve traffic flow, and provide mobility solutions for those unable to drive. Although fully autonomous vehicles are still under development, the progress illustrates AI's potential to redefine transportation.

▶ **Business problem:** Many traffic accidents caused by human error and inefficiencies in traffic management.

▶ **Business goal:** Improve road safety, enhance traffic flow, and provide innovative mobility solutions.

▶ **AI solution:** Develop AI-powered autonomous vehicles that can navigate safely using data from sensors and cameras.

Agriculture: Precision Farming

AI-powered precision farming tools analyze satellite images and data from sensors to optimize agriculture's planting, watering, and harvesting processes, as shown in Figure 1.4. This approach allows for more efficient use of resources like water and fertilizers, improving crop yields while minimizing environmental impact. John Deere, for example, uses AI and machine learning to enable tractors and other equipment to analyze soil conditions and crop health in real time, automating decisions that maximize efficiency and productivity.

▶ **Business problem:** Inefficient use of resources and declining crop yields due to traditional farming practices.

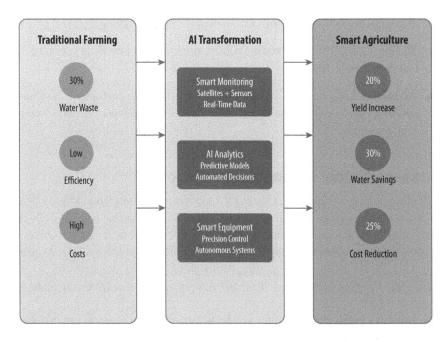

FIGURE 1.4 AI-powered agricultural transformation: from traditional farming to data-driven precision agriculture

▶ **Business goal:** Optimize resource use and improve crop yields through data-driven farming practices.

▶ **AI solution:** Utilize AI and machine learning to analyze satellite images and sensor data for precision farming.

AI's impact now stretches far beyond Silicon Valley's tech bubble, transforming even the most traditional industries. As an AI product leader and professor working with successful entrepreneurs, I've seen firsthand that focusing on concrete business problems—rather than technology for technology's sake—unlocks immense value. From optimizing crop yields in agriculture to preventing equipment failures in manufacturing, AI is proving its worth through measurable, real-world outcomes. The democratization of AI means that organizations of any size or sector can now harness its power to tackle unique challenges. Ultimately, it's not the complexity of the algorithm that matters, but how effectively it addresses genuine customer needs.

Creative Industry: Generative AI in Customized Fashion Design

In the fashion industry, generative AI is revolutionizing the way designers create and customers engage with fashion, as shown in Figure 1.5. A standout example of this is the use of generative adversarial networks (GANs) to design personalized clothing. These AI models learn from vast datasets of fashion items, styles, and trends to generate new designs that cater to individual preferences and emerging fashion trends. Designers input parameters related to color, fabric type, and style into the AI system, which then proposes unique, customized designs. This not only accelerates the design process but also allows for a higher degree of personalization and creativity.

▶ **Business problem:** The slow and resource-intensive process of fashion design and the challenge of meeting diverse consumer preferences at scale.

▶ **Business goal:** Enhance the creativity and efficiency of the fashion design process while providing highly personalized products to customers.

▶ **AI solution:** Use GANs to learn from current fashion trends and consumer preferences to generate unique, customized clothing designs.

This generative AI application empowers fashion brands to offer personalized shopping experiences where customers can have a say in the designs of their clothes,

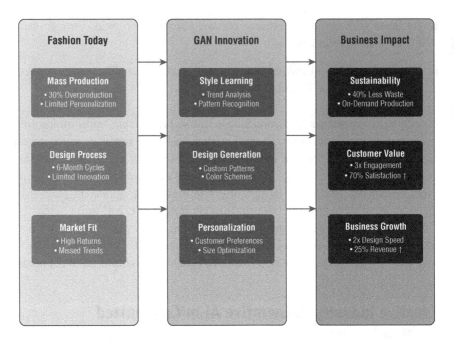

FIGURE 1.5 AI fashion revolution: mass to personalized design

leading to higher satisfaction and loyalty. It also opens up new possibilities for sustainable fashion, as items can be produced on demand, reducing waste associated with overproduction. By integrating generative AI into their design processes, fashion brands can stay ahead of trends, cater to individual customer needs, and drive innovation in a highly competitive industry.

The Revolutionization of Generative AI

Before discussing the emerging technical machine learning concept and the curiosity to learn AI use cases in the next chapter, we must first discuss the burgeoning relevance of generative AI in this context. In the swiftly evolving landscape of AI, generative AI emerges as a beacon of innovation. It offers unprecedented opportunities for businesses to harness its potential in creating content, designs, and simulations. This technology, characterized by its ability to generate new, unique data or content indistinguishable from that created by humans, is not merely an advancement; it's a revolution in how we conceive and execute the creation process across various domains. From drafting textual content to designing complex digital artifacts and simulating environments for testing or training, generative AI applications are vast and varied, pushing the boundaries of what's possible within AI-driven solutions.

For product managers, particularly those navigating the AI domain, the advent of generative AI signifies a pivotal shift in strategy and product development. The ability to automate and enhance creative processes through AI does not just streamline operations; it opens up new avenues for innovation and customization that were previously unthinkable. In content creation, for example, generative AI can produce articles, reports, and marketing copy tailored to specific audiences with remarkable efficiency and accuracy. Similarly, in design, it can generate numerous iterations of digital models, graphics, and user interfaces, facilitating a more dynamic and responsive approach to design challenges. Understanding the potential of generative AI requires a nuanced approach to integrating it into business strategies. Product managers must consider not only the technical capabilities of these AI systems but also how they can be aligned with business objectives to create value. This involves identifying areas within the business where generative AI can have the most significant impact, whether by enhancing product offerings, improving customer experiences, or driving operational efficiencies. Moreover, it necessitates a forward-thinking mindset, anticipating the future needs and preferences of the market to leverage generative AI in developing innovative and relevant solutions.

The strategic implementation of generative AI promises to transform businesses, enabling them to operate more efficiently and innovate more freely. However, it also presents challenges, including ethical considerations around copyright and authenticity and the need for robust data governance to train AI models responsibly. As such, product managers must navigate these challenges with a keen eye on the broader implications of generative AI applications. By doing so, they can steer their organizations toward leveraging this transformative technology to achieve superior business outcomes, ensuring that their products and services remain at the forefront of innovation and relevance in a competitive landscape. This dedicated exploration of generative AI underscores its critical role in shaping the future of AI applications in business, highlighting the strategic insights and actions required for product managers to capitalize on its potential effectively.

Traditional AI vs. Generative AI

As AI continues to evolve, it's crucial to understand the differences between traditional AI and the emerging field of generative AI. Both approaches offer significant advantages but cater to different needs and applications, as shown in Table 1.1. Let's explore these distinctions in a comparative discussion.

Traditional AI	Generative AI
Well-defined problems	Broader, complex challenges
Structured data, historical data	Structured and unstructured data
Improved accuracy and efficiency	New insights, innovation
Fixed parameters, less adaptable	Flexible, scalable, adaptable
Optimization and enhancement	Drives innovation and creativity

Table 1.1 Old vs. New AI: mapping problems to business goals for AI products (core principle: AI should solve real, well-defined business problems)

Well-Defined Problems vs. Broader, Complex Challenges   Traditional AI is designed to solve well-defined problems with clear objectives. These systems excel in specific tasks such as image recognition, language translation, and predictive analytics. The focus is on tackling predefined problems with known parameters, ensuring high precision and reliability. On the other hand, generative AI addresses broader and more complex challenges that extend beyond well-defined tasks. It is engineered to create and innovate, handling problems requiring more creativity and flexibility. This capability includes generating human-like text, creating artwork, composing music, and designing new products.

Historical Data vs. AI-Created Data   Traditional AI relies heavily on historical data to build models. By analyzing historical data, these systems can spot trends and generate precise forecasts. Using meticulously labeled and curated data ensures that traditional AI performs its tasks efficiently and effectively. In contrast, generative AI can create new data. This self-generating capability allows it to produce original content, such as new images, audio, or text that didn't exist before. This ability to generate data opens up new possibilities for innovation and creativity, providing unique solutions that traditional AI might not explore.

Improved Accuracy and Efficiency vs. New Insights and Innovation   The primary goal of traditional AI is to optimize and enhance existing processes. By leveraging historical data, these systems can improve efficiency and accuracy in various operations, such as supply chain management, financial forecasting, and customer service. The focus is on making existing processes more effective. Meanwhile, generative AI provides new insights and drives innovation by exploring possibilities beyond what traditional AI can offer. It generates novel solutions and ideas, pushing the possible boundaries. This capability is particularly valuable in creative fields like design, content creation, and scientific research, where innovation is paramount.

Fixed Parameters vs. Flexibility and Adaptability   Once trained, traditional AI models operate with fixed parameters. Although they perform their designated tasks exceptionally well, they are less adaptable to new, unforeseen scenarios without retraining. This rigidity can be a limitation in dynamic environments where conditions change rapidly. In comparison, generative AI systems are highly flexible and adaptable. They can adjust to new inputs and generate outputs that align with evolving requirements. This adaptability makes them suitable for applications where conditions change frequently, requiring continuous innovation and scalability.

Optimization and Enhancement vs. Driving Innovation and Creativity   At its core, traditional AI focuses on optimization and enhancement. These systems are designed to improve existing processes, making them more efficient and effective. Traditional AI aims to enhance operational efficiency and decision-making by optimizing logistics, enhancing image quality, or streamlining customer interactions. Conversely, generative AI is about driving innovation and creativity. It empowers businesses to develop unique solutions and products, enhancing their ability to compete in a rapidly changing market. Generative AI enables organizations to stay ahead of trends and continuously innovate by generating new ideas and possibilities.

Endnote

1. In this context, business outcomes can be similar to addressing customer needs or making a social impact.

Chapter 2

Curiosity to Learn AI Use Cases and Emerging Technical ML Concepts

In this chapter, we jump into the critical exploration of artificial intelligence (AI) product management, marking curiosity as the essential second step to successful AI product creation in the journey through the AI and machine learning (ML) domains. First, we will lay the foundation by discussing the core principles of ML, which are essential for navigating the complexities of AI. Following this, we will explore the vast landscape of AI, examining the indispensable tools and technologies that drive development and innovation. Delving deeper, we will uncover the frontiers of innovation within deep learning and generative AI (GenAI), showcasing their potential to transform industries and redefine problem-solving. Further, we will demystify the model training process, providing a step-by-step breakdown of how data is transformed into predictive insights. Finally, we will bridge theory with practice, highlighting real-world AI applications that illustrate the tangible impact of AI across various sectors. Through this journey, AI product managers are equipped with the knowledge and insights necessary for leveraging AI technologies to achieve strategic objectives, underscoring the significance of curiosity, lifelong learning, and adaptability in mastering the dynamic field of AI.

> To harness AI's transformative power, product teams must relentlessly pursue mastery of evolving machine learning technologies. This journey includes mastering foundational libraries, capitalizing on advanced cloud-based AI, and exploring the frontiers of deep learning and transfer learning. Such commitment will enable product creators to solve complex business challenges and redefine the boundaries of what is possible.

The Foundation of Machine Learning

In the dynamic world of AI and ML, a successful AI product manager must be driven by a curiosity to learn not only about the various AI use cases but also about emerging technical concepts in ML. First, let's define it.

As shown in Figure 2.1, ML is a subfield of AI that focuses on developing algorithms and statistical models that enable computers to improve their performance on a specific task through learning from data without being explicitly programmed. In other words, it trains computers to learn and make predictions or decisions based on data without intended instructions. This revolutionary approach moves beyond the traditional norms to a model where machines improve and adapt through experience.

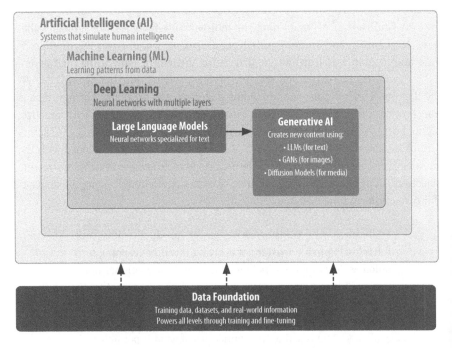

FIGURE 2.1 Evolving models within the AI taxonomy. This diagram illustrates how evolving models, such as those in deep learning, fit into the broader landscape of AI, showcasing the progression and specialization within the field

Source: Adapted from [i]

At its core, the journey into ML begins with data. Whether structured or unstructured, this data is the lifeblood of ML algorithms, offering the raw material from which learning is derived. From sensors capturing real-time inputs to databases storing vast amounts of historical information, the variety and volume of data available today are unprecedented. ML's reliance on data underscores the shift toward evidence-based decision-making in business, where insights and predictions are drawn from actual data rather than intuition.

Types of ML

There are four main types of ML, as listed in Table 2.1, each offering distinct approaches for analyzing data and building predictive models, and they evolved in varied timelines. Let's delve into these categories to understand their unique methodologies and applications.

Year	Paradigm	Key applications
1950s	Supervised learning	Statistical modeling, predictions
1960s	Unsupervised learning	Pattern recognition, data clustering
2000s	Semisupervised learning	Medical diagnosis, hybrid datasets
2010s	Reinforcement learning	Game AI, robotics control

Table 2.1 Four types of ML

Supervised learning: Supervised learning is arguably the most commonly used category of ML. In this approach, algorithms are trained on labeled datasets, meaning the input data is paired with the correct output data. The algorithm learns from this data and makes predictions by generalizing from the training set to unseen situations. There are two main types of problems solved by supervised learning:

▶ Classification: The output variable is a category, such as "spam" or "not spam."

▶ Regression: The output variable is a real value, such as "weight" or "price."

Applications:

▶ Email spam filtering

▶ Risk assessment in insurance

▶ Price prediction in real estate

Unsupervised learning: Unsupervised learning involves training algorithms on data without labeled responses. Here, the system tries to learn the patterns and the structure from the data without any reference to known or labeled outcomes.

▶ Clustering: The process of grouping similar entities together. Common algorithms include k-means, hierarchical clustering, and DBSCAN.

▶ Association: A rule-based method for discovering interesting relations between variables in large databases. It's used for market basket analysis.

Applications:

▶ Market segmentation

▶ Recommender systems

▶ Anomaly detection

Semisupervised learning: Semisupervised learning sits between supervised and unsupervised learning. In this approach, algorithms are trained on a dataset containing labeled and unlabeled data. Typically, there's a small amount of labeled data and a lot of unlabeled data. The systems use the labeled data to learn the structure and make inferences about how to label the unlabeled data.

▶ Self-training: A method where a model is initially trained with a small set of labeled data and then used to classify unlabeled data. The most confident predictions are added to the training set, and the model is retrained.

▶ Transductive learning: This method tries to predict new outputs directly using both the labeled and unlabeled data.

Applications:

▶ Image and speech recognition when only some examples are labeled

▶ Web content classification where tagging all content is impractical

Reinforcement learning: Reinforcement learning is different from the other types as it is based on the concept of agents that take actions in an environment to maximize some notion of cumulative reward. The algorithm learns to achieve a goal in an uncertain, potentially complex environment. In reinforcement learning, an agent makes observations and takes actions within an environment, and in return, it receives rewards. Its objective is to learn to act in a way that will maximize its expected long-term rewards.

▶ **Value-based:** The goal is to maximize a value function, which represents the maximum expected cumulative reward achievable from a state.

▶ **Policy-based:** Directly learns the policy function that maps state to action without needing a value function.

Applications:

▶ Real-time decisions in software, such as recommendation engines

▶ Game playing and robotics

▶ Self-driving cars and resource management

Each of these ML types offers a unique approach to understanding and processing data. They can be used individually or in combination to solve complex real-world problems. The key to successful ML projects lies in choosing the right type of learning and algorithms for your specific task and ensuring that you have the appropriate data to train your models.

The algorithms that power ML models are the architects of this learning process. These mathematical models are adept at identifying patterns and relationships within the data, a capability that is categorized into supervised learning, unsupervised learning, and reinforcement learning (see Figure 2.2).

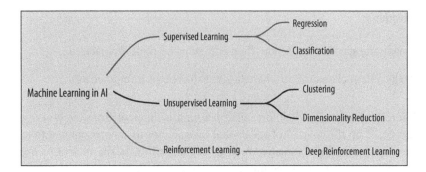

FIGURE 2.2 A mind map illustrating different categories of ML within AI. It shows three core branches: supervised learning, unsupervised learning, and reinforcement learning

Based on labeled data, supervised learning guides algorithms to predict outcomes based on past examples. In contrast, unsupervised learning explores unlabeled data, revealing hidden patterns without predefined categories. Reinforcement learning introduces a dynamic of actions and rewards, crafting models that learn optimal behaviors through trial and error to achieve specific objectives.

The training phase is where the true potential of ML is unveiled. During this phase, models are exposed to datasets, adjusting their internal parameters to learn from the data. This iterative process reduces the discrepancy between the model's predictions and the actual outcomes, enhancing the model's accuracy. After training, the model is tested with new, unseen data to evaluate its predictive capabilities. Once a model has been validated for its performance, it progresses to the inference stage. Here, it applies its learned knowledge to make decisions or predictions, demonstrating its readiness for real-world applications.

The application of ML spans a breathtaking array of domains, reshaping them with its capacity for innovation. Natural language processing (NLP) like Siri and Google Assistant bridges human–machine communication; in computer vision, it endows machines with the gift of sight; in recommendation systems, it personalizes user experiences. ML's applications across healthcare, finance, and beyond are as varied as they are impactful, automating tasks, enhancing decision-making, and igniting innovation.

All these concepts make it evident that the boundaries of what's possible continually expand. This dynamic field not only revolutionizes industries by introducing unprecedented levels of efficiency and innovation but also challenges professionals to stay ahead of the technological curve. It heralds a future where AI's potential is fully harnessed to solve the most pressing challenges. For an AI product manager, understanding these foundational elements is beneficial and imperative. It equips them with the knowledge to navigate the technical complexities of AI, envision new possibilities, and lead the charge in transforming these possibilities into reality.

A Walk Through the AI Landscape

In the rapidly advancing field of AI and ML, AI product managers are at the helm, navigating the complex landscape of technologies that drive innovation. Their role is pivotal, merging the technical intricacies of AI with strategic business visions to craft products that are not only innovative but also technically feasible and aligned with market needs. To excel in this role, an AI product manager must deeply understand the various tools and model architectures that constitute the backbone of AI technology. They should be conversant with high-level APIs like those shown in Figure 2.3:

▶ **SciPy and NumPy:** These Python-based libraries are fundamental for scientific and numerical computing. They support an array of high-level mathematical functions critical in AI and ML algorithms.

▶ **Pandas:** A data manipulation and analysis tool that offers data structures and operations for manipulating numerical tables and time series—a staple for data preprocessing in ML workflows.

▶ **Scikit-learn:** This library is known for its simple and efficient tools for predictive data analysis. It's built on NumPy, SciPy, and Matplotlib and is the go-to choice for starting with classical ML algorithms.

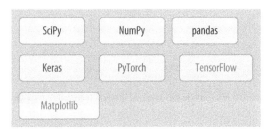

FIGURE 2.3 Examples of high-level APIs

▶ **TensorFlow:** This open-source platform is known for its flexible ecosystem of tools, libraries, and community resources, which enable researchers to push the boundaries of ML and developers to easily build and deploy ML-powered applications.

▶ **Keras:** Operating on top of TensorFlow, Keras is an open-source neural network library that provides a Python interface for artificial neural networks. Keras acts as an interface for the TensorFlow library, easing the complexity of building deep learning models.

▶ **PyTorch:** Developed by Facebook's AI Research lab, PyTorch is an open-source ML library based on the Torch library. It's popular for its ease of use and flexibility, especially in research settings.

▶ **Matplotlib:** A plotting library for the Python programming language and its numerical mathematics extension NumPy. It provides an object-oriented API for embedding plots into applications.

Understanding and utilizing these tools allows AI product managers to transcend the boundaries between abstract AI concepts and practical, scalable, and efficient product solutions. Although there are still more of them, let's talk about the three most used and popular deep learning frameworks.

Three Popular Deep Learning Frameworks

Deep learning has become a cornerstone technology powering many AI innovations. At the heart of this revolution are deep learning frameworks designed to facilitate the development of sophisticated neural network models, each offering unique advantages and capabilities to the field of AI (see Figure 2.4):

FIGURE 2.4 Three essential ML frameworks every AI product manager should be familiar with

Keras: intuitive high-level API for deep learning: Keras is renowned for its user-friendliness and modularity, making it the perfect gateway for those new to deep learning. As a high-level neural network library, Keras acts as an interface for the TensorFlow library, abstracting away much of the complexity in favor of a more intuitive approach. It was designed to facilitate fast experimentation and can run on top of TensorFlow, enabling rapid movement from idea to result. Keras simplifies the process of building deep learning models through its consistent and simple APIs, making it possible to construct a neural network in just a few lines of code (see Keras benefits in Table 2.2). However, despite its simplicity, Keras is powerful enough to support advanced research that requires deep customization and complex neural architectures.

Feature	Description
Easy and fast prototyping	Allows rapid model development and experimentation
Supports multiple network types	Compatible with convolutional, recurrent, and hybrid networks
Clear feedback for user errors	Provides actionable feedback to help users correct errors
Best practices for reducing cognitive load	Designed to be user-friendly and intuitive

Table 2.2 Keras benefits

TensorFlow: comprehensive platform for ML: TensorFlow, developed by Google Brain, is perhaps the most comprehensive library available for developers and researchers alike. Its flexible architecture allows for the easy deployment of computation across a variety of platforms (CPUs, GPUs, TPUs), serving from the research phase right through to production. TensorFlow excels with its broad set of tools and resources that are continually updated by a vast community of contributors and Google developers. Its computational graph approach, where nodes represent mathematical operations and edges represent multidimensional data arrays (tensors) that flow between them, provides a powerful environment for constructing and training complex models. TensorFlow also offers robust support for production tasks and serves as the backbone for many Google services.

From my conversations with industry leaders, I've seen how TensorFlow's scalability and flexibility transform businesses. Take Uber: the company is using it for real-time demand forecasting to optimize rider experience. DeepMind's teams shared how they're leveraging deep learning optimization for healthcare breakthroughs, and Intel's engineers have mastered hardware acceleration for their ML models.

At eBay, API versatility enables both personalized recommendations and sophisticated fraud detection. Qualcomm is doing impressive work optimizing mobile performance. Even Coca-Cola uses the end-to-end ML pipeline for smarter marketing and supply chain decisions.

What's really caught my attention is how Google deploys TensorFlow across platforms—from search algorithms to language translation and autonomous vehicles. Whether it's Dropbox enhancing file management or X (formerly Twitter) boosting user engagement, TensorFlow has proven its worth from research labs to real-world business solutions.

PyTorch: dynamic neural network toolkit: PyTorch, developed by Facebook's AI Research lab, has gained a reputation for being a dynamic and flexible framework that's particularly well-suited to research due to its ease of use and Pythonic integration. Unlike TensorFlow, which uses a static computation graph, PyTorch operates with dynamic computational graphs, meaning that the graph is built on the fly as operations are created. This feature, known as *define-by-run*, allows for more intuitive graph debugging and more natural coding of complex architectures. PyTorch's design is centered around enhancing the speed and flexibility of experimentation—a critical aspect of AI research and iterative development. Additionally, PyTorch offers an extensive library of tools and libraries for computer vision (Torchvision), NLP (TorchText), and more.

Spara AI libraries, such as TensorFlow, and platforms like SageMaker provide the tools and environment necessary for developing, training, and deploying AI models. Now, let's explain them in more detail. TensorFlow, a brainchild of Google's pioneering work in ML, stands at the forefront of AI development. This open-source library has democratized ML, offering a versatile tool suite that empowers developers and product managers to experiment, develop, and deploy AI models with unprecedented ease. TensorFlow's robust, scalable framework is designed to accommodate the complex computations required for ML, making it an indispensable resource for those looking to explore the frontiers of AI capabilities.

On a parallel track, Amazon SageMaker takes the complexity out of ML projects, offering a fully managed platform that encompasses the entire model life cycle. From building and training to deploying and managing models, SageMaker equips AI product managers with a seamless, integrated environment that accelerates the pace of innovation. Its ability to scale effortlessly with the project's demands, coupled with Amazon Web Services cloud infrastructure, ensures that AI applications can be developed and deployed rapidly, meeting the fast-evolving needs of businesses.

The journey of AI development is underpinned by the meticulous process of data labeling, a task that is both critical and labor-intensive. Data labeling tools such as

Labelbox and Supervisely emerge as key allies in this endeavor, simplifying the task of annotating data with the necessary labels to train supervised learning models. They typically provide an intuitive user interface that allows human annotators to interact with the data and apply annotations efficiently; this interface may include features for zooming, panning, and inspecting data details. These platforms enhance the efficiency and accuracy of data labeling, providing intuitive interfaces for annotators and incorporating features that streamline collaboration and quality control. The strategic use of these tools significantly impacts the success of AI projects, enabling the development of precise models aligned with the real-world complexities they aim to address.

Building on this foundation, the evolution of data labeling tools extends into advanced functionalities to further refine the data preparation process. Quality control emerges as a pivotal aspect, with sophisticated mechanisms integrated into labeling platforms for verifying data accuracy and consistency, a critical step for ensuring the reliability of annotations. Moreover, incorporating ML and computer vision technologies enhances the annotator's capabilities, offering predictive prelabeling and suggesting refinements. This synergy between human oversight and algorithmic assistance paves the way for defining comprehensive labeling workflows, tailored guidelines, and real-time progress monitoring, addressing the dynamic needs of AI projects. Additionally, amid growing concerns over data privacy and security, these tools adapt by introducing measures for data anonymization and stringent access controls, safeguarding sensitive information throughout the labeling process.

As the complexities of data labeling expand, so does the versatility of these platforms. Ensuring compatibility with various ML frameworks through support for various export formats is paramount, facilitating seamless integration into the AI development life cycle. In this changing reality, the capacity for customization stands as a critical feature, bridging the gap between diverse project requirements and the capabilities of labeling tools. Customization options allow for tailoring labeling interfaces to meet specific project requirements, thereby enhancing the user experience and operational efficiency. This adaptability caters to the unique needs of different AI projects and significantly boosts productivity and alignment with project goals. Following these threads, integrating labeling tools with data management systems and AI platforms naturally extends their utility. These integration capabilities do not merely add another layer of convenience; they play a vital role in streamlining the end-to-end ML pipeline, emphasizing the tools' essential function in the broader ecosystem of AI development. This integration facilitates a more cohesive workflow, ensuring that data moves efficiently through every phase, from collection and labeling to training and deployment. Such a seamless process marks a significant advancement in optimizing the lifecycles of AI projects.

Furthermore, adopting active learning strategies, where models iteratively suggest the most impactful data points for labeling, exemplifies forward-thinking approaches to optimizing model training. Such strategies not only enhance the efficiency of data annotation but also ensure that the models evolve in a way that is closely aligned with the complexities of real-world data. Ultimately, these advanced features and considerations underscore the indispensable role of data labeling tools in cultivating supervised learning models, driving the advancement of AI technologies by ensuring the quality and relevance of the training data.

Deep Learning and Generative AI—The Frontiers of Innovation

Two main emerging fields in AI are currently at the forefront of transforming how we interact with and leverage technology: deep learning and GenAI (see Figure 2.5). These disciplines are not just expanding the boundaries of what machines can do but redefining the nature of innovation and problem-solving across industries.

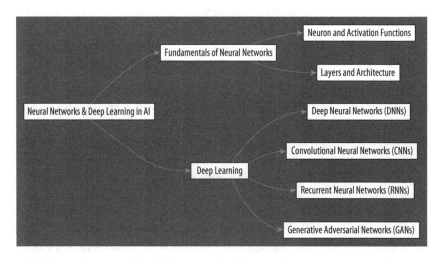

FIGURE 2.5 Neural networks and deep learning: from fundamentals to advanced models

Deep learning, a subset of ML inspired by the structure and function of the human brain, utilizes artificial neural networks with multiple layers (hence "deep") to process data in complex ways. Its algorithms are designed to automatically learn and represent data in increasingly abstract and hierarchical ways, allowing them to make sense of complex patterns and features within the data, as shown in Figure 2.6.

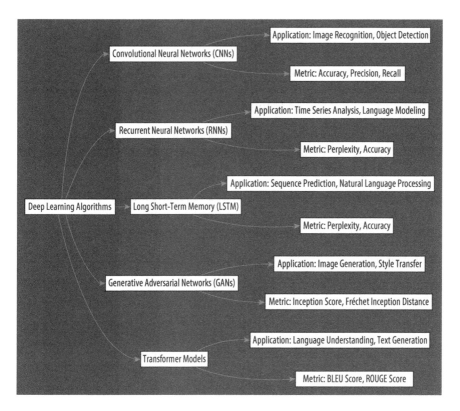

FIGURE 2.6 Deep learning algorithms: key applications and evaluation metrics

Lower layers in the network learn simple features like edges and textures, whereas higher layers learn more complex and abstract features. This hierarchy of features allows deep learning models to capture structures in data. It can be applied to both supervised learning tasks (where labeled data is used for training) and unsupervised learning tasks (where the algorithm discovers patterns and structures in unlabeled data). The approach of deep learning enables the automatic learning of intricate patterns in large datasets, significantly advancing capabilities in image and speech recognition, NLP, and even decision-making processes. Unlike traditional ML techniques that require manual feature selection, deep learning algorithms learn these features directly from data, making them extraordinarily effective for tasks involving unstructured data, such as photos and human language.

Deep learning models are composed of multiple layers of artificial neurons, referred to as *deep neural networks* or *deep networks*. These layers can range from a few to hundreds or even thousands, enabling the modeling of complex relationships in the data. Let's go over a few terms and abbreviations:

▶ **Convolutional neural networks (CNNs)** are a type of deep neural network particularly suited for image and video analysis. They use convolutional layers to learn spatial hierarchies of features.

▶ **Recurrent neural networks (RNNs)** are designed for sequence data and are well-suited for tasks like NLP and speech recognition. They have memory cells that can capture temporal dependencies.

▶ **Long short-term memory (LSTM) and gated recurrent units (GRU)** are specialized RNN architectures capable of learning long-range dependencies in sequential data, making them well-suited for tasks with extended context.

▶ **Autoencoders** are a class of neural networks used for unsupervised feature learning and data compression.

The impact of deep learning is profound, offering transformative potential across various sectors. It has achieved exceptional performance in tasks such as image classification, object detection, facial recognition, and image segmentation. Moreover, it has revolutionized NLP with the introduction of models like transformers, enabling significant advances in machine translation, sentiment analysis, chatbots, and more. Additionally, it has powered speech recognition systems, making voice assistants and transcription services more accurate and accessible. Deep learning is used to develop recommendation algorithms, improving personalized content recommendations on platforms like Netflix and Amazon. It plays a vital role in self-driving cars, helping them perceive their environment and make driving decisions.

GenAI, on the other hand, refers to models that can generate new data that resembles the training data, essentially learning the distribution of that data. This field has given rise to technologies like generative adversarial networks (GANs) and transformers, which have applications ranging from creating realistic images and videos to generating coherent text and music. GenAI can not only augment creative processes but also enhance data augmentation techniques, improving the robustness of AI models by providing diverse training data (see Figure 2.7).

The versatility of GenAI is showcased in its ability to produce novel content, from artwork that blurs the line between human and machine creativity to synthesized

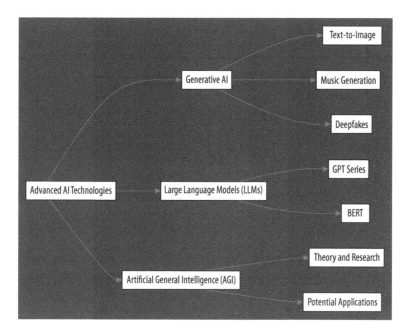

FIGURE 2.7 Advanced AI technologies: GenAI, large language models, and AGI

voices and deepfake videos that are indistinguishable from real ones. Text generation models, like OpenAI's GPT (generative pretrained transformer) series, are capable of generating coherent and contextually relevant textual content. In fact, they are used for tasks like natural language generation, chatbots, and content generation. Also, models like DCGANs and StyleGANs are used to generate images, often with remarkable realism. For this reason, they have applications in creating art, generating realistic faces, and more. In business applications, generative models are revolutionizing marketing by generating personalized content at scale, and in research, they accelerate the discovery process by simulating experimental data.

As we stand on the cusp of these frontiers of innovation, the potential for deep learning and GenAI to redefine industries is clear: unlocking new capabilities that were once the realm of science fiction. For AI product managers, it is essential to have a foundational understanding of the underlying technical concepts of AI and ML. This includes understanding how models are trained, what the different libraries and tools are used for, and how they are being utilized in the development and deployment of AI solutions.

The Model Training Process, Demystified

Developing an ML model is a nuanced and captivating journey, comprising several crucial stages that transform raw data into intelligent systems capable of insightful predictions and decisions. For AI product managers, a clear grasp of this process is key to confidently steering AI projects to success. Let's distill the process into six fundamental steps, as the framework depicts in Figure 2.8:

1. **Data preparation:** This is the foundation of the model training process. It encompasses gathering relevant data from various sources, which could be images, text, or numerical data, and then cleaning it to rectify any issues with noise, missing values, or inconsistencies. The objective is to refine the data into a pristine dataset that can be effectively used for training models.

2. **Feature extraction:** After the initial preparation, the next phase is to extract meaningful features from the data. This involves selecting the most informative attributes that are most likely to predict the outcome. This step is critical as the right features can greatly enhance the model's learning efficiency and overall predictive performance.

3. **Model training:** With clean data and relevant features at hand, we proceed to train the model. This involves choosing a suitable algorithm and allowing it to learn from the data. The algorithm iteratively adjusts its parameters to minimize the error in its predictions, using optimization techniques such as gradient descent.

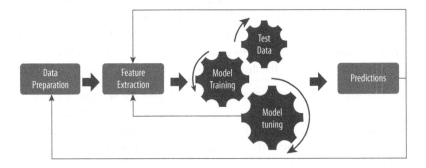

FIGURE 2.8 ML workflow: a cyclical process from data preparation and feature extraction to model training, tuning, testing, and making predictions

4. **Model tuning:** This step fine-tunes the model by tweaking the hyperparameters, which are essential settings that govern the model's learning structure and behavior. Hyperparameter tuning is an art that balances model complexity with predictive power, ensuring that the model performs optimally without overfitting or underfitting.

5. **Test data:** Once the model is trained and tuned, it's evaluated against a test set—a subset of data not seen by the model during training. This crucial phase tests the model's ability to generalize its learning to new, unseen data.

6. **Predictions:** If the model performs well on the test data, it is then ready to make predictions or decisions in a real-world environment. This step involves deploying the model to a production system where it can provide insights, automate tasks, or enhance decision-making processes.

As you can see, demystifying the model training process reveals the depth of work and expertise required to develop effective AI systems. Understanding each step is vital for overseeing the development of AI solutions that are innovative and aligned with business objectives. So, to recap:

▶ Knowing how models are trained, including feeding data into the model, optimizing the model parameters, and evaluating the model's performance, is essential for making informed decisions about developing and deploying AI solutions.

▶ Having a foundational understanding of the various libraries and tools used in developing and deploying AI solutions is essential for making informed decisions about the development and deployment of AI solutions.

Advanced AI

The concept of *advanced AI* often encompasses two pivotal stages in the development of AI: artificial general intelligence (AGI) and super artificial intelligence (SAI), both representing significant leaps beyond the capabilities of today's narrow AI (NAI), as shown in Figure 2.9. Although NAI excels in specific domains, mastering tasks ranging from voice recognition to beating humans in strategic games, its expertise is confined to narrow windows of capability without the broader contextual understanding that human intelligence naturally possesses.

LEVELS OF AI

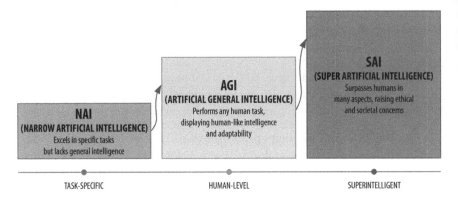

FIGURE 2.9 Levels of AI: hierarchical classification showing NAI, SAI, and AGI, illustrating their relative capabilities and scope of intelligence

AGI, the first horizon in advanced AI, aims to match humans' nuanced and sophisticated intelligence, where machines could theoretically perform any intellectual task that a human being can. It represents the bridging of gaps between a machine's ability to excel in a single task and the versatility of human cognition. The leap from NAI to AGI entails endowing machines with the ability to understand, learn, and apply knowledge in diverse ways, thus requiring not just quantitative increases in processing power or data but a qualitative transformation in the algorithms themselves. Researchers in the field of AGI are drawing from computer science, cognitive sciences, neurology, and philosophy, trying to replicate the depth and plasticity of human thought.

The eventual realization of AGI would be a momentous milestone, but it leads to the concept of SAI—an even more advanced form of AI that surpasses human intelligence across all areas. SAI envisions a future where machines could outthink us in every conceivable way. The implications of such intelligence are profound and multifaceted, sparking intense debate around its ethical constructs, potential risks, and how it could reshape our world. However, SAI also promises groundbreaking advancements in technology and society.

At the heart of advanced AI lies the promise of augmenting human potential and opening doors to untapped possibilities. With AGI, the partnership between humans and machines can enhance decision-making and creativity, propelling industries forward into a new era of efficiency and innovation. With the advent of SAI, humanity could witness the dawning of an age where intelligence transcends human limitations, offering insights and strategies beyond our current comprehension. The path to advanced AI is not merely an extension of our technological progress; it reflects our ambition to redefine what is possible. As we stand on the cusp of these advancements, we anticipate a future where AI serves as a beacon for human potential, heralding an epoch of unparalleled discovery and progress.

Now, Let's Talk About Generative AI and LLM Libraries

GenAI stands as a revolutionary force within the field of AI, pushing the boundaries of what machines can create and comprehend. This subset of AI is all about synthesizing new content, whether images, sounds, text, or even complex data structures, effectively mimicking the variety and nuance seen in human-generated data. It's a leap from the traditional use of AI for analysis and pattern recognition into creation and invention (see Figure 2.10).

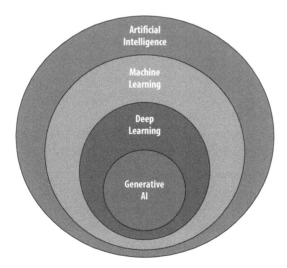

FIGURE 2.10 Hierarchy of AI technologies: GenAI within deep learning, ML, and the broader field of AI

At the heart of GenAI is the power of deep learning, which eschews the rigid frameworks of human-guided instruction and feature engineering that characterized earlier ML approaches. Instead, it harnesses the fluidity of neural networks, vast interconnected systems inspired by the human brain. These networks are composed of layers of nodes that hierarchically process data. Each layer identifies and extracts increasingly complex features as information passes through the network, building a sophisticated understanding of the data without explicit human direction. This process is similar to an artist first sketching the broad strokes of a scene and then gradually adding detail, color, and texture to bring the artwork to life.

The capabilities of GenAI are perhaps best exemplified in the impressive feats of large language models (LLMs). LLMs like OpenAI's GPT series have taken the world by storm, demonstrating uncanny abilities. These models are pretrained on a diverse corpus of text from the internet, allowing them to generate authentic and contextually relevant information. They've been designed not only to predict the next word in a sentence but also to grasp the underlying ideas, themes, and stylistic nuances that give the language depth and richness. As these generative models grow more sophisticated, they expand into other creative and functionality domains. GenAI's ability to generate new data points and creative outputs holds the promise of emulating human creativity and amplifying it. Through providing tools that can automate and enhance the creative process, GenAI offers a collaborative platform where human and machine intelligence can intersect to push the envelope of innovation.

Purpose of GenAI

The purpose of GenAI is threefold, as shown in Figure 2.11: autonomous content generation, advanced problem-solving, and creativity amplification.

1. **Autonomous content generation:** GenAI is designed to independently generate new content by identifying and leveraging recognized patterns within data. This enables the creation of original text, images, and videos that mimic the complexity of human-made examples.

2. **Enhanced problem-solving:** GenAI assists with complex problem-solving by producing a spectrum of possible solutions. It generates numerous potential outcomes, thus providing users with a broad range of options and pathways to explore.

3. **Creativity amplification:** GenAI boosts human creativity by producing unique outcomes, enabling users to discover and harness fresh ideas and possibilities. It acts as a catalyst, expanding the creative capacity of human endeavors.

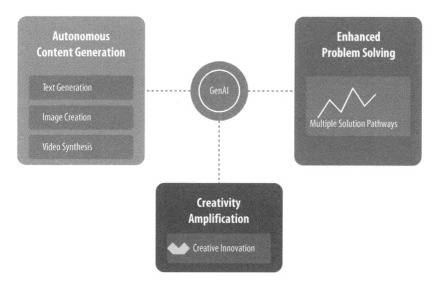

FIGURE 2.11 The purpose of GenAI

Beyond these key functions, the scope of GenAI extends into countless applications, each harnessing the potential to innovate and transform.

As a product manager navigating the dynamic and evolving terrain of GenAI, it's imperative to grasp the multifaceted applications this technology brings to the fore. GenAI is not just about leveraging cutting-edge tech to enhance product offerings; it's a beacon that guides the creation of substantial business value. Understanding the intricacies of this burgeoning field involves recognizing how generative models, distinct from their discriminative counterparts, operate on a foundational level. These models are ingeniously constructed on the transformative architecture known as *transformers*, which serve as the backbone for a variety of innovations in AI.

Delving into the generative models, it's vital to discern how they differ fundamentally from discriminative models. Although discriminative models excel at identifying distinctions and categorizing data, generative models are adept at creating new data instances that mimic the training data, hence generating novel content. This distinction underscores a broader understanding of AI's potential applications, from text and image generation to more complex data synthesis, all powered by the underlying principles of transformer architecture.

Traditional AI vs. Generative AI

Understanding the distinction between traditional AI and GenAI is essential for AI product managers when exploring AI use cases and emerging technical concepts. These two approaches offer different capabilities and applications, each playing a unique role in the AI landscape. Let's delve into a comparative discussion based on the characteristics outlined in Table 2.3.

Characteristic	Traditional AI	Generative AI
Focus	Structured data	Patterns in data, generation
Capabilities	Predict, analyze	Create, adapt
Technology	Simple algorithms	Deep learning, neural networks, transformers
Applications	Optimization	Innovation (images, text, etc.)

Table 2.3 Core differences between traditional AI and GenAI, providing AI product creators with a framework to understand focus, capabilities, technology, and applications as they explore emerging AI and ML concepts

Focus: Structured and Unstructured Data vs. Patterns in Data, Context, and Generation Traditional AI primarily focuses on structured and unstructured data. It is designed to analyze existing data, whether neatly organized in databases (structured) or found in formats like text and images (unstructured). Traditional AI systems excel at making sense of this data, extracting valuable insights, and making predictions based on historical trends. In contrast, GenAI goes a step further by identifying patterns in data and generating new content based on these patterns. This approach is about understanding existing data and creating new data that mirrors the patterns and structures found in the training data. GenAI can generate text, graphics, and other types of information, making it an effective tool for innovation and creativity.

Capabilities: Predict and Analyze vs. Create and Adapt Traditional AI systems are built to predict and analyze. They excel at forecasting future events based on past data and analyzing current datasets to extract actionable insights. For example, traditional AI models can predict customer churn, analyze market trends, or forecast sales, providing businesses with the information needed to make informed decisions. On the other hand, GenAI is designed to create and adapt. It can generate new content that did not previously exist, such as writing new articles, composing music, or creating realistic images. Additionally, GenAI systems are highly adaptable, capable of adjusting to new inputs and generating outputs that align with evolving requirements and contexts.

Technology: Simple Algorithms vs. Deep Learning, Neural Networks, and Transformers Traditional AI often relies on simpler algorithms that are well-understood and have been in use for decades. These include techniques like linear regression, decision trees, and support vector machines. Although these algorithms are powerful and effective for many applications, they are typically less complex than the deep learning models used in GenAI. GenAI, however, leverages advanced technologies such as deep learning, neural networks, and transformers. These models can learn complicated patterns and relationships from data. Deep learning models, for example, are composed of numerous layers that can capture intricate features, making them ideal for tasks requiring high degrees of abstraction and creativity, such as image and word creation.

Applications: Prediction vs. Creation Traditional AI applications are primarily focused on prediction. These systems forecast outcomes, optimize processes, and improve decision-making. For instance, traditional AI is widely used in finance to predict stock prices, healthcare to diagnose diseases, and marketing to personalize customer experiences.

In comparison, GenAI is focused on creation. It can generate new content, innovate designs, and enhance creativity. Applications of GenAI include creating artwork, writing stories, designing products, and even generating synthetic data for training other AI models. This ability to create opens up new entertainment, design, and research possibilities.

Real-World AI: Bridging Theory and Practice

Now, let's transition from theoretical frameworks to the tangible impact of AI, exploring how abstract concepts materialize in practical applications.

Image Recognition for Quality Control

In the competitive manufacturing arena, where the margin for error is increasingly slim, a notable company confronts escalating challenges in maintaining product quality. The advent of defective products undermines brand reputation and inflates costs. In response, the company looks toward AI, specifically image recognition technologies, as a beacon of innovation to revolutionize its quality control processes (see Figure 2.12).

▶ **Business problem:** Escalating quality control issues lead to more defective products.

▶ **Business goal:** Aim to reduce the volume of defective products by 30 percent in the following quarter.

▶ **AI solution:** Develop a sophisticated deep learning model that employs image recognition to inspect and meticulously identify defects during the manufacturing process.

▶ **Technical know-how required:** An AI product manager needs a strong understanding of deep learning, image recognition, and TensorFlow to guide model development and deployment, ensuring a tangible reduction in production errors.

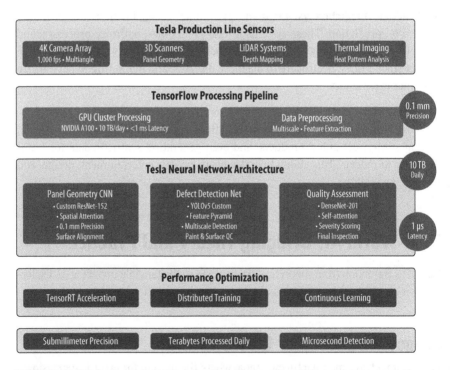

FIGURE 2.12 Tesla's advanced manufacturing AI architecture: from high-speed sensor arrays through neural networks to microsecond-level defect detection in real-time production

AI product managers at Tesla blend deep technical expertise with practical implementation. Their mastery spans TensorFlow deployment, computer vision algorithms, and real-time processing systems. These specialists work with data science teams to fine-tune neural networks to detect submillimeter defects at production speeds—from analyzing complex panel geometries to processing multicamera image feeds.

The impact? Highly optimized AI models that process terabytes of visual data daily, delivering microsecond-level defect detection accuracy. This technical precision transforms manufacturing quality control, proving that sophisticated AI architecture can solve real-world industrial challenges at scale.

Data Augmentation for Small Datasets

A healthcare company striving to leverage AI for diagnostic purposes faces a significant hurdle: a limited dataset of medical images, which constrains the training and eventual effectiveness of its ML models. Recognizing the critical need to enhance its dataset for the advancement of medical diagnostics, the company turns to the innovative solution of data augmentation through generative models, aiming to improve model performance substantially and, by extension, patient outcomes. Figure 2.13 illustrates this system's end-to-end architecture, providing AI product managers with a crucial blueprint that bridges technical implementation and business requirements. The architecture maps the complete workflow from data ingestion through GAN-based generation to clinical validation while highlighting key performance indicators, regulatory checkpoints, and quality metrics that product managers must monitor for successful deployment.

▶ **Business problem:** The restrictive size of the medical image dataset limits the training efficacy of ML models.

▶ **Business goal:** To expand the dataset, thereby boosting the model's accuracy and overall performance.

▶ **AI solution:** A generative model, notably a GAN, is applied to augment the dataset with synthetic yet realistic medical images.

▶ **Technical know-how required:** The AI product creator is expected to have an understanding of GenAI and GANs, complemented by proficiency with data labeling tools for annotating these enhanced images, promoting superior training results.

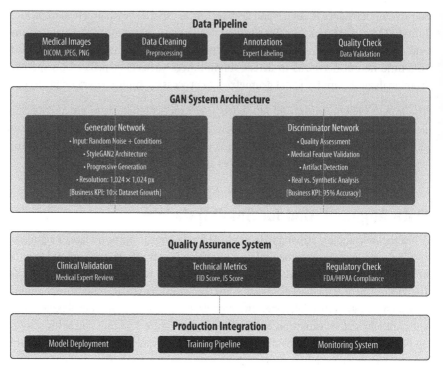

FIGURE 2.13 End-to-End medical GAN system: bridging technical implementation with product management insights

Predictive Maintenance in the Energy Sector

Facing the dual challenges of maintaining operational efficiency and minimizing downtime, a leading operator in the renewable energy sector, specifically wind farms, seeks innovative solutions. Unpredictable turbine failures result in lost productivity and escalating maintenance costs. The operator, therefore, explores the potential of AI, particularly ML models, to forecast these failures and implement predictive maintenance, aiming to transform their operational paradigm.

▶ **Business problem:** Unexpected turbine failures leading to increased downtime and escalated maintenance costs.

▶ **Business goal:** Implement predictive maintenance to foresee and mitigate potential failures, targeting a 20 percent increase in turbine uptime.

▶ **AI solution:** Crafting an ML model designed to analyze sensor data from turbines for early detection of potential failures, facilitating preemptive maintenance actions.

▶ **Technical know-how required:** Expertise in ML algorithms for time-series data analysis, leveraging platforms like Amazon SageMaker for comprehensive model training and deployment.

AI-Driven Customer Service Chatbots (Conversational AI)

Figure 2.14 illustrates an example of the architecture of this system. A retail behemoth is faced with the challenge of scaling its customer service to meet the growing

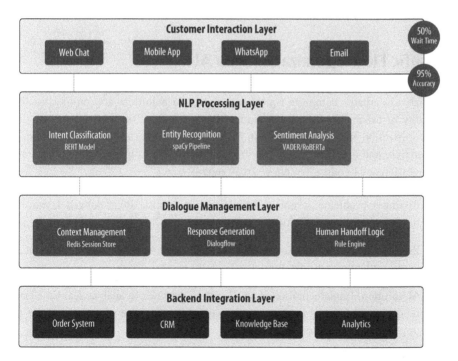

FIGURE 2.14 Multilayer AI chatbot architecture: from customer query to intelligent response through NLP processing and enterprise system integration

demand without compromising response times or quality. Lengthy wait times and inefficient service could tarnish customer satisfaction and loyalty. In pursuit of a solution, the company turns to AI, specifically the development of chatbots powered by NLP, to revolutionize customer service by providing immediate, accurate responses to customer inquiries.

▶ **Business problem:** Increasing customer service inquiries resulting in longer wait times and diminished customer satisfaction.

▶ **Business goal:** Reduce customer wait times by half and enhance service efficiency.

▶ **AI solution:** Introduction of AI-powered chatbots that utilize advanced NLP to comprehend and address customer inquiries instantly.

▶ **Technical know-how required:** A strong command of NLP and chatbot development, focusing on libraries such as NLTK and spaCy and platforms like Google's Dialogflow to create intuitive and responsive bots.

Traffic Flow Optimization with AI

Urban centers globally grapple with the perennial challenge of traffic congestion, which exacerbates commute times, contributes to pollution, and diminishes the quality of urban life. In collaboration with a technology firm, an innovative city administration embarks on a mission to tackle this issue head-on. By harnessing AI to analyze and optimize traffic flow in real time, they aim to significantly alleviate congestion and herald a new era of urban mobility.

▶ **Business problem:** Severe traffic congestion leading to prolonged commute times and increased pollution.

▶ **Business goal:** Enhance urban mobility and alleviate congestion through intelligent traffic flow optimization.

▶ **AI solution:** Implementation of an AI system designed to analyze real-time traffic data, adjust signal timings, and provide dynamic route recommendations to improve overall traffic flow.

▶ **Technical know-how required:** Proficiency in AI for real-time data processing and analytics, focusing on developing applications capable of efficiently handling geospatial data using technologies like TensorFlow for predictive modeling and cloud platforms for scalable deployment solutions.

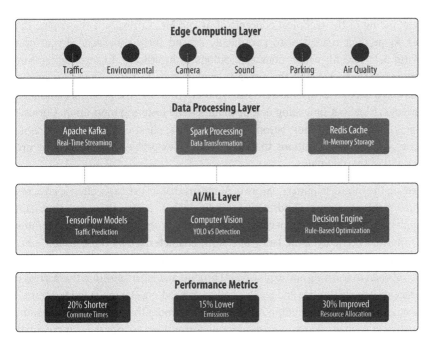

FIGURE 2.15 Barcelona's TensorFlow-powered urban intelligence system: from IoT sensors to real-time traffic control

As shown in Figure 2.15, Barcelona's transformation through AI exemplifies how cities can tackle urban challenges with smart technology. Through a partnership with Cisco, the city implemented an AI-driven traffic management system that harnessed Internet of Things (IoT) sensor data for intelligent traffic control. The AI product manager's expertise in TensorFlow modeling and cloud infrastructure proved crucial for system scalability and performance. The results were compelling: 20 percent shorter commute times and 15 percent lower emissions. This case study demonstrates how technical knowledge combined with cross-functional collaboration can transform AI potential into measurable urban improvements. As later chapters will explore, success in AI implementation requires both deep technical understanding and effective partnership with data science teams.

Embracing Curiosity to Drive AI Innovation and Mastery

The second step toward the goal of successful AI product management, curiosity to learn AI use cases and emerging technical ML concepts, involves a foundational understanding of the technical concepts of AI and ML. Curiosity is the engine that drives AI product managers to continually expand their knowledge. In an ever-evolving field like AI, which finds applications in healthcare, finance, agriculture, entertainment, and beyond, the desire to explore how AI technologies are applied across these sectors is invaluable. This exploration is not just about accumulating knowledge; it's about unlocking new possibilities and fostering innovation. Curiosity compels individuals to look beyond conventional applications of AI, encouraging them to devise novel solutions that address complex problems or streamline processes within their domains.

Moreover, the interdisciplinary nature of AI means that its use cases often span across multiple fields. A curious mindset allows individuals to bridge these domains, gaining diverse insights and perspectives that catalyze cross-disciplinary collaboration and innovation. The dynamic landscape of AI, characterized by the constant emergence of new use cases, demands adaptability—an attribute that curiosity nurtures. By being open to learning and exploring, AI product managers position themselves to embrace new opportunities and tackle challenges head-on, staying at the forefront of AI advancements. Understanding AI use cases does more than enhance professional competency; it opens doors to new career opportunities. As industries increasingly seek professionals versed in AI, curiosity and knowledge in this area become differentiators in the job market, paving the way for career growth and development. Curiosity about AI also prompts individuals to consider the broader implications of AI technologies, including ethical, fairness, and transparency issues. Engaging in these critical discussions contributes to the responsible development and deployment of AI, ensuring that technological advancements benefit society as a whole.

Therefore, embodying curiosity as the second step to successful AI product creation is fundamental for AI product managers. It equips them with the insight to make informed decisions, guiding the development and deployment of AI solutions that not only address business challenges but also achieve significant business goals. In embracing curiosity, AI product managers unlock the full potential of AI, navigating the path to mastery with a keen eye on the future and a commitment to innovation.

Chapter 3

Experimentation Mindset and Room in the Roadmap to Innovate

In this chapter, we will explore the pivotal role of experimentation within artificial intelligence (AI) product management. We will begin by understanding the essence of an experimentation mindset, which is crucial for fostering innovation and adaptability in the rapidly evolving field of AI. Next, we'll identify the key aspects of an experimentation mindset, exploring how these principles can be effectively implemented to drive project success. We'll then examine how experimentation in AI projects is applied, discussing methodologies and techniques that encourage creativity and discovery. Following this, we will discuss integrating experimentation into the AI product roadmap, outlining strategies to embed innovative processes into the life cycle of AI projects. Finally, through real-world case studies, we will illustrate the tangible impacts of embracing an experimentation mindset, demonstrating its value in solving complex challenges and achieving breakthrough results.

> AI initiatives differ fundamentally from traditional software development, as they cannot guarantee specific accuracy levels in the initial model implementation. Instead, product teams must prioritize ongoing experimentation within their roadmaps, developing plans based on observed outcomes to enhance model effectiveness. This approach involves embracing continuous learning and integrating small-scale experiments into daily workflows, ensuring adaptive progress and iterative improvements.

The Experimentation Mindset

An explorer venturing into uncharted territory— that's essentially what it means to be an AI product manager today. Just as explorers need a special mindset to navigate unknown lands, AI product managers need an experimental mindset to navigate the vast landscape of AI (see Figure 3.1). But what does having an "experimentation" mindset really mean? It means understanding AI's technical capabilities and how they can be applied innovatively to solve real-world problems, much like a master chef understanding both ingredients and cooking techniques to create extraordinary dishes. At its core, having an experimentation mindset means adopting an approach and attitude toward problem-solving and decision-making that prioritizes learning, adaptation, and, crucially, the willingness to embrace uncertainty. It is about being open to exploring new ideas and recognizing that the path to innovation often requires venturing into uncharted territory. This mindset understands that breakthroughs frequently emerge from stepping beyond the bounds of conventional thinking and being receptive to novel concepts and unconventional approaches.

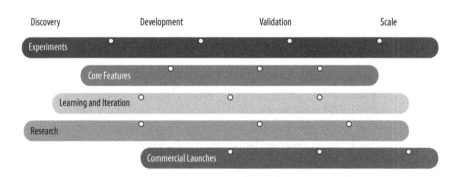

FIGURE 3.1 AI product creation roadmap: from research to launch

An experimentation mindset in AI product management translates to a proactive stance toward problem-solving and decision-making, built on the premise of trial and error, guided by informed hypotheses. It's a recognition that in the journey of developing AI-driven solutions, the paths to success are often not linear but require a willingness to venture into the unknown, to test and iterate. This approach is crucial, for AI projects are characterized by their inherent uncertainties—data variability, model behavior, or the impact of external factors on predictive accuracies. Adopting such a mindset is both a strategic choice and a necessary shift in perspective that aligns with the nature of AI itself. It acknowledges that the complexity of AI problems often precludes straightforward solutions, demanding instead a readiness to explore diverse approaches, to learn rapidly from each attempt, and to adapt strategies in response to new insights and outcomes.

The importance of an experimentation mindset extends beyond the technical aspects of AI development; it fosters an organizational culture that values innovation and continuous improvement. It encourages teams to approach challenges carefully, creating a conducive environment for groundbreaking discoveries and advancements. In essence, the experimentation mindset empowers AI product managers and their teams to confidently navigate the uncertainties of AI projects. It equips them with the resilience to face setbacks as learning opportunities, the agility to pivot based on evidence, and the vision to see beyond immediate challenges. It opens up a world of potential for innovation and impact, inspiring them to push the boundaries of what is possible in AI.

Key Aspects of an Experimentation Mindset

Adopting an experimentation mindset in AI product management is grounded in several key aspects that define the overall approach. Each element plays a vital role in navigating the complex, uncertain terrain of AI and ML projects, fostering a culture of innovation and continuous learning. Here are the critical facets of an experimentation mindset:

▶ **Openness to new ideas:** Central to the experimentation mindset is the willingness to consider and explore new, potentially unconventional ideas. This openness is what allows AI product managers to envision and pursue breakthrough innovations, recognizing that transformative solutions often emerge from thinking outside traditional boundaries.

▶ **Embracing failure as a learning opportunity:** An integral part of experimentation is understanding that not every attempt will lead to success. However, within this mindset, failure is not a setback but a valuable source of information. It provides unique insights essential for refining strategies and improving outcomes, cultivating a culture where setbacks are seen as crucial steps in the learning process.

▶ **Iterative approach:** Embodying an experimentation mindset means preferring an iterative process over a one-shot attempt. This approach involves making small, incremental changes and evaluating their impact, allowing for continuous refinement and adjustment based on real-world feedback and outcomes.

▶ **Data-driven decision-making:** At its core, an experimentation mindset is deeply rooted in data and evidence. It prioritizes data collection, analysis, and use to inform decisions, ensuring that experimentation is guided by concrete information rather than mere speculation.

▶ **Hypothesis testing:** Experimentation is often structured around formulating and testing hypotheses. This systematic method allows AI product managers to make educated guesses about potential solutions and design experiments to validate these hypotheses, facilitating structured learning and insight gathering.

▶ **Curiosity and continuous learning:** A hallmark of the experimentation mindset is relentless curiosity and a commitment to lifelong learning. It involves actively seeking new knowledge, insights, and feedback to expand your understanding and improve decision-making capabilities constantly.

▶ **Adaptability:** Flexibility and the ability to pivot are crucial in an experimentation mindset. This adaptability allows for swift changes in strategy or direction when data and feedback indicate a need for adjustment, ensuring that AI initiatives remain responsive and relevant.

▶ **Tolerance for ambiguity:** Comfort with uncertainty and ambiguity is necessary for those adopting an experimentation mindset. Recognizing that some experiments may not yield immediate or definitive results is essential for maintaining momentum and focus on long-term learning and improvement.

▶ **Continuous improvement:** With an experimentation mindset, the pursuit of perfection is replaced by the pursuit of progression. There's a continuous drive to refine and enhance processes, products, or strategies, leveraging experimentation as a means to achieve ongoing optimization.

▶ **Risk management:** Although experimentation involves taking risks, those with this mindset also understand the importance of managing these risks thoughtfully. This involves setting clear boundaries and being mindful of the potential implications of experimental actions.

▶ **Collaboration:** Finally, an experimentation mindset thrives in environments that encourage collaboration and the sharing of diverse perspectives. It recognizes that collective exploration can lead to richer insights and more innovative solutions.

Together, these aspects form the backbone of an experimentation mindset, guiding AI product managers in their quest to navigate the uncertainties of AI development and leverage experimentation as a powerful tool for innovation and growth.

Experimentation in AI Projects

Experimentation plays a very big role in the development and refinement of AI projects. This process is characterized by systematically exploring various methodologies, models, and configurations to optimize performance and achieve the desired outcomes. Here's a closer examination of how experimentation is done and how it directly influences AI project success:

1. **Trying different approaches:** The journey of innovation in AI is paved with experimentation and the understanding that there is often no one-size-fits-all solution. The diversity of AI applications, from natural language processing (NLP) to computer vision and reinforcement learning, necessitates a broad exploration of methodologies. Each problem or task within the vast spectrum of AI may benefit from a distinct approach, underscoring the importance of being open to trying different models, data processing techniques, and feature engineering methods. This willingness to explore various avenues is crucial for identifying the most effective solution tailored to the unique requirements of each project.

AI models come with an array of hyperparameters that when finely tuned can significantly enhance their performance on specific tasks. Experimenting with these hyperparameters—adjusting them to find the optimal settings—is a critical step in the optimization process. Through such detailed experimentation, you may discover new methods or combinations of techniques, potentially overlooked or underutilized yet highly effective for the problem at hand.

This pursuit of optimization through experimentation seamlessly leads to a broader strategy for tackling complex, multifaceted problems—ones that require a refined understanding that moves beyond generic solutions. Engaging in the trial of various approaches allows AI product managers and their teams to uncover deeper insights into the subtleties and trade-offs characteristic of complex domains. This comparative analysis and evaluation of different AI methodologies illuminate the most suitable, efficient, or accurate approaches for specific use cases. Such a process enriches the understanding of the problem space itself, guiding teams toward more informed decision-making and innovative solutions.

Moreover, given AI's interdisciplinary nature, exploring different approaches encourages cross-disciplinary learning and innovation. It allows teams to borrow and apply techniques from one domain to another, leveraging insights across fields to fuel creativity and problem-solving. This cross-pollination of ideas is a testament to AI's transformative potential, enabling solutions as diverse as the challenges they aim to address.

When embarking on this exploratory journey, several considerations are paramount to ensure the effectiveness and relevance of experimentation:

▶ **Clearly define objectives:** Having clear objectives and metrics for each approach tested is essential. This clarity allows for evaluating their effectiveness and facilitates informed decision-making.

▶ **Resource constraints:** The availability of computational resources, data, and time must be carefully considered. Some approaches may demand more in terms of computation or data volume, impacting feasibility and scalability.

▶ **Performance metrics:** Choosing appropriate performance metrics is critical. These metrics, whether accuracy, precision, recall, F1-score, or mean squared error, should align with the project's goals and provide a meaningful assessment of each approach's impact.

▶ **Documentation and reproducibility:** Keeping detailed records of the experiments, including hyperparameters used, preprocessing steps, and any modifications, ensures that experiments are reproducible and that insights gained are actionable and shareable.

▶ **Ethical and regulatory considerations:** Ethical and regulatory considerations must guide the experimentation process. This is especially pertinent in domains such as healthcare or finance, ensuring that privacy, fairness, and compliance are upheld.

▶ **Collaboration and knowledge sharing:** As stated earlier, experimentation thrives in collaborative environments. Engaging with experts across different areas of AI can enhance outcomes, pooling collective knowledge to navigate the complexities of AI solutions more effectively.

2. **Learning from failures:** As previously highlighted, embracing failure as a pivotal learning opportunity is fundamental in the experimentation journey of AI projects. This concept bears repeating: not every experimental attempt will culminate in success, but each outcome serves as a rich source of insights. Failure, far from being an endpoint, is an invaluable informant that guides the iterative process of refining AI models and strategies.

In the AI landscape, where uncertainty is constant and the complexity of problems often defies straightforward solutions, the ability to learn from failures becomes a superpower. It transforms setbacks into stepping stones, illuminating the path toward optimization and innovation. This perspective is vital for AI product managers and their teams, as it encourages resilience and a proactive approach to problem-solving.

Acknowledging that setbacks are integral to the learning process fosters a culture of experimentation where risk-taking is encouraged, within bounds, and every result is mined for valuable lessons. It shifts the focus from avoiding failure to maximizing the learning derived from each attempt. This shift is crucial in an environment as dynamic and evolving as AI, where the lessons learned from what doesn't work often pave the way for groundbreaking solutions and breakthroughs.

3. **Continuous iteration:** Continuous iteration stands at the heart of AI experimentation, driving the refinement and enhancement of AI models. In an arena where technological advancements occur at a breakneck pace, the ability to iterate rapidly and effectively is indispensable. This iterative process embodies the principle of gradual improvement—each cycle of development, testing, and feedback sharpens the model's accuracy, usability, and relevance. As AI systems interact with real-world data, their capacity to learn and adapt hinges on this constant iteration cycle, making it possible to fine-tune algorithms in response to new insights and evolving challenges.

The significance of continuous iteration extends beyond technical adjustments; it fosters a dynamic environment where learning is ongoing and improvement is perpetual. By embedding iteration into the experimentation process, AI product managers ensure that AI projects remain agile and aligned with the latest developments and user needs. This approach underscores the commitment to leveraging AI not as a static solution but as a growing, evolving entity capable of meeting the complexities of modern problems.

Integrating Experimentation into the AI Product Roadmap

The Nonlinear Roadmap

For product managers, the roadmap in an AI context is less a strict itinerary and more a compass direction (see Figure 3.1). It provides a sense of direction but must allow for diversions and discoveries along the way. A conventional product roadmap might have clear milestones and deliverables; an AI roadmap, by contrast, should be built with flexibility to accommodate the iterative cycles of hypothesis, experimentation, and learning.

The product roadmap is a strategic document that outlines the product's vision, direction, and progress over time, as shown in Figure 3.2. It is a visual, high-level guide communicating the product's direction, milestones, and features to various stakeholders, including the development team, executives, investors, and customers. This document is vital for ensuring that all stakeholders are aligned with the product's strategic goals and priorities, and it helps reduce misunderstandings and misalignments within the organization:

▶ It provides a clear and visual representation of the product's future, making it easier for teams to understand and prioritize their work.

▶ It also helps communicate with external stakeholders, such as customers and partners.

▶ It assists in prioritizing features, enhancements, and bug fixes, allowing the team to focus on the most important and valuable work that aligns with the product's goals.

▶ Roadmaps are a strategic tool for product managers. They help product managers plan and sequence features and improvements, taking into account market trends, competition, and customer feedback.

▶ Furthermore, by outlining the expected timeline for different features or releases, a roadmap effectively helps allocate resources, such as engineering, design, and testing.

▶ Roadmaps can help identify potential risks or bottlenecks in the development process. For example, if a critical feature is scheduled for late in the development cycle, it may risk the project's success.

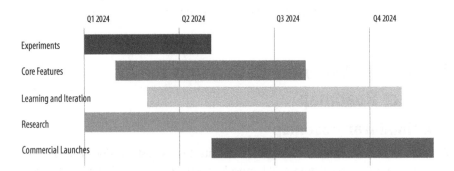

FIGURE 3.2 AI product experimentation timeline: progressing from initial experiments to full commercial launches

▶ Public-facing roadmaps or release notes help manage customer expectations. When customers have insight into what features are in development, it can reduce frustration and improve customer satisfaction.

▶ It can also serve as a tool for collecting feedback and suggestions from internal and external stakeholders.

▶ Product managers can engage with customers and teams to refine the product strategy.

▶ Beyond immediate releases, a product roadmap can illustrate the long-term vision for a product or product line. This is important for motivating the team and stakeholders and aligning with the broader goals.

▶ Plus, having a well-structured roadmap can give your product a competitive advantage. It lets you plan and anticipate market trends, customer needs, and competitive moves.

▶ As development progresses, the roadmap provides a framework for measuring progress and ensuring the product remains on track to meet its goals.

However, in the context of AI, it is essential to create room in the roadmap for innovation, experimentation, and iteration. Experimentation, in particular, requires flexibility in the roadmap to accommodate

1. **Prioritizing experiments:** Continually prioritizing experiments in the roadmap is crucial for improving the model. This may involve trying different models, data processing techniques, or feature engineering methods.

2. **Allocating resources for innovation:** Allocating resources, both time and personnel, for innovation is essential for staying competitive in the fast-paced world of AI. Effective resource allocation can drive innovation, foster creativity, and help organizations harness the transformative power of AI. Areas of focus should include hiring skilled data scientists, investing in data infrastructure, and ensuring sufficient computational resources.

Start with a well-defined innovation strategy that aligns with your overall business objectives. What are your innovation goals in AI? Are you looking to develop new products, improve existing processes, or explore cutting-edge AI technologies? Attract and retain top AI talent. Innovation requires skilled data scientists, machine learning engineers, AI researchers, and domain experts to allocate resources to hire and train the right professionals.

Data is the lifeblood of AI; invest in data infrastructure, data storage, data quality, and data management to ensure that you have a solid foundation for AI innovation. AI models, especially deep learning models, often require significant computational resources. Allocate resources for high-performance computing infrastructure, including GPUs and TPUs, to support AI development. It is important to dedicate a portion of your budget to research and development efforts in AI. This can involve exploring new algorithms, testing innovative techniques, and staying abreast of the latest research in the field.

In addition, collaborate with academic institutions, start-ups, and other organizations in the AI ecosystem: partnerships can bring fresh perspectives, access to talent, and shared resources for innovation. You should also allocate resources for rapid prototyping and experimentation and encourage teams to explore new AI ideas through proof-of-concept projects and pilots. Consider establishing dedicated innovation labs or centers focused on AI, as these spaces can foster creativity and provide a supportive environment for experimentation.

Always protect your AI innovations by allocating resources for patent applications and IP management; this is really important as it can safeguard your competitive advantage. You can implement key performance indicators (KPIs) and metrics to measure the impact of your AI innovation efforts. Regularly assess the return on investment (ROI) to ensure effective resource allocation.

Ensure that your AI innovations are scalable by allocating resources for infrastructure that can handle growth and increased demand as your AI applications gain traction. Invest in ongoing education and training for your AI teams: AI is an evolving field, and continuous learning is essential for innovation. It is important to leverage open-source AI frameworks and libraries to reduce development costs. External resources like cloud services can also be cost-effective for AI development. And finally, you must understand that not all AI innovations will succeed: allocate resources for risk management, and accept that some projects may not yield the expected results.

3. **Flexible planning:** The roadmap should be flexible enough to accommodate changes based on the experiments' results. This may involve revising the priorities, timelines, or resources allocated for different tasks, especially if a particular model or approach needs to be adjusted or replaced based on experimental outcomes.

The results of the experiments may sometimes necessitate changes in the plan. For example, if a particular model is not yielding the desired results, trying a different model or approach may be necessary. Planning on the fly involves being flexible and adaptive to changes based on the results obtained. In the case of such an event:

▶ **Revise the plan:** The plan may need to be revised based on the results of the experiments. This may involve changing the model, approach, or timeline.

▶ **Adapt to changes:** The world of AI is fast-paced and ever-evolving. Adapting to changes, whether new technologies, tools, or approaches, is crucial for staying competitive.

▶ **Continuous improvement:** The work does not end once the model is deployed. Continuous monitoring of the model's performance and ongoing experimentation and iteration are necessary to maintain and improve its effectiveness.

Managing Expectations   One of the most critical roles for a product manager in an AI-driven project is setting and managing stakeholder expectations. Stakeholders need to understand that the path to a successful AI product is not guaranteed and that the timeline may be unpredictable. Product managers should educate stakeholders on the experimental nature of AI product development and the need for a flexible approach.

Collaboration with Data Science Teams   To effectively manage an AI product roadmap, product managers must work in close collaboration with data scientists and understand the complexities of the data science workflow. This includes appreciating the nuances of data preparation, model selection, training, evaluation, and reiteration. By understanding these elements, product managers can better gauge the time and resources required for each stage of product development.

Real-World Case Studies

The following case studies showcase how diverse industries leverage an experimentation mindset to solve complex business problems with AI:

Enhancing E-Commerce with AI-Driven Recommendations

In the competitive e-commerce sector, personalization can dramatically enhance customer engagement and sales. An e-commerce company recognized the need to improve its recommendation system to better cater to individual preferences, aiming to boost overall sales performance and customer satisfaction.

▶ **Business problem:** The company's existing recommendation system was not effectively driving sales.

▶ **Business goal:** Increase sales by 10 percent in the next quarter.

▶ **AI solution:** Develop a recommendation system using collaborative filtering.

▶ **Experimentation mindset:** The AI product manager implemented various models and approaches, learning from each iteration's results to refine the system continually. The product roadmap was adapted to allow room for ongoing experimentation and optimization based on insights gained.

Advanced Fraud Detection in Finance

As financial transactions move increasingly online, the need for robust fraud detection systems becomes more critical. A financial institution facing rising fraudulent transactions sought to harness advanced AI to enhance its detection capabilities, aiming to safeguard customer assets more effectively.

▶ **Business problem:** Increasing incidents of fraudulent transactions.

▶ **Business goal:** Reduce fraudulent transactions by 20 percent within the next quarter.

▶ **AI solution:** Implement a fraud detection model using anomaly detection techniques.

▶ **Experimentation mindset:** The AI product manager experimented with different models, feature engineering methods, and data processing techniques, iteratively improving the model's effectiveness. Innovations were incorporated into the roadmap, allowing the system to evolve based on the results obtained.

Optimizing Supply Chain Logistics

A manufacturing company faced significant supply chain inefficiencies, resulting in higher operational costs and delivery delays (see Figure 3.3). Seeking to streamline operations, the company turned to AI to optimize logistics and enhance supply chain management. With an experimentation mindset, the product manager applied this AI-driven framework to drive iterative improvements, reducing costs and improving delivery timelines.

▶ **Business problem:** Inefficiencies in the supply chain leading to increased costs and delayed deliveries.

▶ **Business goal:** Improve supply chain efficiency by 15 percent.

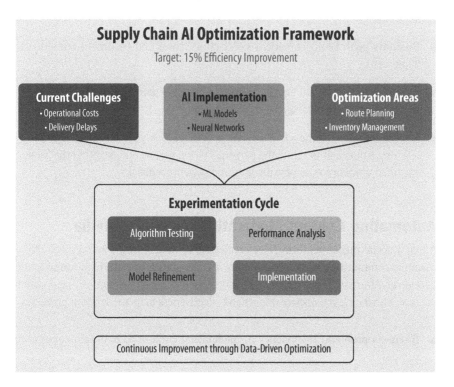

FIGURE 3.3 AI-powered supply chain optimization: a framework for efficiency and continuous improvement through data-driven experimentation

▶ **AI solution:** Deploy a machine learning model to optimize routing and inventory management.

▶ **Experimentation mindset:** Various algorithms, including neural networks and simulation models, were trialed to determine the best solution for specific logistical challenges, with continuous feedback loops refining the approach.

Personalizing Patient Care in Healthcare

To enhance patient care, a healthcare provider aimed to utilize AI to develop more personalized treatment plans based on individual health data. This initiative was driven by the goal to improve patient outcomes and increase patient engagement and satisfaction.

▶ **Business problem:** Need to improve patient outcomes through more personalized care.

▶ **Business goal:** Enhance patient satisfaction scores and treatment outcomes by 20 percent.

▶ **AI solution:** Implement an AI system that analyzes patient data to predict health risks and suggest personalized treatment plans.

▶ **Experimentation mindset:** Different predictive analytics models were tested, learning from each to refine the personalization engine and adapting the product roadmap to incorporate new insights and patient feedback.

Automating Content Moderation for Social Media

A major social media platform faced challenges in moderating content efficiently to maintain community standards (see Figure 3.4). To address this, the platform sought to develop an AI-driven tool to automate the detection and management of inappropriate content, enhancing the responsiveness and effectiveness of its moderation processes.

▶ **Business problem:** Inefficiency in moderating content to maintain community standards.

▶ **Business goal:** Increase the accuracy of automated content moderation by 25 percent.

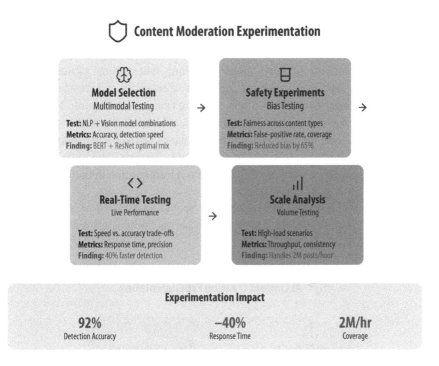

FIGURE 3.4 AI content moderation pipeline systematic experimentation from model testing to scaled deployment, showing safety metrics and performance impact

▶ **AI solution:** To detect inappropriate content, develop an AI tool using generative AI/NLP and image recognition.

▶ **Experimentation mindset:** The A I product manager led experiments with different generative AI/NLP models and image recognition techniques, iterating based on performance metrics to continually enhance the tool's accuracy.

Revolutionizing Content Creation: A Case Study in Marketing Innovation with Generative AI

In an era where marketing teams struggle with content creation bottlenecks, this case study explores how an AI product manager employs an experimentation mindset to transform digital content production through generative AI. Faced with excessive resource consumption and delayed campaigns, the team sets an ambitious goal to automate 30 percent of content creation within six months. The approach combines systematic platform testing, metric-driven validation, and careful attention to legal and ethical considerations.

Through structured experimentation—including split testing against human-created content and quantitative measurement of creativity and engagement—the AI product manager demonstrates how building experimentation into the product roadmap can drive meaningful automation while maintaining quality and trust (see Figure 3.5). This case illuminates the delicate balance between leveraging AI innovation and ensuring human oversight in content creation, providing valuable insights for product managers navigating similar digital transformation initiatives.

▶ **Business problem:** The marketing team spends excessive time and resources creating a high volume of digital content across multiple channels, leading to delayed campaigns and increased costs.

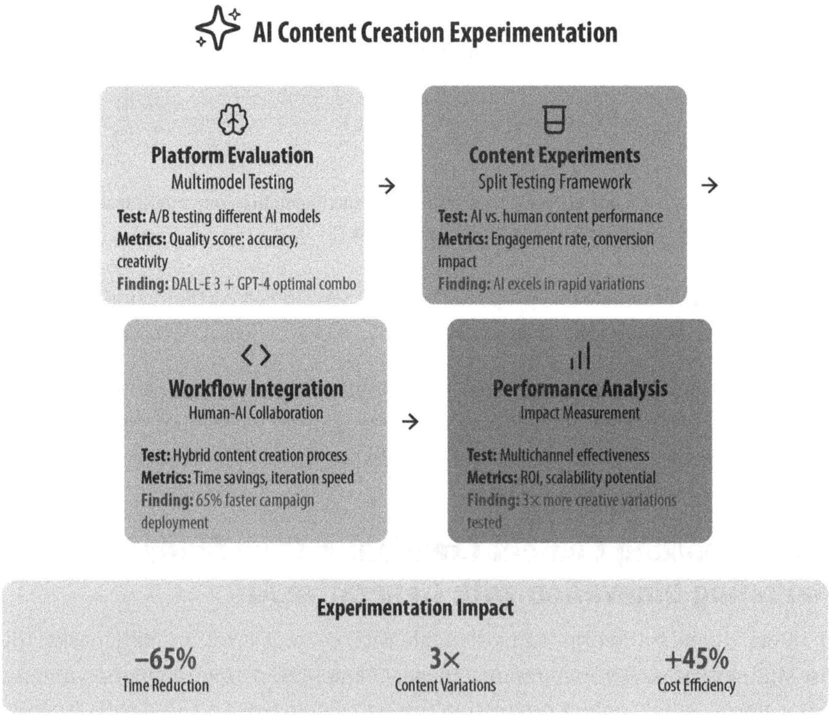

✨ AI Content Creation Experimentation

Platform Evaluation
Multimodel Testing

Test: A/B testing different AI models
Metrics: Quality score: accuracy, creativity
Finding: DALL-E 3 + GPT-4 optimal combo

→

Content Experiments
Split Testing Framework

Test: AI vs. human content performance
Metrics: Engagement rate, conversion impact
Finding: AI excels in rapid variations

→

Workflow Integration
Human-AI Collaboration

Test: Hybrid content creation process
Metrics: Time savings, iteration speed
Finding: 65% faster campaign deployment

→

Performance Analysis
Impact Measurement

Test: Multichannel effectiveness
Metrics: ROI, scalability potential
Finding: 3× more creative variations tested

Experimentation Impact

−65%	3×	+45%
Time Reduction	Content Variations	Cost Efficiency

FIGURE 3.5 AI content creation experimentation framework systematic testing approach showing experimentation stages and measured impact on content production

▶ **Business goal:** To automate 30 percent of content creation within six months to speed up campaign deployment and reduce operational costs.

▶ **AI solution:** Implement a generative AI system that can produce initial drafts of both text and visual content, which can be further refined by human designers and copywriters.

▶ **Experimentation mindset:** The AI product manager pilots various generative AI platforms, measuring the efficiency and quality of generated content against human-made benchmarks:

  ▶ Develops a metric system to quantify the creativity and engagement of AI-generated content through consumer feedback and interaction rates

  ▶ Sets up a structured experimentation process where each content piece is split-tested against human-created content to iteratively train and improve the AI's output

  ▶ Works closely with the legal department to establish clear guidelines for AI-generated content and ensure adherence to copyright and trademark laws

  ▶ Establishes an ethical framework to ensure transparency about the use of AI in content creation to maintain consumer trust

Experimentation Mindset: The Foundation for AI Innovation

The third step to successful AI product creation, an experimentation mindset and room in the roadmap to innovate, is vital for cultivating a culture that thrives on flexibility, creativity, and continuous improvement. This tenet underscores the importance of being open to experimenting with different approaches, learning from failures, and continually iterating to refine the effectiveness of AI models. By embracing this mindset, an AI product manager can develop solutions that address immediate business challenges and pave the way for groundbreaking innovations.

Embracing an experimentation mindset involves a readiness to test various strategies and accept the fact that not all will succeed on the first try. This openness is crucial, as it allows AI product managers to uncover unique solutions and make informed adjustments to their strategies. It's about being agile, adapting to results in real time, and not being afraid to pivot when necessary. Such flexibility is essential in the fast-paced realm of AI, where new technologies and methodologies can quickly shift the landscape. Moreover, making room in the product roadmap for innovation is equally crucial. This strategic space allows for the exploration of creative ideas that may not have immediate applications but could potentially transform the market landscape. Balancing steady progress with the freedom to explore and experiment is key to fostering a dynamic and innovative product development environment.

Traditional AI vs. Generative AI

In AI product management, fostering an experimentation mindset is crucial for driving innovation and achieving breakthrough results. As we delve into this discussion, we must compare traditional AI and generative AI based on their characteristics to understand how each supports the experimentation process and innovation roadmap, as shown in Table 3.1.

Category	Traditional AI (old AI)	Generative AI (new AI)
Experimentation	Focused on refining existing approaches	Encourages exploration of new possibilities
Roadmap	Fixed; milestone-driven	Dynamic; adaptable with branching options
Risk tolerance	Low; prioritizes known outcomes	High; embraces uncertainty for breakthroughs
Change adaptability	Slow; struggles with disruptions	Fast; thrives in evolving environments
Creativity	Limited; focuses on optimization	High potential for innovative solutions

Table 3.1 Embracing generative AI: experimentation and flexibility redefining innovation

Experimentation: Refining Existing Approaches vs. Exploration of New Possibilities

Traditional AI typically focuses on refining existing approaches. This involves enhancing and optimizing known methods and algorithms to improve accuracy, efficiency, and performance. Traditional AI relies heavily on historical data and established techniques, making it ideal for scenarios that aim to improve on proven strategies incrementally. In contrast, generative AI is centered around exploring new possibilities. It pushes the boundaries of what AI can do by generating new content, designs, or previously unimaginable solutions. Generative AI's ability to create new data and patterns opens up vast avenues for innovation, allowing AI product managers to experiment with uncharted ideas and concepts.

Roadmap: Fixed; Milestone-Driven vs. Dynamic; Adaptable with Branching Options

Traditional AI projects often follow a fixed, milestone-driven roadmap. This approach ensures a structured path with clear objectives and checkpoints. Although this method provides a sense of security and predictability, it can sometimes limit flexibility and adaptability, which are crucial for dealing with the dynamic nature of AI development.

On the other hand, generative AI thrives on a dynamic and adaptable roadmap with branching options. This flexibility allows AI product managers to pivot and explore different directions based on experimental outcomes. A dynamic roadmap embraces the uncertainty inherent in innovative projects, making it possible to adjust plans in real time to capitalize on discoveries and opportunities.

Risk Tolerance: Low; Prioritizes Known Outcomes vs. High; Embraces Uncertainty for Breakthroughs

Traditional AI generally has a low-risk tolerance, prioritizing known outcomes and minimizing uncertainties. This cautious approach suits applications where reliability and consistency are paramount, such as financial forecasting or healthcare diagnostics. Conversely, generative AI embraces a high-risk tolerance, recognizing that uncertainty is a gateway to breakthroughs. By accepting and managing higher levels of risk, generative AI encourages bold experimentation and innovation. This approach is critical for developing new solutions and pushing the edges of AI's accomplishments, especially in creative fields such as art, music, and design.

Change Adaptability: Slow; Takes Time with Disruptions vs. Fast; Thrives in Evolving Environments

Traditional AI tends to be slower in adapting to changes. Integrating new data, retraining models, and adjusting to disruptions requires significant time and effort. This slower pace can be a drawback in rapidly evolving industries where agility is critical. In contrast, generative AI is designed to adapt quickly and thrive in evolving environments. Its flexibility and ability to generate new data make it highly responsive to change. This adaptability is crucial for product managers who must stay ahead of market trends and continuously innovate to meet emerging demands.

Creativity: Limited; Focuses on Optimization vs. High Potential for Innovative Solutions

Traditional AI focuses on optimization and improving existing processes. Although it is highly effective in enhancing performance and efficiency, its creativity is limited to the scope of its predefined tasks and historical data. Generative AI, however, offers a high potential for innovative solutions. Its creative capabilities extend beyond optimization to generate new ideas, designs, and content. This high level of creativity makes generative AI a powerful tool for innovation, enabling AI product managers to develop unique and groundbreaking products.

Crafting Success Through Experimentation and Innovation

The fusion of an experimentation mindset with flexible roadmap planning emerges as a fundamental requirement for successful AI product creation. As this chapter has demonstrated through practical case studies and detailed analysis, the most effective AI initiatives are those that systematically build innovation space into their roadmaps while embracing experimentation as a core development principle. This approach—whether applied to traditional AI optimization or cutting-edge generative AI applications—enables product managers to transform uncertainties into opportunities and setbacks into valuable insights. By deliberately creating room for exploration within structured development frameworks, organizations can maintain the delicate balance between systematic progress and innovative discovery. The result is not just better AI products, but a sustainable approach to innovation that adapts to emerging technologies while consistently delivering value. As the field continues to evolve, this combination of experimental thinking and flexible planning will remain essential for those seeking to create AI products that truly make an impact.

Part II

Implementation & Integration

Bridging Research and Reality in AI Development

Implementation & Integration

Bridging Research with Reality in AI Deployment

Chapter 4

Integrating the MDLC with the SDLC

To successfully build and deploy AI solutions, the model development life cycle (MDLC) must be integrated with the software development life cycle (SDLC), as represented visually in Figure 4.1. In the fast-evolving world of technology, AI models and software systems must work seamlessly together to deliver optimal results. The MDLC encompasses problem definition, data collection, feature engineering, model training, and evaluation. At the same time, the SDLC includes phases like requirement analysis, system design, implementation, testing, deployment, and maintenance. Integrating these life cycles ensures that AI models are technically sound and embedded within robust software frameworks that can support their deployment and ongoing operation.

FIGURE 4.1 Visual representation of the integration between the MDLC and the SDLC, illustrating how AI model development must be aligned with traditional software engineering practices for successful deployment of AI solutions

The need for this integration stems from the distinct but complementary nature of MDLC and SDLC. Whereas MDLC focuses on developing predictive models and algorithms, SDLC provides a structured approach to building and maintaining software applications. AI models might fail to meet business requirements or align with software system constraints without proper integration, leading to suboptimal performance or project failure. Therefore, aligning MDLC with SDLC involves coordinated efforts between data scientists, machine learning (ML) engineers, software developers, and other stakeholders.

Effective integration requires parallel execution of the MDLC and SDLC phases, ensuring that data preparation, model development, and software design are synchronized. This collaboration extends to testing and validation, where the AI model's performance and the software application's functionality are thoroughly evaluated. Moreover, deployment and monitoring must be conducted to maintain the performance and reliability of AI-enhanced software applications. By following best practices and addressing integration challenges proactively, organizations can leverage the full potential of AI technologies, ensuring that AI models are seamlessly incorporated into production environments and contribute to achieving business goals.

AI product managers play a crucial role in integrating the distinct mindsets of data scientists and software developers. Data scientists are driven by a research-oriented approach, delving into a realm of exploration, experimentation, and innovation. Their primary focus includes discovering new algorithms, extracting insights from data, and pushing the boundaries of what is possible with data science. In contrast, software developers prioritize implementation and operational excellence, concentrating on stability, scalability, and efficiency. They work to ensure that the innovative solutions created by data scientists can be effectively translated into robust, scalable, and efficient software products. Bridging the SDLC and the MDLC is not only about aligning processes but also about integrating these diverse mindsets. AI product managers ensure that the innovative capabilities of data science are harnessed and translated into practical, reliable, and scalable applications by fostering a collaborative environment where both exploration and implementation thrive, achieving both groundbreaking innovation and operational success.

Understanding the MDLC

The MDLC is a structured framework that guides the development of AI models from inception to deployment. For AI product managers, understanding the MDLC is essential to ensure that AI models are technically robust and aligned with business objectives. This understanding allows them to efficiently manage the integration of AI models into the larger software development process while ensuring that these models provide concrete commercial value.

The MDLC consists of several stages (see Figure 4.2):

▶ **Problem definition:** The first stage articulates the AI model's business problem. This stage sets the foundation for the project, ensuring that subsequent stages are focused and aligned with business needs. To connect technological goals with strategic business objectives, AI product managers collaborate with stakeholders to define the AI effort's scope, objectives, and success criteria.

▶ **Data collection and preparation:** High-quality data is the cornerstone of any successful AI model. This stage involves gathering relevant data from various sources, cleaning it to remove inconsistencies, and preprocessing it to make it suitable for model training. AI product managers ensure that the data is accurate, complete, and reflective of real-world scenarios, facilitating communication between data engineers and scientists.

▶ **Data exploration and analysis:** In this stage, data scientists explore the dataset to uncover insights and patterns. This exploratory phase is crucial for understanding

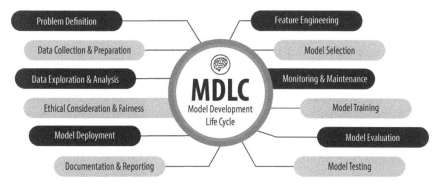

FIGURE 4.2 Key stages of the MDLC, illustrating the end-to-end process from problem definition to model deployment, monitoring, and maintenance

the underlying structure of the data and identifying any anomalies or trends. AI product managers oversee this process, ensuring that the insights gained guide the subsequent steps of feature engineering and model selection.

▶ **Feature engineering:** In this stage, relevant features are selected, transformed, or created from the raw data. Feature engineering directly influences the model's ability to learn and make accurate predictions. AI product managers work closely with data scientists to ensure that selected features align with the business problem and enhance model performance.

▶ **Model selection:** The appropriate AI model or algorithm is chosen based on the problem type and data characteristics. This decision is guided by the nature of the business problem and the specific requirements of the task. AI product managers facilitate this selection process by providing insights into business requirements and constraints.

▶ **Model training:** During this phase, the selected model learns about the relationships and patterns found in the data. Optimization techniques such as cross-validation and hyperparameter tuning refine the model. AI product managers monitor this process, ensuring the training meets defined success criteria and business objectives.

▶ **Model evaluation:** A separate validation dataset assesses the model's performance. Evaluation metrics like accuracy, precision, recall, and mean squared error are calculated. AI product managers ensure that the evaluation metrics align with business goals and that the model meets predefined success criteria.

▶ **Model testing:** The model is tested on a separate set to ensure its robustness and reliability. This step validates the model's ability to perform well on new, unseen data. AI product managers oversee this phase, ensuring that the model meets all performance and reliability standards before deployment.

▶ **Model deployment:** When the model is integrated into a production environment, it can make judgments or predictions in real time. Deployment involves creating APIs or embedding the model into software applications. AI product managers coordinate with software developers and IT teams to ensure a smooth deployment.

▶ **Monitoring and maintenance:** AI models require continuous monitoring to maintain performance over time. Monitoring involves tracking key performance metrics and detecting issues like model drift. Maintenance activities may include retraining the model with new data or updating features. AI product managers establish robust monitoring frameworks to ensure long-term success.

▶ **Ethical considerations and fairness:** Ensuring that the model is fair, unbiased, and complies with ethical standards is critical for maintaining trust and credibility. AI product managers integrate ethical considerations into every stage of the MDLC and ensure compliance with legal and regulatory requirements.

▶ **Documentation and reporting:** Comprehensive documentation of the model development process, including data sources, model parameters, and performance metrics, is essential for transparency and reproducibility. AI product managers ensure that documentation is maintained and accessible to all stakeholders.

Stages of SDLC

The SDLC helps create software applications methodically. It offers a disciplined framework to guarantee that software projects are finished on schedule, stay within budget, and meet the specified functionality and quality benchmarks. Understanding the SDLC is crucial for AI product managers as it allows them to effectively integrate AI models into software systems, ensuring seamless operation and alignment with business goals.

The SDLC typically comprises several distinct phases, varying depending on the methodology employed. However, a common SDLC framework generally includes the following stages, as shown in Figure 4.3:

▶ **Requirement analysis:** This initial phase involves gathering and documenting the software requirements from various stakeholders, including clients, end users, and business analysts. The AI product manager collaborates closely with

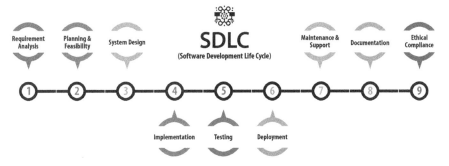

FIGURE 4.3 Stages of the SDLC, outlining the process from requirement analysis to deployment, maintenance, documentation, and ethical compliance

these stakeholders to understand the specific needs and expectations, translating them into detailed specifications and use cases. This stage is critical as it sets the foundation for all subsequent phases by clearly defining what the software must achieve. Key activities include requirement elicitation, analysis, validation, and documentation.

▶ **Planning and feasibility:** During the planning and feasibility phase, the project team evaluates the feasibility by considering technical, financial, and organizational factors. AI product managers are essential in this stage to determine whether it is feasible to include AI models in the software. This involves estimating resources, timelines, and costs and identifying potential risks. The project plan developed in this phase outlines the project schedule, resource allocation, milestones, and risk management strategies. Effective planning ensures that the project is well-organized and sets realistic expectations for all stakeholders.

▶ **System design:** The system design phase involves creating the software's architecture, components, and modules. AI product managers work closely with system architects and developers to design a high-level architecture that integrates AI models. This phase produces high-level design documents outlining the overall system architecture and detailed design documents specifying the components, data structures, and interfaces. The goal is to ensure that all software components will work together seamlessly and that the AI models are effectively integrated into the software infrastructure.

▶ **Implementation (coding):** At this stage, developers write the software's actual code based on the design specifications. AI product managers ensure that the code integrates AI models effectively and adheres to coding standards and best practices. This phase involves frequent collaboration between AI engineers and software developers to implement AI functionalities and ensure they operate as intended within the software environment. The implementation phase often follows an iterative approach, where code is developed, reviewed, and refined in cycles to address issues and improve quality.

▶ **Testing:** The testing phase verifies that the software works as expected and is free of defects. Several levels are carried out, such as user acceptance testing (UAT), system testing, integration testing, and unit testing. AI product managers ensure that the AI models are thoroughly tested within the software application to validate their performance and accuracy. This phase involves creating test plans, designing test cases, executing tests, and documenting the results. Identifying and fixing bugs before deployment is crucial to ensure the reliability and robustness of the software.

▶ **Deployment:** After extensive testing and validation, the software is deployed to a production environment and made available to end users. AI product managers coordinate with IT and operations teams to ensure the deployment process is seamless and that the AI models are fully operational. Deployment activities may include configuring the production environment, migrating data, and providing user training to ensure a smooth transition to the new system. Effective deployment minimizes disruption to business processes and ensures that the software and AI models deliver their intended value.

▶ **Maintenance and support:** After deployment, the software enters the maintenance phase, which is continuously monitored and updated to address any issues or enhancements. AI product managers are in charge of monitoring AI models' performance in real-world settings to ensure they continue to satisfy business needs. Maintenance activities include applying software updates, fixing bugs, adding new features, and optimizing performance. Continuous monitoring helps detect and resolve issues early, ensuring that the software remains reliable and effective.

▶ **Documentation:** Throughout the SDLC, comprehensive documentation ensures transparency, consistency, and effective stakeholder communication. Documentation includes requirements specifications, design documents, test plans, user manuals, and maintenance guides. AI product managers ensure that all aspects of the AI models and their integration into the software are thoroughly documented. This documentation is valuable for future maintenance, troubleshooting, and enhancement efforts, facilitating knowledge transfer among team members.

▶ **Ethical and regulatory compliance:** Ensuring ethical and regulatory compliance is critical to the SDLC, particularly for AI-powered software. AI product managers are responsible for ensuring that the software conforms to ethical norms that guard against bias and guarantee justice, as well as pertinent data privacy laws like the General Data Protection Regulation (GDPR) and the Health Insurance Portability and Accountability Act (HIPAA). This involves conducting ethical reviews, implementing data protection measures, and regularly auditing the software to ensure compliance with legal and ethical guidelines.

Synchronizing the MDLC and SDLC for Seamless Integration

Synchronizing the MDLC with the SDLC is vital for successfully integrating AI models into software applications (see Figure 4.4). This synchronization ensures that AI models are effectively incorporated into the software, enhancing functionality and aligning with business goals. AI product managers are crucial in bridging the gap between these two life cycles, ensuring that the AI and software development teams work harmoniously. The first step in synchronization is understanding the distinct yet complementary phases of the MDLC and SDLC. Although the MDLC focuses on creating and optimizing AI models, the SDLC is concerned with the overall development of the software application. By aligning these phases, AI

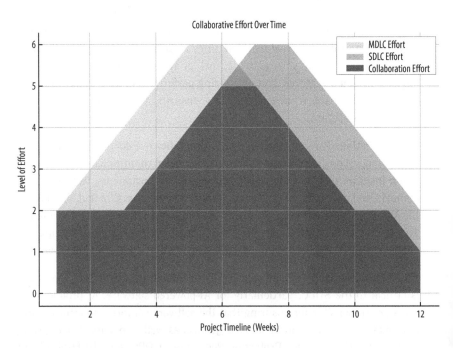

FIGURE 4.4 Collaboration dynamics between the MDLC and SDLC over a 12-week project, highlighting phases of intensified joint effort to ensure seamless integration and optimized deployment

product managers can facilitate a seamless integration process that leverages the strengths of both life cycles:

▶ **Parallel execution:** One effective approach to synchronization is executing the MDLC and SDLC phases in parallel. For instance, while the software development team works on the application's architecture and design, the AI team can simultaneously focus on data preparation and model development. This parallel execution ensures that both teams progress concurrently, reducing delays and improving efficiency. AI product managers must coordinate these parallel activities, ensuring that both teams are aligned on goals and timelines.

▶ **Data flow and preparation:** The data preparation phase in the MDLC should align with the SDLC software application's data requirements. This involves integrating data sources needed for AI model training into the software's architecture. AI product managers must ensure that data engineers and software developers collaborate to make the necessary data accessible to the AI models. This collaboration is crucial for creating a unified data flow supporting model training and application functionality.

▶ **Model integration:** Once AI models are developed and tested, they must be integrated into the software application. This integration can be facilitated through APIs or service endpoints, which allow the software to interact with the AI models. AI product managers oversee this integration, ensuring that the models are seamlessly embedded into the software's architecture. This requires close collaboration between AI engineers and software developers to address any technical challenges that may arise during integration.

▶ **Testing and validation:** Synchronizing the MDLC and SDLC testing phases ensures that AI models and software applications work together harmoniously. This involves thorough model testing within the MDLC and integration testing within the SDLC. AI product managers must ensure that the AI models are evaluated for accuracy and performance while testing the software for functionality and user experience. Joint testing sessions can help identify and resolve any issues related to model performance within the software environment.

▶ **Deployment and monitoring:** The software application and the integrated AI models are moved to a production environment during deployment. AI product managers must coordinate with IT and operations teams to ensure seamless deployment and not disrupt business processes. Once deployed, continuous monitoring of both the AI models and the software application is necessary to maintain performance and reliability. AI product managers should establish monitoring frameworks to track key performance metrics and detect issues like model drift or data shift.

▶ **Feedback loops:** Establishing feedback loops between the MDLC and SDLC teams is crucial for continuous improvement. Changes or enhancements to AI models may impact software functionality and vice versa. AI product managers should facilitate regular team communication to address evolving requirements or performance issues. This iterative feedback process ensures that the AI models and the software application are continuously refined and optimized.

▶ **Version control:** Implementing version control for AI models and software code is essential for maintaining consistency and tracking changes. AI product managers should ensure that both teams use version control systems to manage model versions and software releases. This practice helps maintain a coherent development process and allows for efficient rollback if issues arise.

▶ **Documentation:** Comprehensive documentation is critical for synchronizing the MDLC and SDLC. This includes documenting the model development process, data sources, model parameters, software design, integration points, and testing procedures. AI product managers must ensure that documentation is maintained and accessible to both AI and software development teams, facilitating transparency and knowledge sharing.

▶ **Regulatory compliance and security:** It is essential to ensure that MDLC and SDLC processes comply with relevant regulations and security standards. AI product managers must work with the legal and security teams to ensure that data handling, model deployment, and software development adhere to legal and ethical guidelines. This includes implementing data protection measures, conducting security audits, and regularly reviewing compliance requirements.

▶ **Training and support:** For AI models to be successfully integrated into software applications, stakeholders and end users must receive sufficient training and assistance. AI product managers must ensure that training materials and user guides are developed and that support mechanisms are in place to assist users in adapting to the new system. This helps maximize the adoption and effectiveness of AI-powered software.

Ensuring Effective Communication and Collaboration Between Teams

Effective communication and collaboration between AI development and software development teams are critical to successfully integrating the MDLC with the SDLC. AI product managers are essential in enabling this form of cooperation by ensuring that both teams cooperate to coordinate actions and accomplish shared objectives.

Opening direct lines of contact between the teams working on the SDLC and MDLC is the first step in promoting successful communication. Regular meetings, video conferences, and collaboration tools can facilitate ongoing discussions and information sharing. AI product managers should consistently use these channels to inform all team members about project progress, challenges, and updates. Establishing a shared communication platform, such as Slack or Microsoft Teams, can help streamline communication and ensure that everyone is on the same page.

Shared objectives and project goals are crucial for aligning the efforts of both teams. AI product managers must ensure that both the AI development and software development teams understand and share the same objectives. To avoid misunderstandings and guarantee that both teams are working toward the same objectives, it is important to clearly define the scope and expected outcomes of the AI-powered software application. A joint project kickoff meeting with members from both teams can set the tone for collaboration and alignment, discussing project goals, requirements, timelines, and responsibilities.

Creating shared documentation is another important strategy for fostering collaboration. AI product managers should ensure that both teams have access to comprehensive documentation that outlines the model development process, including model architecture, data requirements, and training techniques. This documentation should include software design specifications, integration points, and testing procedures. Shared documentation helps reduce misunderstandings, provides a reference for all team members, and facilitates transparency and knowledge sharing.

Regular status meetings or stand-ups are essential for maintaining alignment and addressing any issues that may arise during the project. AI product managers should organize these meetings to provide updates on progress, challenges, and dependencies. These meetings allow both teams to discuss their work, identify integration issues, and collaborate on solutions. Regular check-ins help keep the project on track and promptly address any potential roadblocks. Cross-functional team members can bridge the gap between AI development and software development. AI product managers should consider including team members with expertise in AI/model development and software development. These cross-functional members can facilitate communication, provide insights into both areas, and help resolve technical challenges that may arise during integration. Individuals who understand both domains can significantly enhance collaboration and ensure a smoother integration process.

Joint testing efforts ensure that the integrated AI models and software applications work seamlessly. AI product managers should facilitate collaboration between the testing teams from both domains, ensuring that the AI models are thoroughly tested within the software environment. This includes integration testing, performance testing, and UAT. Collaborative testing efforts help identify and resolve issues early, ensuring that the final product meets technical and business requirements.

Continuous improvement requires establishing a feedback loop. AI product managers should encourage team members to share feedback on the integration process, identify areas for improvement, and suggest solutions. Regularly reviewing the feedback and implementing necessary changes helps refine the integration process and improve team collaboration.

Best Practices for Integrated Development and Deployment

Integrating the MDLC with the SDLC requires adherence to best practices to ensure the smooth development and deployment of AI-powered software applications. AI product managers are critical in implementing these practices to achieve seamless integration and alignment with business goals:

▶ **Establishing clear objectives and requirements:** The first step in ensuring successful integration is establishing clear and detailed objectives and requirements for the AI model and the software application. AI product managers should work closely with stakeholders to define the AI solution's business goals, success criteria, and performance metrics. This precision guarantees that both development teams know the intended results and can collaborate effectively to achieve them.

▶ **Collaborative planning:** Effective integration starts with collaborative planning. AI product managers should collaborate with software developers, ML engineers, data scientists, and other relevant parties to produce a thorough project plan. This plan should outline the timelines, milestones, resources, and responsibilities for the MDLC and SDLC phases. Collaborative planning helps identify dependencies, anticipate potential challenges, and align the efforts of both teams.

▶ **Parallel development:** To streamline the integration process, AI product managers should promote parallel development of AI models and software components. Although the software development team focuses on building the application's architecture and user interfaces, the AI team can work on data preparation, model training, and validation. This parallel approach reduces development time and ensures that both teams progress toward the project goals simultaneously.

▶ **Regular synchronization meetings:** Maintaining regular synchronization meetings is crucial for aligning both teams. AI product managers should schedule frequent meetings to discuss progress, share updates, and address any issues that may arise. These meetings provide a platform for both teams to communicate their needs, coordinate efforts, and ensure that the integration process stays on track. Effective communication during these meetings helps resolve conflicts and make informed decisions.

▶ **Unified testing strategies:** Implementing unified testing strategies is essential for validating the performance and functionality of integrated AI models and software applications. AI product managers should ensure that both AI and software development teams collaborate on creating comprehensive test plans that cover unit testing, integration testing, system testing, and UAT. Collaborative testing endeavors facilitate the early detection and resolution of integration problems, guaranteeing that the end product satisfies quality benchmarks and business demands.

▶ **Scalable and robust architecture:** Designing a scalable and robust architecture is the best practice for integrating AI models into software applications. AI product managers should work with system architects to ensure that the software architecture can accommodate the computational requirements of AI models. This includes designing efficient data pipelines, scalable computing resources, and robust APIs for model integration. A well-designed architecture ensures that the AI models can operate efficiently within the software environment.

▶ **Continuous monitoring and maintenance:** Maintenance post-deployment and ongoing monitoring are essential to preserve the dependability and efficiency of AI-driven software applications. AI product managers should establish monitoring frameworks to track key performance metrics, detect model drift, and identify any issues that may arise in the production environment. Regular maintenance activities, such as retraining models with new data and updating software components, help sustain the integrated solution's effectiveness.

▶ **Documentation and knowledge sharing:** Comprehensive documentation ensures transparency and facilitates knowledge sharing among team members. AI product managers should ensure that all aspects of the integration process, including model development, software design, testing procedures, and deployment steps, are thoroughly documented. This documentation is valuable for future maintenance, troubleshooting, and enhancements. Promoting knowledge sharing through training sessions and workshops also helps build a collaborative and informed team.

▶ **Adhering to ethical and regulatory standards:** Ensuring that the integrated solution complies with ethical and regulatory standards is a critical best practice. AI product managers should work with legal and compliance teams to ensure that data handling, model deployment, and software development adhere to relevant regulations, such as GDPR or HIPAA. Implementing measures to address ethical concerns, such as bias mitigation and fairness, helps build trust and credibility in the AI-powered solution.

▶ **Stakeholder engagement and feedback:** Engaging stakeholders throughout the development and deployment process is essential for ensuring that the integrated solution meets business needs. AI product managers should facilitate regular feedback sessions with stakeholders to gather insights, address concerns, and incorporate suggestions. This continuous engagement helps align the project with stakeholder expectations and achieve a successful outcome.

Overcoming Common Challenges in Integrating the MDLC and SDLC

Integrating the MDLC with the SDLC can present several challenges. Effectively addressing these challenges is crucial for AI product managers to ensure the successful development and deployment of AI solutions within software applications. Here, we explore some common challenges and strategies to overcome them:

1. **Bridging the communication gap:** One of the most significant challenges in integrating the MDLC and SDLC is bridging the communication gap between data scientists, ML engineers, and software developers. These teams

often have different terminologies, goals, and workflows, leading to misunderstandings and misaligned priorities.

Strategy: AI product managers should establish clear communication channels and foster a culture of collaboration. Regular cross-functional meetings, shared documentation, and collaborative tools can help bridge this gap. Encouraging team members to understand each other's roles and responsibilities also enhances mutual respect and collaboration.

2. **Aligning goals and objectives:** The MDLC and SDLC teams might have different priorities. Data scientists might focus on model accuracy and performance, whereas software developers prioritize scalability, maintainability, and user experience. Aligning these goals is essential for successful integration.

Strategy: AI product managers should facilitate joint planning sessions to align the goals and objectives of both teams. Defining shared success metrics encompassing AI performance and software quality can help unify the teams' efforts. Continuous alignment through regular updates and progress reviews ensures that both teams stay focused on common objectives.

3. **Managing data requirements:** Data management is a critical component of the MDLC, and ensuring that the data requirements align with the software application's needs can be challenging. Solving issues with data integration, quality, and governance is necessary.

Strategy: AI product managers should work closely with data engineers to ensure that data pipelines are designed to meet the needs of AI models and software applications. Implementing robust data governance practices and ensuring data quality through validation and cleaning processes are essential. Collaboration between data scientists and software developers is key to addressing data-related challenges.

4. **Ensuring model interpretability and explainability:** AI models, particularly complex ones like deep learning models, can be challenging to understand and comprehend. This lack of transparency can hinder gaining stakeholder trust and meeting regulatory requirements.

Strategy: AI product managers should prioritize model interpretability and explainability throughout the MDLC. Techniques such as feature importance analysis, model-agnostic interpretability methods (for example, local interpretable model-agnostic explanations [LIME] and Shapley additive explanations [SHAP]), and clear documentation of model decisions can enhance transparency. Engaging stakeholders early in the development process and providing them with understandable explanations of model behavior helps build trust.

5. **Handling model drift and data drift:** Once deployed, AI models can experience performance degradation due to model drift (changes in the model's accuracy over time) or data drift (changes in the underlying data distribution). Continuous monitoring and maintenance are required to address these issues.

   Strategy: AI product managers should implement monitoring frameworks to track key performance metrics and detect signs of model or data drift. Establishing processes for regular model retraining and updating based on new data is essential. Automated alert systems can help identify issues early, allowing for timely intervention.

6. **Balancing innovation and stability:** AI projects often involve rapid experimentation and innovation, whereas software development processes prioritize stability and reliability. Balancing these contrasting needs is a common challenge.

   Strategy: AI product managers should adopt agile methodologies for iterative development and continuous feedback. Creating a sandbox environment for experimentation can enable rapid innovation without compromising the stability of the main software application. Clear guidelines for when to move from experimentation to production ensure a balanced approach.

7. **Regulatory and ethical compliance:** Ensuring compliance with regulatory and ethical standards is a critical challenge in integrating AI models into software applications. This entails following data privacy regulations, guaranteeing equity, and reducing biases in AI algorithms.

   Strategy: AI product managers should collaborate with the legal, compliance, and ethics teams to understand and implement the necessary regulations and ethical guidelines. Regular audits, ethical reviews, and bias mitigation techniques should be part of the development process. Transparent documentation and stakeholder engagement are crucial for demonstrating compliance and building trust.

Case Studies of Successful MDLC and SDLC Integration

Understanding how integrating the MDLC and the SDLC works in real-world scenarios can provide valuable insights and practical examples for AI product managers. Here, we explore several case studies demonstrating the successful integration of the MDLC and SDLC, highlighting the strategies and outcomes.

Predictive Maintenance in Manufacturing

A large manufacturing company aimed to cut equipment downtime by 30 percent and maintenance costs by 20 percent using predictive maintenance (see Figure 4.5).

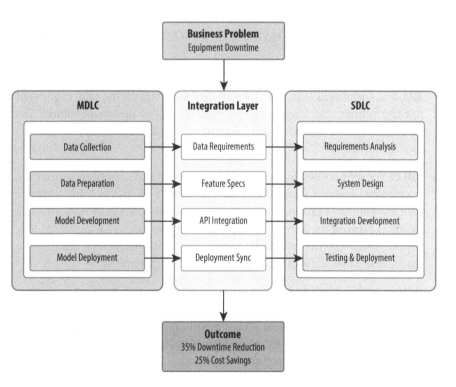

FIGURE 4.5 ML and software engineering in enterprise systems in manufacturing

The AI product manager led the integration of an AI-based predictive model into the existing maintenance system, aligning the MDLC and SDLC processes. The data science team developed a predictive model from historical data, and the software team ensured seamless system integration and real-time data flow. The result: downtime was reduced by 35 percent and maintenance costs by 25 percent, exceeding targets and boosting operational efficiency.

▶ **Business problem:** A large manufacturing company faced frequent equipment breakdowns, leading to significant downtime and increased maintenance costs. The company wanted to implement a predictive maintenance system to anticipate equipment failures before they occurred.

▶ **Business goal:** Reduce equipment downtime by 30 percent and lower maintenance costs by 20 percent within the next year.

▶ **Solution:** The AI product manager spearheaded the integration of an AI-based predictive maintenance model into the company's existing maintenance management software.

▶ **MDLC:** The data science team collected historical maintenance records, sensor data, and operational logs. They then cleaned and prepared the data, engineered relevant features, and developed an ML model to predict equipment failures. The model was trained, evaluated, and validated using historical data to ensure accuracy and reliability.

▶ **SDLC:** The software development team designed and implemented the predictive maintenance system's architecture, ensuring that it could seamlessly integrate with the company's existing software. APIs were developed to facilitate real-time data flow between the AI model and the maintenance management system. The system underwent rigorous testing, including unit, integration, and UAT, to ensure that it met all functional and performance requirements.

▶ **Outcome:** The integrated predictive maintenance system reduced equipment downtime by 35 percent and lowered maintenance costs by 25 percent, exceeding the company's initial goals. The AI model's predictions allowed the maintenance team to schedule preventive maintenance activities proactively, leading to improved operational efficiency and cost savings.

Personalized Customer Experience in E-Commerce

To address low customer engagement and high churn, the e-commerce platform embarked on a strategic initiative to integrate a personalized recommendation system. This case study outlines the challenges, goals, and collaborative approach across the MDLC and SDLC. By leveraging customer data and aligning technical development with business objectives, the project successfully delivered a scalable solution that exceeded performance targets and transformed the customer experience (see Figure 4.6).

▶ **Business problem:** An e-commerce platform struggled with low customer engagement and high churn rates. The company wanted to implement a recommendation system to provide personalized product suggestions and enhance the customer experience.

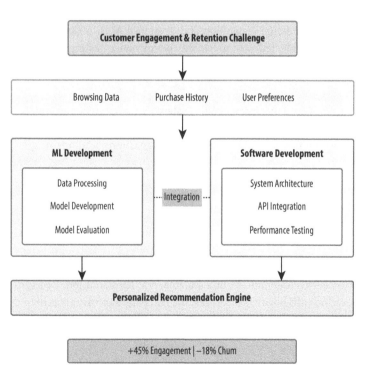

FIGURE 4.6 Architecting success: 45 percent higher engagement through ML–software integration

▶ **Business goal:** Over the next six months, increase customer engagement by 40 percent and reduce churn by 15 percent.

▶ **Solution:** The AI product manager led the project to integrate a recommendation engine into the e-commerce platform, leveraging customer data to deliver personalized product suggestions.

▶ **MDLC:** The data science team collected and prepared information from various sources, including purchase history, browsing habits, and customer preferences. They developed and trained a collaborative filtering model to generate personalized recommendations. The model was evaluated for precision and recall to ensure that it provided accurate suggestions.

▶ **SDLC:** The software development team integrated the recommendation engine into the e-commerce platform. They designed the system architecture to support real-time recommendation generation and developed APIs to facilitate data exchange. The team conducted comprehensive performance testing to ensure the recommendation system could handle the platform's high traffic and provide timely suggestions.

▶ **Outcome:** The personalized recommendation system increased customer engagement by 45 percent and reduced churn rates by 18 percent, surpassing the company's targets. Customers received tailored product suggestions, leading to higher satisfaction and increased sales.

Fraud Detection in Financial Services

Facing rising fraudulent transactions that jeopardized financial security and customer trust, a financial services company launched a strategic initiative to deploy an AI-driven fraud detection system. This case study details the integration of the MDLC and SDLC to develop and implement a scalable, real-time solution. By aligning technical innovation with business priorities, the company successfully achieved significant reductions in fraud while maintaining operational reliability and customer confidence (see Figure 4.7).

▶ **Business problem:** A financial services company faced increasing fraudulent transactions, resulting in financial losses and compromised customer trust. The company intended to deploy an AI-driven fraud detection system to identify and halt fraudulent behavior in real time.

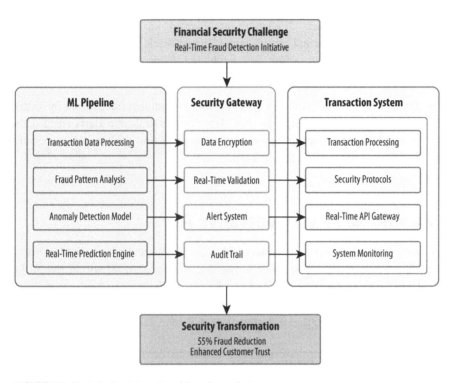

FIGURE 4.7 Dual pipeline integration: ML–software fusion

▶ **Business goal:** Reduce fraudulent transactions by 50 percent within the next year while maintaining a low false-positive rate.

▶ **Solution:** The AI product manager directed the integration of a fraud detection model into the company's transaction processing system.

▶ **MDLC:** The data science team collected transaction data, account information, and historical fraud cases. They cleaned and preprocessed the data, engineered features indicative of fraudulent behavior, and developed an anomaly detection model. The model was trained and validated to ensure high accuracy and a low false-positive rate.

▶ **SDLC:** The software development team integrated the fraud detection model into the transaction processing system. They created APIs for real-time data input and fraud alerts. The system architecture was designed to handle high transaction volumes and provide immediate feedback. Extensive testing, including security and load testing, was conducted to ensure the system's reliability and robustness.

▶ **Outcome:** The fraud detection system reduced fraudulent transactions by 55 percent, exceeding the company's goal. The system's real-time alerts enabled the fraud prevention team to take swift action, protecting the company's financial assets and maintaining customer trust.

Traditional AI vs. Generative AI

Understanding the distinction between old AI approaches and generative AI is crucial for AI product managers when exploring the integration of AI within the MDLC and SDLC. These two approaches offer different capabilities and applications, each playing a unique role in AI development and deployment. Let's dive into a comparative discussion based on the characteristics outlined in Table 4.1.

Aspect	Old AI approach	Generative AI approach
Technology	Basic AI models	Advanced deep learning, neural networks
Data management	Siloed data	Integrated data, real-time analytics
Prompt engineering	Limited user role	Continuous feedback, prompt refinement
Speed	Slower development	Faster, AI-driven automation

Table 4.1 Integrating the MDLC with the SDLC: bridging traditional AI and generative AI for seamless development and innovation

Technology: Basic AI Models vs. Advanced Deep Learning and Neural Networks

Traditional AI primarily utilizes basic AI models, which, although effective for many applications, often lack the sophistication and adaptability required for more complex tasks. These models generally rely on simpler algorithms that can handle structured and unstructured data to provide predictive insights and automate specific processes. However, they are limited in their capacity for continuous improvement and handling dynamic, real-time data.

In contrast, generative AI leverages advanced deep learning and neural networks. These technologies enable the development of models that can learn intricate patterns from large datasets and generate new content. This capability is crucial for creating AI solutions that are not only reactive but also proactive and adaptive. By integrating generative AI into the MDLC and SDLC, organizations can develop more sophisticated applications that leverage real-time data analytics and provide enhanced user experiences.

Data Management: Siloed Data vs. Integrated Data, Real-Time Analytics

In traditional AI, data management often involves working with siloed data, which can lead to fragmented insights and inefficiencies. This approach may hinder the seamless integration of AI models into broader software systems, resulting in slower development and deployment cycles.

Generative AI approaches emphasize integrated data management and real-time analytics, facilitating a more cohesive and comprehensive view of data across the organization. This integration supports the continuous feedback and refinement processes for prompt engineering and model optimization. By aligning data management practices with the SDLC, AI product managers can ensure that AI models are effectively embedded within software applications, leading to more robust and reliable solutions.

Prompt Engineering: Limited User Role vs. Continuous Feedback, Prompt Refinement

Old AI approaches often involve limited user interaction, focusing on predefined tasks with minimal scope for real-time adjustment. This can result in models that are less responsive to changing requirements and user feedback.

Generative AI transforms this dynamic by incorporating continuous feedback and prompt refinement into the development process. This approach allows for more interactive and user-centric AI solutions, where models can be iteratively improved based on ongoing input from users and stakeholders. This continuous loop enhances the model's relevance and performance, ensuring that it remains aligned with evolving business needs and technological advancements.

Speed: Slower Development vs. Faster, AI-Driven Automation

Traditional AI development can be a slow and iterative process, often constrained by the limitations of the models and data management practices in use. This can result in longer development cycles and delays in deploying AI solutions within software systems.

Generative AI, powered by AI-driven automation, significantly accelerates the development process. By automating many aspects of model training, data processing, and integration, generative AI enables faster deployment of AI-enhanced software applications. This speed and efficiency are critical for staying competitive in today's fast-paced technological landscape, allowing organizations to iterate and innovate rapidly.

Chapter 5

Scaling Research to Production

Turning artificial intelligence (AI) research into real-world applications is essential and challenging for AI product managers. AI research often starts with innovative ideas and experimental models in controlled environments, focusing on exploring theoretical possibilities and proving concepts. However, the true value of AI lies in transforming these research insights into reliable, scalable, and user-friendly applications. This process, known as scaling research to production, is key to turning AI innovations into practical solutions that solve business problems and improve operational efficiency.

The importance of scaling research to production is multifaceted. Groundbreaking research is only the first step; the real impact comes when these advancements tackle real-world challenges, enhance user experiences, and streamline operations. This transition involves navigating various technical, organizational, and strategic challenges. AI product managers are crucial in bridging the gap between theory and practice. A significant challenge in this transition is ensuring that the AI models and algorithms developed during research are robust and scalable enough for real-world application. Research settings often use idealized datasets and controlled variables, which differ greatly from production environments' noisy and variable data. AI product managers must ensure that models are rigorously validated, extensively tested, and optimized to perform reliably under these conditions. This involves implementing comprehensive testing, fine-tuning performance, and establishing ongoing monitoring to maintain accuracy and efficiency.

Integration with existing systems and workflows presents another layer of complexity. This often requires substantial engineering efforts, including developing APIs, creating data pipelines, and designing user interfaces. AI product managers must collaborate closely with data engineers, software developers, and IT departments to ensure that AI solutions are smoothly incorporated into the organization's infrastructure and meet operational requirements.

Addressing ethical and regulatory considerations is also crucial in the journey from research to production. AI models must comply with data privacy regulations, mitigate biases, and ensure fairness and transparency in their operations. AI product managers must incorporate these considerations into the development and deployment process, fostering trust and accountability in AI applications. The process of scaling research to production is iterative and requires continuous refinement. AI models must be regularly updated and adjusted to maintain effectiveness and relevance as they encounter new data and use cases. This cycle of testing, feedback, and iteration is essential for sustaining the value and impact of AI solutions in a constantly changing business environment.

As we stand amid the AI revolution, our charter as product teams is clear: to seize the raw potential of emerging AI technologies and mold it into tangible assets for our users and our business. The AI revolution demands innovation, and product teams must embrace the potential of emerging tools and research, relentlessly translating breakthroughs into tangible value. Our journey begins in the laboratories and forums where AI research flourishes. We must have the insight to discern which breakthroughs have the potential to revolutionize our products and which may not align with our vision. Bringing AI from research to production is not a solo venture; it demands a symphony of expertise. We must cultivate a collaborative ecosystem, unifying engineers, data scientists, business strategists, and user experience designers to breathe life into AI innovations.

In this dynamic environment, AI product managers play a pivotal role in bridging the gap between cutting-edge research and practical application. They not only drive AI innovation forward but also skillfully translate complex evolving technological capabilities into products that solve real-world problems and deliver measurable value to end-users. This requires more than just technical expertise; it demands a research mindset—a way of thinking that embraces curiosity and a commitment to continuous learning. The AI revolution demands innovation. Product teams must embrace the potential of emerging tools and research, relentlessly translating breakthroughs into tangible value for users and businesses.

Importance of Developing a Research Mindset

In the AI industry, the role of an AI product manager extends beyond managing projects and timelines. It requires a profound understanding of the research that drives innovation and practical applications. Developing a research mindset is crucial for AI product managers as it enables them to navigate the complexities of AI projects, foster innovation, and drive evidence-based decision-making. A research mindset emphasizes critical thinking and continuous learning. In the context of AI, this means staying updated with the latest advancements, understanding new algorithms, and being aware of emerging trends. By regularly engaging with cutting-edge research, AI product managers can ensure that their projects leverage the most effective and efficient techniques. This proactive approach enhances the quality of AI solutions and positions the organization at the forefront of technological innovation.

Critical thinking is a core component of a research mindset. It involves questioning assumptions, analyzing data critically, and evaluating the validity of different approaches. For AI product managers, this means rigorously assessing whether a particular AI model or technique suits the problem. It necessitates a deep comprehension of the advantages and disadvantages of various AI techniques and the capacity to make decisions that are in line with organizational objectives. Moreover, a research mindset fosters a culture of problem-solving. AI projects often involve addressing complex challenges that do not have straightforward solutions. AI product managers can break down these challenges into manageable parts by adopting a research-oriented approach, exploring multiple solutions, and iterating toward the most effective outcome. This iterative problem-solving process is crucial in developing robust AI models that perform well in real-world scenarios.

Evidence-based decision-making is another significant benefit of a research mindset. In AI product management, decisions should be grounded in solid empirical evidence rather than intuition or anecdotal experience. By relying on data and rigorous analysis, AI product managers can make more accurate predictions, optimize models more effectively, and ultimately deliver reliable and impactful solutions. This approach enhances stakeholder confidence, as data-based decisions are more likely to gain support.

In the quick-paced world of AI, a dedication to lifelong learning is crucial. AI product managers must regularly engage with the latest research papers, attend industry conferences, and participate in workshops to stay abreast of new developments. This continuous learning keeps them updated with the latest tools and techniques and inspires new ideas and approaches that can be applied to their projects. Innovation thrives in environments where a research mindset is prevalent. AI product managers can foster a culture of creativity by encouraging team members to explore new ideas, question existing paradigms, and experiment with novel approaches. This culture of innovation is critical for developing AI solutions that are not only effective but also ground-breaking, giving the organization a competitive edge in the market.

Strategies for Developing a Research Mindset

Developing a research mindset is crucial for AI product managers to transform theoretical AI advancements into practical, impactful solutions. This mindset encourages critical thinking, continuous learning, and innovative problem-solving. Here's how AI product managers can cultivate this mindset effectively:

▶ **Reading research papers regularly:** Keeping up with the latest research is essential for AI product managers. Reading research papers on a regular basis will keep you up to date on the most recent advances and trends in AI. Start by identifying research papers relevant to your field or the topics you are interested in. Utilize academic journals, conference proceedings, and online repositories like Google Scholar, PubMed, and arXiv. Dedicate consistent time for reading these papers, approaching the process actively by highlighting key points, taking notes, and questioning the content. Understanding the typical structure of research papers—abstract, introduction, methodology, results, discussion, and conclusion—can help you navigate and comprehend them more effectively. Begin by reading the abstract for an overview and then delve into the introduction for context and motivation behind the research. The methodology section explains how the research was conducted, which is crucial for understanding the data collection and analysis methods. The results section presents the findings, and the discussion interprets these results in the broader context of the field. The conclusion summarizes the key takeaways. Pay attention to citations and references to explore related research, enhancing your understanding of the topic.

▶ **Attending conferences and workshops:** Attending conferences and workshops can help AI product managers network with researchers and other experts, share ideas, and stay current on the latest technological developments. Conferences provide platforms for presenting the latest findings and discussing innovative ideas. Attending these events exposes AI product managers to up-to-date research, diverse perspectives, and new approaches.

Presenting your research at conferences provides valuable expert feedback and critique, helping refine your work and develop a more critical mindset. Additionally, these experiences improve communication and presentation skills, which are essential for effectively conveying complex ideas. Conferences typically include keynote speeches, workshops, and panel discussions, offering insights into the latest trends and methodologies. These sessions can inspire ambitious projects and encourage thinking outside the box.

▶ **Cultivating curiosity:** Curiosity drives exploring new ideas and approaches, encouraging a deeper understanding of problems and solutions. AI product managers should cultivate a curious mindset to explore uncharted territories, challenge assumptions, and innovate. This curiosity broadens knowledge, drawing from diverse subjects and disciplines to inform and enrich work. Curiosity also fosters resilience, motivating perseverance in facing challenges and setbacks.

Staying curious promotes lifelong learning, encouraging acquiring new skills, techniques, and knowledge. It leads to well-informed decision-making and fosters adaptability in a rapidly evolving research landscape. Curious researchers are often better communicators and collaborators, open to sharing knowledge and learning from others.

▶ **Embracing complexity in AI and data science:** AI and data science are inherently complex fields. Embracing this complexity, rather than fearing it, is essential for AI product managers. Tackling difficult problems head-on helps develop a deeper understanding and leads to innovative solutions. Additionally, it promotes a development attitude in which obstacles are viewed as chances to grow and learn. Finding creative solutions to issues and gaining a deeper understanding is facilitated by not being scared to tackle challenging subjects.

▶ **Taking part in ongoing education:** The field of AI is dynamic and always changing. Product managers who deal with AI must commit to lifelong learning to keep current with these breakthroughs. This involves reading research papers, attending conferences, participating in workshops, and engaging with the broader AI community. Continuous learning ensures staying ahead of the curve and bringing cutting-edge knowledge and techniques into projects. Dedicate yourself to ongoing education through formal coursework, online learning platforms, or self-directed study to keep your skills and knowledge up to date.

▶ **Building a network of experts:** Networking with other professionals in the AI field provides access to diverse perspectives, new ideas, and collaborative opportunities. AI product managers should actively engage with their peers, participate in professional organizations, and join online communities. This network offers support, feedback, and inspiration, enhancing the research mindset and professional growth. Engaging with the broader AI community through conferences, social media, or professional organizations provides access to knowledge and experience. Building a network of peers and mentors fosters collaboration, inspiration, and professional growth.

Transitioning from Research to Production

Translating AI research into production involves several key considerations that ensure successful deployment and operational efficiency. AI product managers must navigate challenges and strategically align their efforts to bridge the gap between theoretical research and practical application (see Figure 5.1):

▶ **Understanding the research:** The first step in translating research into production is thoroughly understanding the research and its implications. AI product managers must grasp the research's core concepts, methodologies, and findings. This includes understanding the strengths, limitations, and potential applications of the AI models developed during the research phase. By comprehensively understanding the research, AI product managers can identify how it can be adapted and applied to solve specific business problems.

FIGURE 5.1 From concept to creation: the journey of transforming research into a market-ready product

▶ **Evaluating the research:** Evaluating the research involves assessing its feasibility, scalability, and alignment with business goals. AI product managers must determine whether the research outcomes are robust enough to handle real-world data and scenarios. This assessment includes evaluating the quality and quantity of data used in the research, the performance metrics achieved, and the model's ability to generalize to new, unseen data. The evaluation process helps identify gaps or limitations that need to be addressed before moving to production.

▶ **Adapting the research:** Research findings frequently need to be modified to meet the unique requirements and limitations of the business situation. This adaptation may entail modification to connect the AI models, algorithms, or approaches with the organization's data architecture, operational requirements, and user needs. Data scientists, engineers, and domain specialists need to work with AI product managers to customize research results for the real world. This step guarantees the theoretical soundness and practical applicability of the AI solution.

▶ **Developing a prototype:** It is essential to construct a prototype before scaling up to full production. AI product managers can evaluate the viability and efficacy of the modified research in a controlled setting by using a prototype as a proof of concept. The prototype development phase involves these steps:

(A) Implementing the AI model on a small scale

(B) Integrating it with the necessary data pipelines

(C) Testing its performance on real-world data

This phase helps identify potential issues and areas for improvement, providing valuable insights for the final deployment.

▶ **Iterative testing and improvement:** Iterative testing and improvement are essential to refining the AI model and ensuring its robustness in production. This process involves continuously testing the prototype, collecting feedback, and making necessary adjustments to enhance performance. AI product managers must implement a strict testing strategy covering many kinds of testing, including performance, integration, and unit testing. This iterative approach helps identify and address weaknesses or limitations, ensuring that the AI solution is reliable and effective.

▶ **Ensuring scalability and performance:** Scalability and performance are critical factors in translating research into production. AI product managers must ensure that the AI solution can handle large volumes of data, high user loads, and diverse scenarios without compromising performance. This involves optimizing the model, improving computational efficiency, and ensuring that the underlying infrastructure can support the production requirements. Monitoring and maintaining performance metrics is crucial to sustaining the AI solution's effectiveness.

▶ **Addressing ethical and regulatory considerations:** Ethical and legal issues are crucial when implementing AI solutions in the real world. AI product managers are responsible for ensuring the AI models respect fairness and transparency, minimize biases, and conform to data privacy laws. This entails implementing data governance procedures, carrying out bias audits, and ensuring that the AI solution complies with regulatory and industry standards. These factors promote accountability and trust, which are necessary to adopt AI solutions effectively.

▶ **Implementing continuous monitoring and maintenance:** Ongoing maintenance and monitoring are crucial to guaranteeing the AI after the solution's continued effectiveness and applicability are put into production. AI product managers must establish monitoring frameworks to track the performance of the AI model, spot irregularities or drifts, and make any necessary changes or adjustments. Frequent maintenance keeps the AI solution updated with changing business requirements and helps handle new problems.

Understanding the Research

Understanding the research is crucial in the journey from theoretical AI advancements to practical applications. This involves a deep dive into the research methodologies, findings, and implications for AI product managers to determine how they can be effectively translated into real-world solutions:

▶ **Thorough analysis of research findings:** The first step in understanding the research is to analyze the findings thoroughly. AI product managers need to comprehend the core concepts, methodologies, and results presented in the research. This includes understanding the specific problem the research aims to solve, the data used, the algorithms applied, and the outcomes achieved. By doing so, AI product managers can identify the strengths and limitations of the research, which is essential for assessing its potential applicability to business problems.

▶ **Evaluating research methodologies:** Evaluating the methodologies used in the research is critical. This involves scrutinizing the research design, data collection methods, preprocessing techniques, and model training processes. AI product managers must assess whether the research methodologies are robust and appropriate for the problem. Understanding the methodologies also helps replicate the research in a production environment and make necessary adaptations to fit the organization's specific needs.

▶ **Identifying research gaps and limitations:** Every research study has its limitations and gaps. AI product managers must identify these to understand the feasibility of applying the research findings in real life. This includes recognizing any biases in the data, limitations in the model's performance, or constraints in the research environment that may not translate well to production. AI product managers can foresee future difficulties and create plans to overcome them by identifying these gaps.

▶ **Assessing data requirements and availability:** Research often relies on specific datasets, which may not be readily available or applicable in a production environment. AI product managers need to assess the research's data requirements, including the type, quality, and volume of data needed to replicate the results. They must ensure that the organization can access comparable data or collect and preprocess data to align with the research requirements. This step is crucial for ensuring the scalability and robustness of the AI solution in production.

▶ **Understanding model performance metrics:** Understanding the performance metrics used in the research is essential for evaluating the model's effectiveness. AI product managers must be familiar with metrics such as accuracy, precision, recall, F1-score, and area under the curve (AUC) to assess the model's performance. These metrics provide insights into how well the model performs on the research data and its potential to generalize to new, unseen data in a production environment. AI product managers should also consider the context in which these metrics were evaluated and whether they align with the business objectives.

▶ **Translating research outcomes to business goals:** Finally, AI product managers must translate the research outcomes into actionable insights that align with the organization's business goals. This involves mapping the research findings to business problems and determining how the AI solution can add value. For instance, if the research demonstrates a new algorithm for fraud detection, the AI product manager should assess how it can be integrated into the existing fraud detection system to enhance its accuracy and efficiency.

Developing Prototypes and Iterative Testing

Developing prototypes and conducting iterative testing are crucial steps from AI research to production. These processes allow AI product managers to validate the feasibility and effectiveness of AI models in controlled environments before scaling them to full production.

Importance of Prototyping

Testing an AI model's initial viability requires prototyping (see Figure 5.2). A prototype, a condensed version of the finished product, enables AI product managers to test various strategies and evaluate the model's effectiveness using actual data. This step helps identify potential issues early, providing a foundation for further refinement and development.

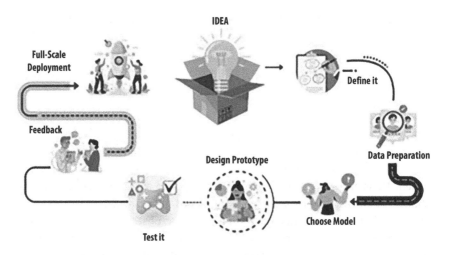

FIGURE 5.2 From spark to scale: the end-to-end journey of bringing an idea to full-scale deployment

Steps in Developing a Prototype

1. **Define objectives and requirements:** Clearly outline the prototype's objectives. Determine which key performance indicators (KPIs) will be used to measure its success. Recognize the goals and the business problem the prototype is intended to address.

2. **Select and prepare data:** Collect and prepare the information needed for the prototype. Ensure that the data reflects the kinds of real-world situations that the AI model will face in its production environment. This includes cleaning the data, handling missing values, and performing feature engineering to enhance the model's performance.

3. **Choose the right model:** Select an appropriate AI model based on the problem type and data characteristics. Depending on the specific use case, this could be a classification, regression, clustering, or another model type. Utilize algorithms and techniques that have shown promise in the research phase.

4. **Develop the prototype:** Implement the selected model using the prepared data. Use a development environment that allows for rapid prototyping and experimentation. Focus on achieving a functional model that can be evaluated against the defined objectives.

5. **Initial testing:** Conduct initial tests to assess the prototype's performance. Evaluate its accuracy, precision, recall, and other relevant metrics. Point out any problems right now or places that need work. Before proceeding to more extensive testing stages, ensure the prototype satisfies the fundamental requirements.

6. **Iterative testing and improvement:** Once the prototype is developed, iterative testing is crucial for refining and optimizing the model. This process involves multiple testing cycles, feedback, and adjustments to enhance the model's performance and reliability.

7. **Unit testing:** Begin with unit testing to verify that individual components of the model function correctly. This includes testing individual functions, data preprocessing steps, and other modular parts of the prototype. Unit testing helps isolate and fix specific issues early in the development process.

8. **Integration testing:** After unit testing, integrated testing ensures that different model components work together seamlessly. This involves testing the interactions between the model, data pipelines, and any external systems or APIs it relies on. Integration testing helps identify and resolve issues related to system interoperability.

9. **Performance testing:** Conduct performance testing to evaluate the prototype's efficiency and scalability. This includes assessing its response time,

computational requirements, and ability to handle large volumes of data. Performance testing ensures that the model can meet the demands of a production environment.

10. **User acceptance testing (UAT):** Engage end-users or stakeholders in user acceptance testing to validate that the prototype meets their needs and expectations. UAT provides valuable feedback on the model's usability, relevance, and effectiveness in solving the intended business problem.

11. **Feedback and iteration:** Collect feedback from all testing phases to refine and improve the prototype. This iterative process involves adjusting the model, retraining with updated data, and reevaluating its performance. Continue this cycle until the model consistently meets or exceeds the defined objectives and KPIs.

12. **Preparing for full-scale deployment:** After iterative testing and refinement, the prototype should be robust, reliable, and ready for full-scale deployment. AI product managers must ensure that all identified issues are resolved and that the model performs well under production conditions. This preparation includes finalizing the model, documenting the development process, and planning for ongoing monitoring and maintenance.

Generative AI and Traditional AI within Scaling Research to Production

Generative AI represents a groundbreaking innovation capable of creating new content, designs, and simulations that mimic human creativity. This type of AI produces high-quality, unique outputs, which are invaluable in marketing, design, and entertainment. For example, generative AI can automate the creation of personalized marketing content, significantly reducing the time and effort required to produce engaging materials. It could result from multiple iterations of digital models, graphics, and user interfaces, enabling a more dynamic and flexible approach to design challenges. Various processes are involved in bringing generative AI from research to production. AI product managers are essential in this integration because they ensure that the generated content satisfies customer expectations and quality standards. This requires rigorous testing and validation, continuous feedback loops, and fine-tuning based on real-world performance. Product managers must manage data quality, consider ethical considerations, and ensure that the AI models are scalable and robust.

On the other hand, traditional AI focuses on tasks like classification, prediction, and data analysis, providing reliable and precise outcomes essential for business operations. To produce precise predictions and classifications, traditional AI models are built to evaluate enormous volumes of data. They are widely used in finance, healthcare, and logistics sectors for fraud detection, disease diagnosis, and supply chain optimization. For instance, a traditional AI model in finance can analyze transaction data to detect fraudulent activities, provide real-time alerts, and reduce financial losses.

Transformers and Scaling Research to Production: A Case Study

One of the most significant examples of scaling AI research to production is the development and deployment of transformer models. This is particularly highlighted in the paper "Attention Is All You Need."[1] Transformers have brought about a revolution in natural language processing (NLP) by enabling more efficient and accurate models. A key innovation in transformers is the self-attention mechanism, which allows the model to weigh the importance of different words in a sentence, thereby improving context understanding. This example underscores the importance of effectively scaling AI research to production and the role of transformer models in this process.

Scaling this research into production has been pivotal in developing advanced AI applications, such as OpenAI's ChatGPT.

ChatGPT's success showcases the importance of effective scaling from research to production, as it leverages the power of transformers to provide human-like text generation capabilities. This transformation underscores why AI product managers must prioritize scalability and robustness in their development processes to achieve impactful real-world applications.

Scaling traditional AI from research to production necessitates ensuring that the models are accurately trained and tested on real-world data. This task demands precise tuning to handle specific tasks efficiently, managing vast datasets, and continuously optimizing the models to maintain high accuracy and reliability. In this process, AI product managers play a crucial role. They oversee data collection and preprocessing, define acceptance criteria, and manage the deployment and monitoring phases. Their responsibility is to ensure that the AI models comply with regulatory requirements and ethical standards, continuously evaluating and adjusting the models to maintain their effectiveness.

AI product managers hold the key to balancing traditional AI's precision and dependability with the creative potential of generative AI. They are instrumental in transforming theoretical AI advancements into practical, user-centric applications that drive business value. By focusing on data quality, clear acceptance criteria, comprehensive ramp-up plans, and cross-functional collaboration, product managers can effectively scale AI research to production, ensuring that AI technologies deliver significant business value and drive innovation.

Traditional AI vs. Generative AI

Understanding the evolution from traditional AI to generative AI is crucial for AI product managers scaling AI research into production-ready solutions. The transition involves adopting new technologies and ensuring they are robust, scalable, and efficiently integrated into real-world applications. Based on Table 5.1, let's explore how these AI paradigms differ in the context of scaling research to production.

Feature	Old AI	New AI
Computation resource	Primarily used CPUs	Primarily uses GPUs
Scalability	Scalability limited and costly	Highly scalable with cost-effective solutions
Speed and efficiency	Slower due to manual processes and less efficient hardware	Faster due to parallel processing and more efficient hardware

Table 5.1 Key differences between old and new AI: scaling research to production for seamless deployment

Computation Resource: CPUs vs. GPUs

Traditional AI models predominantly relied on central processing units (CPUs) for computation. Although effective for simpler tasks, CPUs often struggled with the intensive computational demands of more complex AI models, leading to slower processing times and limited scalability. This limitation made moving AI research into production challenging, as the computational power required to handle large-scale real-world data was often insufficient.

In contrast, generative AI harnesses the power of graphics processing units (GPUs) designed to handle parallel processing more efficiently. GPUs significantly accelerate the training and deployment of deep learning models, enabling the rapid execution of complex computations. This advancement is pivotal for AI product managers, as it allows for the seamless transition of advanced AI research into scalable, production-ready solutions that can handle large amounts of data and deliver faster results.

Scalability: Limited and Costly vs. Highly Scalable and Cost-Effective

Scaling traditional AI was often a costly endeavor, with limited scalability options. The manual processes involved in managing and deploying these models added to the complexity and expense. Organizations faced challenges adapting these models to varying data sizes and operational demands, often hindering their practical application.

Generative AI, however, is inherently more scalable and cost-effective. Leveraging advanced hardware like GPUs and sophisticated algorithms, generative AI models can be scaled efficiently to meet the demands of large-scale production environments.

This scalability ensures that AI models can be deployed across diverse applications and industries, providing consistent performance regardless of data size or complexity. For AI product managers, this means a smoother, more cost-effective path from research to production, with the ability to rapidly iterate and improve AI models as new data and requirements emerge.

Speed and Efficiency: Slower and Less Efficient vs. Faster and More Efficient

Traditional AI development was often slow due to reliance on manual processes and less efficient hardware. The iterative nature of AI research and the need for constant tweaking and optimization meant that moving from research to production could be lengthy and cumbersome. This inefficiency limited the ability to respond quickly to new opportunities or challenges in the market.

Generative AI transforms this landscape by offering faster development cycles through parallel processing and more efficient hardware. AI-driven automation further streamlines the development and deployment process, enabling quicker iterations and more rapid improvements. For AI product managers, this increased speed and efficiency is pertinent for maintaining a competitive edge, as they can deploy robust AI solutions faster, adapt to changing conditions, and continually refine models to enhance performance.

Case Studies of Scaling AI Research to Production

To illustrate the process of scaling AI research to production, let's explore some real-life examples of innovative AI models successfully transitioning from research to practical applications. These examples highlight the critical steps and considerations involved in this journey.

Implementing a New Algorithm for E-Commerce Recommendations

This case study examines how a leading e-commerce platform transformed its recommendation system through the practical application of cutting-edge AI research. By bridging the gap between academic innovation and real-world implementation, the company not only enhanced its customer experience but also demonstrated the tangible business value of AI-driven personalization. As the project's orchestrator, the AI product manager played a pivotal role in identifying promising research, aligning technical capabilities with business needs, and guiding the systematic implementation from prototype to production (see Figure 5.3).

▶ **Business problem:** An e-commerce company wants to improve its recommendation system to enhance customer experience and increase sales.

▶ **Research:** The AI product manager identifies a recent research paper that proposes a novel algorithm for recommendation systems and shows promising results in academic settings.

▶ **Adapting the research:** The data science team and the AI product manager modify the algorithm to meet the unique requirements and limitations of the business's e-commerce platform. This involves modifying the algorithm to handle the company's unique data structure and user behavior patterns.

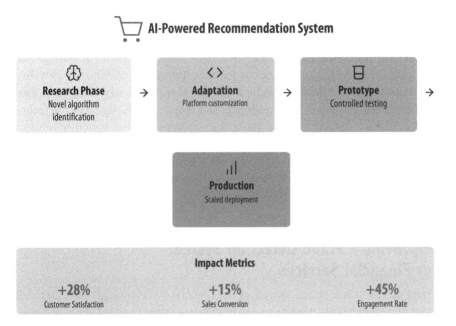

FIGURE 5.3 AI recommendation system pipeline from research to production, showing key metrics and business impact

▶ **Developing a prototype:** A prototype of the new recommendation system is developed and tested in a controlled environment. The prototype is integrated with the company's existing data pipelines and evaluated using historical data.

▶ **Iterative testing and improvement:** The prototype undergoes multiple rounds of testing, including unit testing, integration testing, and UAT. Feedback from these tests is used to refine the algorithm, improve its accuracy, and ensure that it performs well under real-world conditions.

▶ **Scaling to production:** Once the prototype consistently meets the defined objectives, it is deployed to the production environment. Continuous monitoring and maintenance are established to ensure the recommendation system remains effective and adapts to changing user behaviors.

▶ **Outcome:** The new recommendation system improves the consumer experience and boosts sales and customer happiness by offering more precise and customized recommendations.

Instacart systematically transforms cutting-edge research into production features through its AI Lab, where product managers bridge collaboration between researchers and engineers to enhance grocery recommendation systems. For instance, the development of deep learning models for substitute item recommendations drew on academic advancements in sequential prediction, which were adapted to meet Instacart's real-world business constraints and shopper needs. By balancing technical feasibility, business priorities, and a deep understanding of customer behavior, product managers played a key role in translating theoretical models into a practical real-time substitution system. This approach reportedly led to a significant increase in customer acceptance of substitute items, demonstrating the impact of aligning research with business goals.

Improving a Fraud Detection System for Financial Services

Fraud detection is a critical focus area for financial institutions, as inaccuracies in identifying fraudulent transactions can lead to significant financial losses and erode customer trust. This case study explores how a financial organization leveraged advanced AI techniques and cutting-edge research to enhance its fraud detection capabilities. By tailoring a novel feature-engineering approach to its specific needs, the institution developed and deployed a more accurate and reliable fraud detection system, demonstrating the power of AI in solving complex business challenges.

▶ **Business problem:** A financial institution needs to improve the accuracy of its fraud detection system to reduce financial losses and enhance customer trust.

▶ **Research:** The AI product manager identifies a recent study that introduces a new feature-engineering technique for improving the accuracy of fraud detection models.

▶ **Adapting the research:** The feature-engineering process is tailored to the financial organization's needs. This involves customizing the approach with the institution's transaction data and fraud detection requirements.

▶ **Developing a prototype:** A prototype fraud detection system incorporating the new feature-engineering technique is developed. The prototype is tested using historical transaction data to accurately evaluate its ability to detect fraudulent activities.

▶ **Iterative testing and improvement:** The prototype is subjected to iterative testing, including performance and UAT. Feedback from these tests is used to fine-tune the model, enhance its precision and recall, and ensure that it can handle the volume and variability of real-world transactions.

▶ **Scaling to production:** The improved fraud detection system is deployed in the production environment after thorough testing and validation. Ongoing monitoring and maintenance ensure that the system performs effectively and adapts to new fraud patterns.

▶ **Outcome:** By drastically lowering the number of false positives and negatives, the improved fraud detection system improves the accuracy of identifying fraudulent transactions. This improves the financial institution's ability to prevent fraud and protect customer accounts.

Enhancing Customer Support with AI Chatbots

This case study examines how a company enhanced its customer support through AI chatbot implementation. By adapting academic NLP research into a practical solution, the team developed a system that effectively handles customer queries while reducing agent workload. The AI product manager orchestrated the transition from research to production, resulting in improved response times and customer satisfaction (see Figure 5.4).

▶ **Business problem**: A telecommunications company aims to improve its customer support services by implementing AI chatbots to handle common customer queries and issues.

▶ **Research:** The AI product manager finds a research paper demonstrating the effectiveness of a new NLP model for chatbot applications.

▶ **Adapting the research:** The NLP model is adapted to understand and respond to the queries and issues encountered by the company's customers. This involves training the model on the company's customer service data to ensure that it provides accurate and relevant responses.

▶ **Developing a prototype:** A prototype chatbot is developed and integrated with the company's customer support platform. The prototype is tested with a limited set of real customer queries to evaluate its performance and identify areas for improvement.

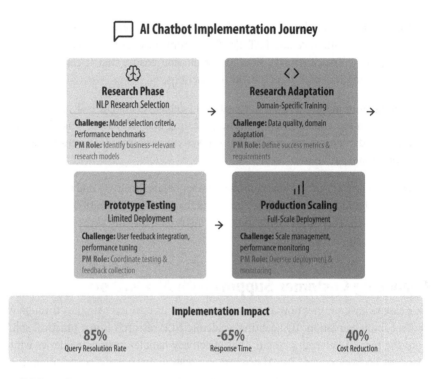

FIGURE 5.4 Research-to-production AI journey from academic research to deployed AI solution, showing product manager orchestration and business impact

▶ **Iterative testing and improvement:** The chatbot undergoes several iterative testing and feedback collection rounds. Based on this feedback, enhancements are made to the model's accuracy, response time, and user interaction. User acceptability testing is also done to ensure the chatbot satisfies customer service standards.

▶ **Scaling to production:** Once the prototype chatbot achieves the desired performance levels, it is scaled up and deployed across the company's customer support channels. Continuous monitoring is established to track the chatbot's performance and adjust it as needed.

▶ **Outcome:** The AI chatbot effectively handles many customer queries, reducing the workload on human customer support agents. This results in increased customer satisfaction, quicker response times, and cost savings for the business.

Levis transformed its customer support experience by implementing an AI-powered chatbot that assists customers in finding their perfect fit. Leveraging advanced NLP, the team developed an intelligent assistant capable of understanding detailed style preferences and offering personalized fit recommendations. Under the leadership of the AI product manager, the chatbot evolved from a simple size guide to an interactive stylist, providing tailored denim suggestions that blend size data, customer preferences, and current style trends. This innovation not only enhances customer confidence in their orders but also reduces the need for support inquiries related to fit and sizing, creating a more seamless and satisfying shopping experience.

Optimizing Supply Chain Management with Predictive Analytics

This case study examines how a manufacturing company transformed its supply chain management by implementing AI-driven predictive analytics. Through systematic adaptation of academic research into practical application, the company successfully deployed a system that optimizes inventory levels and forecasts demand patterns. The AI product manager played a crucial role in bridging research innovation with operational needs, leading to significant improvements in forecast accuracy and inventory efficiency.

- ▶ **Business problem:** A manufacturing company seeks to optimize its supply chain management by predicting demand fluctuations and managing inventory more effectively.

- ▶ **Research:** The AI product manager identifies a research study introducing a new predictive analytics model for supply chain optimization.

- ▶ **Adapting the research:** The predictive analytics model is tailored to the particular needs of the company's supply chain operations. This involves adjusting the model to account for the company's product lines, sales data, and market trends.

- ▶ **Developing a prototype:** A prototype predictive analytics system is developed and tested using the company's historical sales and inventory data. The prototype is evaluated for its accuracy in predicting demand and optimizing inventory levels.

▶ **Iterative testing and improvement:** The prototype undergoes iterative testing, including performance and integration testing. Feedback from these tests refines the model and improves its predictive accuracy. UAT ensures that the system meets the company's operational requirements.

▶ **Scaling to production:** The predictive analytics system is deployed in the production environment after thorough testing and refinement. Continuous monitoring is implemented to track the system's performance and adjust predictions as needed.

▶ **Outcome:** The optimized supply chain management system leads to more accurate demand forecasts, reduced inventory costs, and improved product availability. This enhances the company's operational efficiency and customer satisfaction.

Endnote

1   Vaswani, A., Shazeer, N., Parmar, N., Uszkoreit, J., Jones, L., Gomez, A. N., Kaiser, Ł., & Polosukhin, I. (2017). Attention is all you need. Advances in Neural Information Processing Systems, 30. Retrieved from `https://proceedings.neurips.cc/paper/2017/file/3f5ee243547dee91fbd053c1c4a845aa-Paper.pdf`

Chapter 6

Acceptance Criteria in the World of AI

Acceptance criteria are crucial in guiding the development and deployment of artificial intelligence (AI) systems, setting the standards that models must meet to succeed. Unlike traditional software development, where criteria are mostly about functionality, AI systems need a more detailed approach. This is because AI models must be evaluated on what they do and how well they perform, considering metrics like precision, recall, and the balance between false positives and false negatives.

Think of it this way: traditional software is like assembling furniture—you follow precise instructions, and if all the parts fit, the job is done. AI, however, is more like teaching a student. It's not enough to pass the test; they need to understand, adapt, and thrive in different situations. Acceptance criteria in AI are how we measure this ability—whether the model can consistently perform under varying conditions and deliver value in the real world.

In this chapter, we'll delve into the unique aspects of acceptance criteria in AI. We'll discuss the practical application of precision and recall, how to effectively use the confusion matrix, and why a ramp-up plan is a game-changer after implementation. By mastering these components, AI product managers can confidently ensure that their models work correctly and perform effectively in real-world situations. This chapter provides a practical understanding of setting, evaluating, and achieving acceptance criteria through theoretical insights and real-life examples, empowering you to translate AI research into functional, impactful applications.

In traditional software development, acceptance criteria are clear and straightforward, outlining what makes a feature complete. But in the world of AI, these criteria are far more complex. They must address not just the functionality of the AI model but also its performance, tailored to the specific model type and deeply intertwined with the business context. This demands a reimagining of success, pushing us to innovate and deliver AI solutions that are not only technologically advanced but also profoundly impactful and relevant.

Understanding Acceptance Criteria in AI

In AI, acceptance criteria are essential for ensuring that AI models meet the necessary standards to be deemed successful. Unlike traditional software, where acceptance criteria are primarily about functional requirements, AI systems require a more comprehensive approach. Here, we will explore the concept of acceptance criteria in AI, highlighting the unique challenges and considerations involved. Your role in understanding and implementing these criteria is crucial to the success of AI system development:

▶ **Functional requirements and performance metrics:** In AI, acceptance criteria begin with defining the system's functional requirements. These requirements outline what the AI model should do, such as recognizing images, processing natural language, or predicting outcomes. However, functional requirements alone are insufficient. AI models must also meet specific performance metrics to operate effectively in real-world scenarios. Key performance metrics include precision, recall, accuracy, and F1-score, each providing insights into different aspects of the model's performance.

▶ **Precision and recall:** Precision and recall play a pivotal role in AI acceptance criteria. Precision, determined by dividing all positive predictions by the percentage of true positive forecasts, showcases the model's accuracy. On the other hand, recall quantifies the percentage of actual positives among all genuine positive forecasts, reflecting the model's ability to identify all relevant instances in the dataset. Understanding and balancing these metrics is crucial, as they are key indicators of the model's performance and can be prioritized based on specific business needs.

▶ **The confusion matrix:** The confusion matrix is a vital tool in assessing AI models. It is a table comparing real and anticipated values, clearly showing how well a classification model performs. The matrix includes four key values: true positives (correctly predicted positives), false positives (incorrectly predicted positives), true negatives (correctly predicted negatives), and false negatives (incorrectly predicted negatives). AI product managers can develop realistic and significant acceptance criteria by thoroughly understanding the model's strengths and shortcomings through the confusion matrix analysis.

▶ **Complexity of AI acceptance criteria:** Acceptance criteria in AI are inherently more complex than in traditional software development. This complexity arises from the unique challenges of assessing whether the AI system functions correctly and how well it performs under various conditions. AI models learn from data, and numerous factors, including data quality, feature selection, and training processes, can influence their performance. Therefore, acceptance criteria must encompass a range of performance metrics to ensure robustness and reliability. We understand the complexity of your work, and this chapter is here to help you navigate it.

▶ **Behavior and outcomes:** Beyond performance metrics, acceptance criteria must describe the expected behavior and outcomes of the AI system in different scenarios. This includes defining how the system should respond to various inputs and conditions. For instance, acceptance criteria in an AI-powered customer service chatbot might include responding accurately to user queries, handling unexpected inputs gracefully, and maintaining a certain response time.

▶ **Iterative updates and continuous improvement:** Acceptance criteria for AI systems are not static; they must evolve as the system learns and improves. As new data becomes available and the model is exposed to different scenarios, continuous monitoring and iterative updates are necessary to maintain performance standards. This iterative process of updating acceptance criteria is fundamental to ensuring that the AI system remains effective and aligned with business goals, highlighting the dynamic nature of AI system development.

Defining Functional Requirements and Performance Standards

Determining functional requirements and performance standards is a critical first step in guaranteeing the effective implementation of AI systems. Unlike traditional software development, which focuses primarily on functional specifications, AI systems necessitate a nuanced approach emphasizing performance metrics. This subsection delves into establishing these critical acceptance criteria for AI projects:

▶ **Functional requirements:** Functional requirements specify what the AI system should do and how it should perform specific tasks. These requirements outline the core functionalities that the system must deliver to meet business objectives.

For example, functional requirements in an image recognition system might include accurately identifying and classifying different objects within images. For an AI chatbot, functional requirements might cover understanding user queries, providing accurate responses, and handling multiple user interactions simultaneously. Clearly defining functional requirements is a collaborative process that involves stakeholders. It's about understanding the business needs and user expectations and ensuring that the AI system aligns with the business strategy and delivers tangible value. Functional requirements should be specific, measurable, and aligned with the business goals to provide a clear roadmap for the development team.

▶ **Performance standards:** Performance standards are essential for evaluating the effectiveness of AI models. These standards go beyond basic functionality to assess how well the model performs its tasks. Key performance metrics for AI systems include precision, recall, F1-score, and inference speed. Each indication helps to guarantee that the AI system performs successfully in real-world scenarios by providing insights into diverse aspects of the model's performance.

  ▶ **Precision:** The precision of the model is determined by dividing all of its positive predictions by the percentage of true positive forecasts. It shows how accurately the model predicts favorable outcomes. High precision is essential in applications like fraud detection or medical diagnostics, where false positives might have serious repercussions.

  ▶ **Recall:** The ratio of accurate positive forecasts among all real positive occurrences is known as recall. It reflects the model's ability to identify all relevant cases. High recall is essential in applications where missing positive instances, such as security surveillance or disease outbreak detection, can be costly.

  ▶ **F1-score:** The F1-score is a statistic that balances precision and recall by taking the harmonic mean of the two. It is especially beneficial when precision and recall are required to balance a specific application.

  ▶ **Inference speed:** Inference speed measures how quickly the AI model can predict. This metric is critical in real-time applications, such as autonomous driving or real-time financial trading, where timely decisions are essential.

▶ **Behavior and outcomes:** Defining expected behavior and outcomes for the AI system is another vital component of acceptance criteria. This includes specifying how the system should respond to different inputs and conditions. For instance, an AI-powered recommendation engine should provide relevant product suggestions based on user behavior and preferences. In contrast, an AI-driven fraud detection system should accurately flag suspicious transactions while minimizing false positives.

Behavioral requirements should consider various scenarios and edge cases to ensure that the AI system can gracefully handle unexpected situations. This includes defining error-handling protocols, failover mechanisms, and response strategies for scenarios where the model's confidence is low.

▶ **Data quality and input conditions:** The quality of the input data strongly impacts the effectiveness of AI models. The standards for data quality, including data formats, sources, and preparation procedures, should be outlined in the acceptance criteria. Ensuring the quality of input data is crucial for developing robust and dependable models. To ensure that the model can effectively understand varied user inputs, acceptance requirements in a natural language processing (NLP) application can, for instance, state the necessity for a wide and representative dataset containing various dialects and accents.

▶ **Scalability and load testing:** Scalability and load testing are critical for AI systems that handle large datasets or high user loads. Acceptance criteria should include scalability requirements to ensure that the system can grow with increasing demands. Load testing helps verify that the AI system performs well under peak conditions, maintaining its accuracy and efficiency.

▶ **User experience (UX) considerations:** Acceptance criteria for AI applications with user interfaces should cover UX aspects like design, navigation, and user interaction requirements. Providing a smooth and simple UX is essential for AI systems to be adopted and successful. For example, an AI-driven customer care platform should have an intuitive user interface that simplifies it so that users can engage with the system and receive prompt, correct answers to their questions.

Managing Data Quality, Scalability, and Compliance

In AI, managing data quality, ensuring scalability, and maintaining compliance are critical to the acceptance criteria. These elements are fundamental to the success of AI models, as they directly impact the model's performance, reliability, and adherence to legal and ethical standards. This section explores these three essential aspects in detail:

▶ **Quality of data:** The foundation of successful AI models is high-quality data. Inaccurate forecasts, skewed results, and general model failure can result from poor data quality. Therefore, acceptance criteria for AI systems must include stringent data quality requirements.

Key aspects of data quality management include:

▶ **Data accuracy:** Ensure that the data used for training and testing the AI model is accurate and error-free. Inaccurate data can mislead the model, resulting in poor performance.

▶ **Data completeness:** The dataset should be comprehensive and include all relevant features to train the model effectively. Missing data can create gaps in the model's learning process, leading to unreliable predictions.

▶ **Data consistency:** Data should be consistent across different sources and periods. Inconsistencies can confuse the model and degrade its performance.

▶ **Data relevance:** The data must be relevant to the problem the AI model is designed to solve. Irrelevant data can introduce noise, making it harder for the model to identify important patterns.

▶ **Data preprocessing:** Data preprocessing steps, such as cleaning, normalization, and feature engineering, should be clearly defined. Proper preprocessing is crucial for transforming raw data into a format suitable for model training.

▶ **Scalability:** Scalability is another critical factor in the acceptance criteria for AI systems. AI models must handle increasing amounts of data and user interactions without performance degradation. Ensuring scalability involves:

▶ **Load testing:** Conducting tests to evaluate how the AI system performs under different demand levels. This helps identify potential bottlenecks and ensures that the system can scale efficiently.

▶ **Resource utilization:** Monitoring and optimizing computational resources, such as central processing units (CPU), graphics processing unit (GPU), and memory. Efficient resource utilization ensures that the system can handle large-scale operations without excessive costs.

▶ **Distributed computing:** Implementing techniques to manage large datasets and complex computations. This involves using a framework like Apache Hadoop or Spark to distribute tasks across multiple nodes, enhancing scalability.

▶ **Elasticity:** Designing the system to be elastic allows it to automatically scale up or down based on the current workload to scale up or down based on the current workload automatically. This ensures optimal performance and cost efficiency.

▶ **Performance optimization:** Continuously optimize the model and system performance through pruning, quantization, and more efficient algorithms.

▶ **Compliance:** Compliance with legal, ethical, and regulatory standards is paramount in AI development. Acceptance criteria must ensure that the AI system adheres to all relevant guidelines and regulations. Key aspects of compliance include:

▶ **Data privacy:** Implementing data protection mechanisms, gaining required consent, and anonymizing sensitive information are all critical to ensure that the AI system complies with data privacy standards, including the General Data Protection Regulation (GDPR), the California Consumer Privacy Act (CCPA), and the Health Insurance Portability and Accountability Act (HIPAA).

▶ **Bias and fairness:** Addressing potential biases in the data and model to ensure fair and unbiased outcomes. This includes conducting bias audits, using fairness metrics, and implementing bias mitigation strategies.

▶ **Transparency and explainability:** Ensuring that the AI system's decision-making process is visible and understandable. Stakeholders must comprehend the model's decision-making process to establish credibility and responsibility.

▶ **Security:** Implementing strong security measures to protect the AI system and its data from cyberattacks. This includes encryption, access controls, and regular security audits.

▶ **Regulatory compliance:** Adhering to industry-specific regulations that govern the use of AI. For example, AI systems in healthcare must comply with FDA guidelines, whereas financial AI systems must adhere to SEC regulations.

▶ **Integration and interoperability:** Integrating existing systems and ensuring interoperability are important considerations in managing scalability and compliance. Acceptance criteria should include requirements for:

   ▶ **Seamless integration:** The AI system should integrate seamlessly with the organization's IT infrastructure, including databases, software applications, and hardware. This ensures smooth operation and minimizes disruption.

   ▶ **Interoperability:** The AI system should be compatible with other systems and platforms, allowing for data exchange and collaboration. This enhances the system's functionality and utility.

   ▶ **API standards:** Defining and adhering to API standards to ensure consistent and reliable communication between the AI system and other components.

By rigorously managing data quality, ensuring scalability, and maintaining compliance, AI product managers can develop robust AI systems that perform reliably and ethically in real-world applications. These acceptance criteria help bridge the gap between research and production, ensuring that AI innovations deliver tangible business value while adhering to legal and ethical standards.

Developing a Ramp-Up Plan for AI Deployments

Introducing a new AI system into the real world is like preparing for a big event—you want everything to go as smoothly as possible. That's why developing a ramp-up plan is so important (see Figure 6.1). Think of it as a gradual rollout strategy that eases your AI model from the controlled environment of development into the complexities of full-scale operation. A ramp-up plan allows you to start small, monitor performance, make necessary adjustments, and address any issues that pop up along the way. This not only boosts the model's performance over time but also builds confidence among stakeholders. In this section, we'll walk through the key components and strategies to create an effective ramp-up plan, so you can deploy your AI systems with confidence and set them up for long-term success.

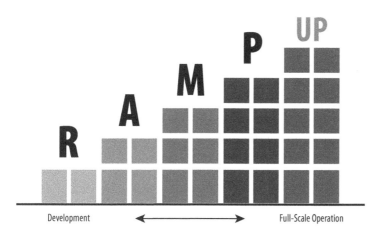

Development ←————————————→ Full-Scale Operation

FIGURE 6.1 A stepped visualization showing the gradual ramp-up progression from AI development to full-scale operation, emphasizing phased deployment and increasing scale of implementation

Importance of a Ramp-Up Plan

A ramp-up plan is essential for several reasons:

1. **Risk mitigation:** Gradually scaling the AI system helps identify and mitigate risks before they affect a large user base.

2. **Performance optimization:** It allows for the continuous optimization of model performance based on real-world data and feedback.

3. **Resource management:** It helps manage computational and human resources more effectively, avoiding sudden spikes in demand.

4. **User adoption:** It facilitates user training and adaptation to the new system, enhancing UX and satisfaction.

Key Components of a Ramp-Up Plan

▶ **Baseline model deployment:** The first phase involves deploying a baseline model to establish initial performance metrics. This stage is crucial for setting a reference point for future improvements.

Actions:

▶ Train the model on available data.

▶ Evaluate baseline precision, recall, and other relevant metrics.

▶ Deploy the model in a controlled or test environment to limit impact.

▶ **Data augmentation and quality improvement:** Improving the quality and amount of training data is critical for optimizing model performance. This phase focuses on expanding the dataset and refining data quality.

Actions:

▶ **Data collection:** Increase the dataset size by collecting more examples, focusing on underrepresented classes or cases where the model performs poorly.

▶ **Data cleaning:** Remove noisy or irrelevant examples to enhance data quality.

▶ **Feature engineering:** Modify or add features based on initial performance insights to help the model make better predictions.

▶ **Model tuning and regularization:** Optimizing the model to balance precision and recall is a critical step in the ramp-up plan. This phase involves fine-tuning model parameters and applying regularization techniques.

Actions:

▶ **Hyperparameter tuning:** Adjust model hyperparameters to find the best balance between precision and recall.

▶ **Regularization techniques:** Implement dropout or L2 regularization techniques to prevent overfitting and improve generalization.

▶ **Model complexity adjustment:** Simplify or increase model complexity based on performance analysis.

▶ **Advanced techniques and iteration:** Leveraging advanced techniques and continuous iteration is essential for refining model performance. This phase includes ensemble methods and custom loss functions to enhance precision and recall.

Actions:

▶ **Ensemble methods:** Combine multiple models to improve overall performance.

▶ **Custom loss functions:** Create loss functions that optimize the balance of precision and recall based on business objectives.

▶ **Active learning:** Iteratively label more data the model is uncertain about to improve predictions.

▶ **Continuous monitoring and improvement:** Establishing ongoing processes for monitoring and enhancing model performance ensures sustained effectiveness. This phase involves setting up systems for continuous feedback and iteration.

Actions:

▶ **Performance monitoring:** Monitor model performance in the live environment to detect degradation.

▶ **Feedback loops:** Implement systems to collect user feedback or ground truth data for continuous retraining and updates.

▶ **Periodic review:** Regularly review model performance against business objectives and adjust strategies as needed.

▶ **Addressing false positives and false negatives:** An essential component of the ramp-up technique is maximizing the ratio of false positives to false negatives. Depending on the application, the impact of these errors can vary significantly (see Figure 6.2).

▶ **False positives:** Occur when the model incorrectly predicts a positive outcome. In applications like fraud detection, false positives can lead to unnecessary investigations and resource wastage.

▶ **False negatives:** Happen when the model does not make a successful prediction. False negatives can have major effects in applications such as medical diagnostics, including missed diagnoses.

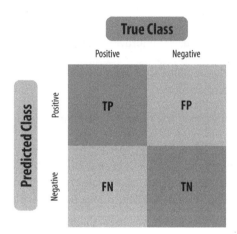

FIGURE 6.2 Confusion matrix showing true positives (TP), false positives (FP), false negatives (FN), and true negatives (TN), essential metrics for evaluating AI model performance and reliability

Confusion Matrix

Understanding false positives and false negatives is a fundamental step in mastering classification algorithms.

The significance of this lies in its real-world impact. Imagine a medical diagnostic system that incorrectly classifies a patient as healthy when they're not (a false negative) or flags a healthy patient as sick (a false positive). The former could lead to missed treatments with serious consequences, while the latter might cause unnecessary anxiety and costs. These errors aren't just technical—they directly affect lives, finances, and trust in the system. Grasping the balance between these outcomes is critical for building models that are not only accurate but also meaningful in their application.

To aid in this understanding, the confusion matrix is an invaluable tool. It's a table that provides a comprehensive evaluation of a classification algorithm's performance, summarizing both correct and incorrect predictions. While it's a staple for data scientists and machine learning (ML) practitioners, it's equally critical for AI product managers. Why? Because understanding the confusion matrix empowers product managers to bridge the gap between technical teams and business stakeholders. It allows them to grasp the trade-offs between false positives and false negatives, align these outcomes with business priorities, and set realistic performance expectations for AI systems. Whether the goal is reducing operational costs, improving customer experience, or ensuring compliance, the insights from a confusion matrix are indispensable for informed decision-making and effective product strategy.

Here's a breakdown of the confusion matrix components:

▶ **True positives (TP):** The positive class is accurately predicted by the model.

▶ **True negatives (TN):** The negative class is accurately predicted by the model.

▶ **False positives (FP):** A Type I error occurs when the model forecasts the positive class inaccurately.

▶ **False negatives (FN):** A Type II error occurs when the model predicts the negative class inaccurately.

Example Confusion Matrix   Consider a medical diagnostic test for detecting a disease. Let's say we tested 100 patients, and the results are as follows:

▶ Fifty patients have the disease (positive cases).

▶ Fifty patients do not have the disease (negative cases).

After applying the diagnostic test, we get the results shown in Table 6.1.

	Predicted positive	**Predicted negative**
Actual positive (disease)	TP = 45	FN = 5
Actual negative (no disease)	FP = 10	TN = 40

Table 6.1 Confusion matrix

From this confusion matrix, we can see:

▶ **True positives (TP):** Forty-five patients were correctly diagnosed with the disease.

▶ **True negatives (TN):** Forty patients were correctly identified as not having the disease.

▶ **False positives (FP):** Forty patients were incorrectly diagnosed with the disease.

▶ **False negatives (FN):** Five patients were incorrectly identified as not having the disease.

Strategies to Address False Positives and False Negatives

▶ **Threshold adjustment:** Adjusting the decision threshold to find a balance that minimizes the impact of false positives and negatives. For instance, lowering the threshold might reduce false negatives but increase false positives, whereas raising it might have the opposite effect.

▶ **Cost-sensitive learning:** Implementing algorithms considering the costs of false positives and negatives. This approach weighs the errors differently based on their impact on the specific application, such as higher costs for missed diagnoses in medical applications.

▶ **Postprocessing rules:** Business rules are applied after the model prediction to further refine the results based on domain-specific knowledge. For example, in fraud detection, a transaction flagged as fraudulent by the model might undergo additional checks before final action.

By understanding and utilizing the confusion matrix, AI product managers can better evaluate and improve their models, ensuring that they effectively balance false positives and false negatives to meet the specific needs of their applications.

Optimizing Precision and Recall

The ramp-up plan should include strategies for continuously optimizing precision and recall based on real-world performance. These strategies involve:

▶ **Incremental improvements:** Making small, incremental changes to the model and evaluating their impact on performance

▶ **A/B testing:** Running controlled experiments to compare different model versions and determine the best-performing one

▶ **User feedback:** Collecting and implementing user comments to help the model become more relevant and accurate

Generative AI and Traditional AI within Acceptance Criteria in AI

Generative AI is a game-changer in the AI landscape, capable of creating new, unique content that mimics human creativity. This type of AI shines in fields like marketing, design, and content creation. For example, generative AI can whip up personalized marketing copy, create multiple versions of digital designs, and even simulate environments for training purposes. To integrate generative AI, we need to set acceptance criteria that focus on the quality, creativity, and relevance of the content it produces. AI product managers are crucial here, ensuring that the models are rigorously tested and meet high quality and user expectations. This involves a lot of iteration and fine-tuning based on real-world performance and feedback.

Conversely, traditional AI is about precision and reliability, handling tasks like classification, prediction, and data analysis. It's widely used in finance, healthcare, and logistics sectors to detect fraud, diagnose diseases, and manage supply chains. For traditional AI, acceptance criteria often emphasize accuracy, precision, recall, and performance metrics. These models must be tested rigorously against diverse datasets to ensure that they work well in real-world situations.

AI product managers are the linchpins in defining and managing acceptance criteria for both types of AI. They connect the dots between what the AI models can do and what the business needs. For generative AI, this means ensuring that the content is high-quality and bias-free. Traditional AI means optimizing the models for the right balance of precision and recall, minimizing errors. AI product managers set clear, measurable criteria, oversee data collection and preprocessing, and ensure that everything meets ethical standards. The strategic implementation of these criteria ensures that AI models are reliable and aligned with business goals. AI product managers manage the integration of AI into business, ensuring that models are robust, scalable, and compliant with regulations. They work closely with data scientists and developers, continuously monitor and improve AI models, and ensure that ethical considerations are always in play.

The evolution of acceptance criteria in AI systems represents a fascinating progression spanning three key phases, as shown in Figure 6.3, each with its own unique evaluation framework. Traditional software relied on binary pass/fail testing through feature and requirement checklists. ML/AI systems introduced quantitative metrics like precision and recall using confusion matrixes. Modern generative AI expanded

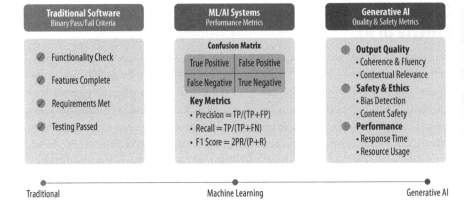

FIGURE 6.3 Evolution of acceptance criteria across software development paradigms: from traditional binary testing to advanced AI evaluation metrics

to include qualitative measures of output coherence and relevance, along with safety considerations and performance metrics. This progression reflects the increasing complexity of AI systems, transitioning from simple binary validation to comprehensive evaluation frameworks measuring both quantitative and qualitative aspects.

Balancing the innovative potential of generative AI with the reliability of traditional AI is no small feat. AI product managers need to make smart decisions about which type of AI to use based on the specific business needs and resources available. By focusing on comprehensive acceptance criteria, robust testing, and continuous improvement, AI solutions can ensure real business value and drive innovation, turning theoretical advancements into practical applications that enhance user experiences and achieve business goals.

Traditional AI vs. Generative AI

As shown in Table 6.2, acceptance criteria are essential in guiding the development and deployment of AI systems, ensuring that they meet the necessary standards for success. Unlike traditional software, where acceptance criteria are primarily about functionality, AI systems require a more detailed approach due to the complexity of evaluating model performance.

Criteria	Old AI	New AI
Precision and recall	Central focus for simpler tasks	Balanced with complex metrics and perception
Fluid metrics	Limited by model complexity	Emphasized; includes real-time performance
Ethical considerations	Less focus due to simpler applications	Strong focus on reducing toxicity, bias, and hallucinations

Table 6.2 Acceptance criteria in the world of AI: old vs. new AI

Here, we will delve into how acceptance criteria differ for traditional AI and generative AI, emphasizing their unique requirements and the role of AI product managers in defining and managing these criteria.

Precision and Recall: Central Focus vs. Balanced Metrics

Precision and recall are central metrics in traditional AI, especially for simpler tasks like classification and prediction. These models focus on achieving high precision (the accuracy of positive predictions) and high recall (capturing all relevant instances). For example, in fraud detection, traditional AI aims to maximize recall to identify as many fraudulent activities as possible while maintaining precision to reduce false positives.

Generative AI, however, requires a more balanced approach. Although precision and recall are still important, additional complex metrics like the F1-score, which balances precision and recall, are crucial. Generative AI models, such as those used for content creation, must be accurate and produce high-quality, contextually relevant outputs. AI product managers must ensure that these models are evaluated on broader metrics to maintain quality and relevance in their outputs.

Fluid Metrics: Limited by Complexity vs. Emphasized Real-Time Performance

Traditional AI metrics are often constrained by model complexity. The focus is on achieving specific performance benchmarks within the limitations of the model's architecture. These models typically undergo extensive offline testing to meet predefined standards before deployment. However, their ability to adapt to changing conditions in real time is limited.

In contrast, generative AI strongly emphasizes fluid metrics, including real-time performance. These models must dynamically adapt to new inputs and continuously learn from real-world data. For instance, a generative AI model used in an interactive art application must generate high-quality images based on user input in real time. AI product managers need to implement robust monitoring and feedback systems to ensure that these models maintain performance and adapt effectively to evolving requirements.

Ethical Considerations: Simpler Applications vs. Reducing Toxicity, Bias, and Hallucinations

Ethical considerations in traditional AI were often less emphasized, primarily due to the more uncomplicated nature of the applications. However, the need for ethical oversight has grown as AI applications become more complicated and integrated into critical decision-making processes. Traditional AI acceptance criteria now increasingly incorporate fairness, transparency, and accountability.

Given its potential to create new content, generative AI faces significant ethical challenges. These models must be designed and evaluated to minimize toxicity, bias, and hallucinations (generating misleading or false information). For example, a generative AI used in moderation must accurately filter out harmful content while avoiding censorship of legitimate expression. AI product managers are essential in defining ethical standards, conducting regular audits, and ensuring compliance with regulatory requirements to build trust and credibility in AI applications.

Case Studies of Acceptance Criteria in the World of AI

These examples highlight the practical challenges and solutions that AI product managers navigate.

Fraud Detection in Financial Services

▶ **Business requirements:** A financial institution aims to enhance its fraud detection system to reduce losses from fraudulent transactions. The goal is to use the model's ability to detect fraud while minimizing false positives, which can inconvenience customers and create operational burdens (see Figure 6.4).

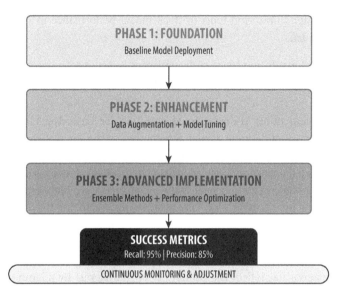

FIGURE 6.4 AI-driven fraud detection: a risk-balanced implementation approach

Acceptance Criteria:

▶ **Minimum recall:** Ninety-five percent to ensure that most fraudulent activities are caught.

▶ **Minimum precision:** Eighty-five percent to reduce the number of false positives.

▶ **False positive rate:** Below 5 percent to maintain customer satisfaction.

Ramp-Up Plan:

▶ **Baseline model deployment:** Deploy an initial model trained on historical transaction data to establish baseline metrics.

▶ **Data augmentation:** Collect more transaction data, especially from underrepresented fraud cases, to improve model accuracy.

▶ **Model tuning:** Adjust hyperparameters and apply regularization techniques to balance recall and precision.

▶ **Advanced techniques:** Use ensemble methods to combine multiple models and improve overall performance.

▶ **Continuous monitoring:** Monitoring tools to track model performance in real time and adjust as needed.

▶ **Outcome:** The financial institution successfully enhances its fraud detection system, reducing fraudulent losses and maintaining customer trust.

Block's approach to implementing AI-driven fraud detection for Cash App highlights the critical importance of defining robust acceptance criteria for real-world AI deployments. In AI systems, acceptance criteria go beyond traditional software measures like binary pass/fail checks and instead focus on performance metrics tied to business goals. Block's implementation reportedly aimed to achieve high detection accuracy (recall) while maintaining a low false positive rate, balancing the dual objectives of safeguarding billions in annualized payments and providing a seamless UX. Its iterative implementation process—progressing from baseline models to more sophisticated methods, including ensemble approaches—emphasizes the need for evolving acceptance criteria that reflect the complexity of AI systems. By aligning these criteria with measurable business outcomes, Block was able to enhance its fraud detection system, transforming it from a regulatory necessity into a competitive differentiator. This underscores how well-defined AI acceptance criteria can drive both technical precision and strategic business impact.

Personalized Marketing in E-Commerce

▶ **Business requirements:** An e-commerce company aims to improve its recommendation system to increase sales and customer engagement. The objective is to provide more accurate and personalized product recommendations to users (see Figure 6.5).

Acceptance Criteria:

▶ **Minimum precision:** Ninety percent to ensure that recommendations are relevant.

▶ **Minimum recall:** Eighty percent to capture a wide range of customer interests.

▶ **Click-through rate (CTR):** At least 5 percent to measure engagement.

Ramp-Up Plan:

▶ **Baseline model deployment:** Launch a basic recommendation model using collaborative filtering techniques.

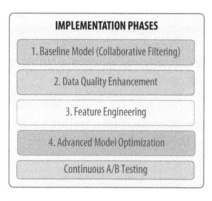 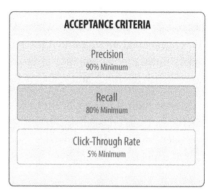

BUSINESS OBJECTIVE
Improve Sales and Customer Engagement through Personalized Recommendations

IMPLEMENTATION PHASES
1. Baseline Model (Collaborative Filtering)
2. Data Quality Enhancement
3. Feature Engineering
4. Advanced Model Optimization
Continuous A/B Testing

ACCEPTANCE CRITERIA
Precision
90% Minimum

Recall
80% Minimum

Click-Through Rate
5% Minimum

EXPECTED OUTCOMES
↑ Sales | ↑ User Engagement | ↑ Time on Platform | ↑ Purchase Frequency

FIGURE 6.5 From metrics to value: building AI acceptance criteria into e-commerce recommendations

▶ **Data quality improvement:** Enhance the dataset by including more user behavior data, such as browsing history and past purchases.

▶ **Feature engineering:** Add features like user demographics and real-time behavior tracking to improve recommendation accuracy.

▶ **Model optimization:** Apply matrix factorization and neural collaborative filtering to refine the model.

▶ **Continuous improvement:** Use A/B testing to compare different model versions and iteratively improve recommendations based on user feedback.

▶ **Outcome:** The e-commerce company sees a significant increase in sales and customer engagement, with users spending more time on the platform and making more purchases.

AI acceptance criteria fundamentally differ based on business risk profiles. Block's fraud detection system demands exceptional recall (for example, 95 percent or greater) and minimal false positives because missing fraud has severe consequences. In contrast, e-commerce recommendation engines prioritize precision (for example, 90 percent) over recall (for example, 80 percent), as a missed product suggestion carries minimal risk.

The feedback loops also differ critically: fraud detection measures success through the absence of negative events, whereas recommendation systems benefit from direct user engagement metrics and A/B testing. This contrast exemplifies how AI product leaders must align acceptance criteria not just with technical capabilities but with business risk tolerance and value creation mechanisms.

In essence, high-stakes applications like fraud detection require stringent, protective criteria, whereas engagement-driven systems like recommendations thrive on iterative, user-feedback-driven metrics. Success lies in matching acceptance criteria to each AI application's unique risk-reward profile.

Predictive Maintenance in Manufacturing

▶ **Business requirements:** A manufacturing firm seeks to implement a predictive maintenance system to reduce equipment downtime and maintenance costs. The goal is to predict equipment failures before they occur and schedule timely maintenance (see Figure 6.6).

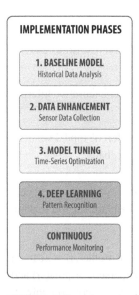
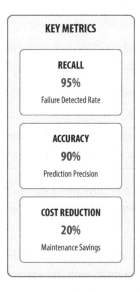

FIGURE 6.6 Metrics to operations: building AI acceptance criteria for predictive maintenance

Acceptance Criteria:

▶ **Minimum recall:** Ninety-five percent to ensure that most potential failures are detected.

▶ **Prediction accuracy:** Above 90 percent to reduce unnecessary maintenance.

▶ **Maintenance cost reduction:** At least a 20 percent decrease in costs.

Ramp-Up Plan:

▶ **Baseline model deployment:** Develop an initial predictive model using historical maintenance and sensor data.

▶ **Data collection and cleaning:** Gather more sensor data and clean the dataset to remove noise and irrelevant information.

▶ **Model tuning:** Optimize the model using time-series analysis and ML algorithms.

▶ **Advanced techniques:** Incorporate deep learning methods for better pattern recognition and anomaly detection.

▶ **Monitoring and maintenance:** Monitor model performance and update it with fresh data to ensure correctness and reliability.

▶ **Outcome:** The manufacturing firm significantly reduces equipment downtime and maintenance costs, improving overall operational efficiency.

This industrial AI implementation demonstrates how acceptance criteria must adapt to operational technology environments. Unlike fraud detection's focus on risk mitigation, predictive maintenance requires a balanced approach across three key metrics: technical reliability (95 percent recall), operational precision (90 percent accuracy), and business value (20 percent cost reduction).

What sets this case apart is its direct connection between AI performance and equipment reliability. False positives translate to unnecessary maintenance costs, whereas false negatives result in expensive failures—creating a clear framework where acceptance criteria directly tie to operational and financial outcomes.

The key insight for AI product leaders: industrial AI applications demand acceptance criteria that create a direct line of sight from model performance to operational improvements, with success measured in both technical accuracy and tangible business results.

Creative Design with Generative AI

▶ **Business requirements:** An advertising agency seeks to use generative AI to create innovative design concepts for marketing campaigns, aiming to enhance creativity and efficiency (see Figure 6.7).

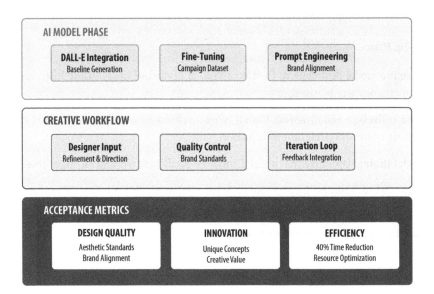

FIGURE 6.7 Balancing art and automation in creative AI

Acceptance Criteria:

▶ **Design quality:** Generated designs must meet aesthetic and branding guidelines.

▶ **Innovation:** AI-generated designs should offer unique and innovative concepts.

▶ **Efficiency:** Reduce the time required to develop initial design concepts by at least 40 percent.

Ramp-Up Plan:

▶ **Baseline model deployment:** Deploy a generative AI model like DALL-E to generate initial design concepts based on text prompts.

▶ **Quality evaluation:** Assess the generated designs against branding and quality standards.

▶ **Model customization:** Fine-tune the AI model using a dataset of past successful campaigns to align outputs with the agency's style.

▶ **Workflow integration:** Integrate AI-generated designs into the agency's creative workflow, allowing designers to refine and build on AI suggestions.

▶ **Feedback loop:** Implement a feedback system where designers provide input on AI outputs to refine the model further.

▶ **Outcome:** The advertising agency boosts its creative process, producing innovative design concepts more quickly and efficiently, ultimately enhancing client satisfaction and driving business growth.

This creative AI implementation represents a paradigm shift in how we define AI acceptance criteria. As we explored earlier in comparing traditional and generative AI acceptance criteria, whereas fraud detection systems measure success through clear numerical thresholds (95 percent recall) and recommendation engines through explicit user engagement (5 percent CTR), creative AI exists in a more nuanced space requiring a hybrid evaluation framework. The uniqueness lies in its three critical dimensions: quantitative metrics demonstrated by a 40 percent time reduction in design concept generation, qualitative standards ensuring aesthetic quality and brand alignment, and innovation metrics measuring novel concept generation and creative differentiation.

What sets this case apart is its dual-track validation approach, where the technical track ensures model performance through fine-tuning and prompt engineering, and the creative track maintains artistic integrity through designer collaboration and quality control. This balanced framework demonstrates how AI acceptance criteria must evolve beyond binary success metrics when dealing with inherently subjective creative processes.

The key lesson for AI product leaders is clear: in creative domains, acceptance criteria must bridge the gap between computational efficiency and creative excellence, establishing new standards for how we measure AI system success in subjective domains.

Part III

Sustainable Excellence & Innovation

Achieving Breakthrough Performance with Responsible Innovation

Chapter 7

Patience and Plan to Surpass Human-Level Performance

Integrating artificial intelligence (AI) into business operations is transformative but often involves phases where AI may initially underperform compared to human capabilities. This early struggle is not a deterrent but a critical part of the innovation process. Understanding this can help avoid the pit known as the *innovator's dilemma*, where promising projects are prematurely terminated due to short-term performance issues. For example, a company implementing AI chatbots for customer service might initially find these bots less effective than human agents. Early interactions may lead to slower responses and occasional errors, causing customer frustration. However, this phase highlights AI's potential. As the AI system learns from each interaction, it improves, eventually surpassing human performance by efficiently handling more queries and providing consistent, 24/7 support. Prematurely terminating the project during its initial struggles overlooks the long-term benefits and innovation that AI can bring once it matures and adapts to the business's specific needs.

This chapter emphasizes the need for patience and strategic planning to harness AI's potential and achieve and surpass human-level performance, instilling confidence in the long-term benefits of AI projects (see Figure 7.1). We explore why patience

FOUNDATION	HUMAN PARITY	SUPERHUMAN
Initial Performance	Matching Performance	Enhanced Performance
60–80% of Human Level	Equal to Human Level	Exceeding Human Level
• Model Training	• Process Integration	• Advanced Capabilities
• Data Collection	• Fine-tuning	• Continuous Learning
3–6 Months	6–12 Months	12+ Months

STRATEGIC PATIENCE + SYSTEMATIC PLANNING = SUCCESS

FIGURE 7.1 AI evolution framework: the journey from initial deployment to superhuman performance, emphasizing strategic patience and systematic planning as key success factors

is essential, considering factors such as task complexity, data requirements, and the incremental nature of AI advancements. We outline strategic planning steps to ensure continuous improvement and eventual success of AI initiatives. Through case studies and real-world examples, we show how a well-structured plan and patience can transform underperforming AI projects into strong, human-level performers. This equips AI product managers with the insights and strategies to champion AI innovations and drive significant business value.

> The pursuit of human-level AI demands patience. Researchers and developers are charting new territory, tackling complex technical and ethical hurdles. Although progress can be swift, true breakthroughs require perseverance, resilience, and a willingness to learn from setbacks on the path to transformative innovation. This journey underscores the innovator's dilemma—the risk for established players to be disrupted by those willing to embrace the potential and uncertainty of AI's future.

The Importance of Patience in AI Development

Integrating AI into business operations demands significant patience. Achieving and surpassing human-level performance in AI involves overcoming numerous challenges that require time, dedication, and a strategic approach. Here's why patience is essential in AI development:

▶ **Complexity of tasks:** Tasks that humans perform effortlessly, such as understanding context and making nuanced decisions, are highly complex for AI systems to replicate. Developing models capable of these tasks involves extensive research and numerous iterations of experimentation and improvement. This process can take years, necessitating a long-term commitment. AI product creators must set realistic expectations and communicate the complexity and time required to stakeholders, breaking tasks into milestones and keeping the team focused on incremental progress.

▶ **Data requirements:** Effective AI models rely on large volumes of high-quality data. Collecting, cleaning, and annotating this data is time-consuming but crucial (see Figure 7.2). It can take years to gather a comprehensive and representative dataset to train a robust AI model. Patience is required to ensure that the data

DATA COLLECTION

DATA CLEANING

DATA ANNOTATING

OTHER TASKS

Data scientists
spend 60% of their
time on cleaning
data.

FIGURE 7.2 Data reality check: data scientists spend 60 percent of their time on cleaning and preparation, underscoring why building a robust AI system requires patience and proper data governance

foundation is solid. AI product managers must ensure that the data pipeline is well-managed and that the importance of high-quality data is understood across the organization, working with data engineers and scientists to establish efficient data governance practices.

▶ **Algorithm development:** Creating AI algorithms that mimic human-like reasoning and decision-making is iterative and complex. Researchers must continually experiment with different approaches, test hypotheses, and refine algorithms. Significant advancements require sustained effort over time. AI product managers must coordinate these efforts, support the team, and keep the development process on track, fostering an environment that promotes experimentation and creativity.

▶ **Computational resources:** Training sophisticated AI models demands substantial computational power. Setting up the necessary infrastructure, including powerful hardware and efficient data pipelines, involves considerable time and investment. Organizations must be patient as they build and scale these resources. AI product managers advocate for the necessary resources and ensure that the infrastructure supports the long-term AI strategy.

▶ **Incremental progress:** Progress in AI is often incremental, with each small advancement contributing to the overall goal of human-level performance. Researchers build on existing work, making gradual improvements to models and algorithms. This steady progress requires a long-term perspective and an appreciation for the cumulative impact of incremental advancements. AI product managers must maintain momentum, celebrate small victories, and keep the team focused on the long-term vision.

▶ **Ethical considerations:** As AI systems approach human-level performance, addressing ethical considerations such as fairness, bias, and transparency becomes increasingly important. Ensuring AI systems follow ethical standards and prevent unforeseen outcomes necessitates substantial consideration and patience. AI product managers must integrate ethical considerations at all stages of AI development.

▶ **User adoption and acceptance:** Achieving human-level performance in AI also involves gaining user trust and acceptance. Users need time to become familiar with AI systems, understand their capabilities, and build confidence in their reliability. Patience is essential to facilitate smooth integration and user adoption. AI product managers must manage change, educate users, and respond to concerns to promote acceptability.

▶ **Regulatory compliance:** AI systems must comply with strict regulatory standards in certain industries. Ensuring that AI models meet these requirements involves rigorous testing, validation, and documentation. This process can be lengthy but is necessary to ensure the AI system's legality and ethical soundness. AI product managers must stay informed about regulatory changes and ensure that AI systems comply with all relevant standards.

▶ **Continuous learning:** AI systems must continuously learn and adapt to new information and changing conditions. This ongoing learning process requires patience and a commitment to long-term improvement. Continuous monitoring, updating, and refining of AI models are essential to maintaining and enhancing their performance over time. AI product managers must establish continuous learning and improvement processes.

Strategic Planning for AI Implementation

Implementing AI systems effectively requires meticulous strategic planning (see Figure 7.3). This involves setting realistic expectations, aligning resources, and maintaining a clear vision for long-term success. Here are the unique aspects of strategic planning for AI implementation:

▶ **Define the problem:** Define the problem or opportunity that AI will address. This ensures that all stakeholders are aligned and provides a clear direction for the AI project. AI product managers facilitate stakeholder discussions to pinpoint exact issues and set clear project objectives.

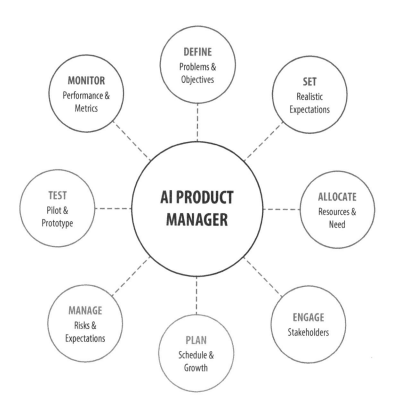

FIGURE 7.3 Strategic planning for AI implementation

▶ **Set realistic expectations:** Establish realistic expectations regarding the AI system's development timeline and performance. Communicate potential challenges and the incremental nature of AI improvements. AI product managers are crucial in managing stakeholder expectations and providing transparent progress updates.

▶ **Resource allocation:** Allocate the necessary resources, including budget, personnel, and technology. A well-planned allocation ensures that the AI project has the support it needs to succeed. AI product managers work with leadership to secure the required resources and ensure that they are used efficiently.

▶ **Stakeholder engagement:** Engage stakeholders to ensure their buy-in and support. Provide them with regular progress reports, and include them in critical decision-making procedures. AI product managers liaise between the AI development team and other departments, fostering collaboration and alignment.

▶ **Scalability planning:** Plan for scalability from the outset. Consider how the AI system will handle increased data volumes, user loads, and additional features. AI product managers must ensure that the system architecture supports future growth and adapts to changing business needs.

▶ **Risk management:** Early detection of possible threats allows for the development of mitigation methods. This includes technical risks, data privacy concerns, and ethical issues. AI product managers lead risk assessment efforts and proactively implement risk management plans to address potential challenges.

▶ **Pilot testing and prototyping:** Conduct pilot tests and develop prototypes to validate the AI system's functionality and effectiveness before full-scale deployment. AI product managers supervise these pilot periods, collecting feedback and making the required changes to improve the system.

▶ **Ethical and regulatory compliance:** Ensure that the AI system complies with ethical standards and regulatory requirements. This involves setting up ethical review processes and conducting regular audits. AI product managers lead efforts to maintain compliance and address ethical concerns during development.

▶ **Performance metrics and monitoring:** Define clear performance metrics to evaluate the AI system's success and effectiveness. Implement continuous monitoring to track performance and identify areas for improvement. AI product managers establish monitoring frameworks and ensure that the system's performance aligns with business goals.

Understanding the Innovator's Dilemma in AI

The innovator's dilemma, introduced by Harvard Professor Clayton Christensen in 1997, explains how market leaders can lose dominance by focusing solely on meeting existing customer needs. The parallel with AI development is striking: both disruptive innovations and AI solutions follow an S-curve, starting with underperformance (Phase 1), advancing to parity (Phase 2), and eventually achieving breakthrough performance (Phase 3) (see Figure 7.4).

As Christensen observed with disk drives, steel mini-mills, and excavators, for example, disruptive solutions often begin with significant limitations, appearing inadequate for mainstream use. Similarly, whereas traditional solutions improve linearly along familiar performance metrics, AI advances exponentially along new

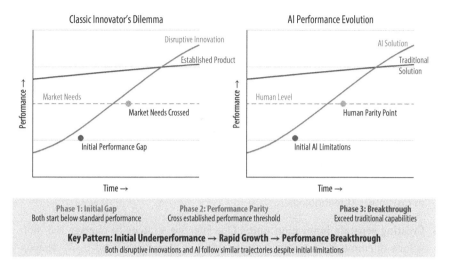

Classic Innovator's Dilemma

AI Performance Evolution

FIGURE 7.4 The parallels between AI evolution and the classic innovator's dilemma: both start with inferior performance before rapidly overtaking established solutions

dimensions. This shift creates a critical crossover point—where AI evolves from an inferior solution to a competitive, then superior one, as represented by "Market Needs Crossed" and "Human Parity Point" in the graphs.

For AI product creators, the lesson is clear: success in AI requires a willingness to launch and iterate on products that may initially seem inadequate by traditional standards. The key is identifying markets where AI's early limitations are acceptable and its unique strengths are valuable and then scaling as its capabilities mature. By embracing AI's exponential improvement curve, organizations can disrupt markets, align with emerging needs, and redefine industry benchmarks—just as Christensen's framework prescribes for managing disruptive innovations.

Here's how AI product managers can navigate this dilemma and ensure long-term success:

▶ **Recognizing initial underperformance:** When AI systems are first implemented, they often underperform compared to human-level performance. The models are still learning from the data and refining their predictions. AI product managers must recognize that this initial phase is a natural part of the development process and set realistic expectations with stakeholders.

▶ **Commitment to long-term vision:** Organizations must commit to a long-term vision for AI development, understanding that significant improvements will come over time. AI product managers are critical in championing this vision, ensuring that the organization remains focused on the ultimate goals despite early setbacks.

▶ **Balancing sustaining and disruptive innovations:** Established companies excel at sustaining innovations and incremental improvements to existing products and services. However, disruptive innovations, like AI, often start by serving niche markets before improving and gaining broader adoption. AI product managers need to balance the pursuit of sustaining innovations with strategic investment in disruptive AI technologies.

▶ **Creating separate innovation units:** One effective strategy to manage the innovator's dilemma is to create separate units or teams dedicated to AI development. These teams can operate with more flexibility and less pressure to deliver immediate results, allowing them to focus on long-term innovation. AI product managers should advocate for establishing these units and ensure that they are adequately supported.

▶ **Iterative development and feedback:** Implementing an iterative development process allows AI systems to improve through continuous feedback and refinement. AI product managers must establish robust feedback mechanisms, collect user insights, and make iterative improvements to the AI models. This approach helps gradually bridge the performance gap and gain user trust.

▶ **Risk management and experimentation:** Encouraging a culture of experimentation is crucial for overcoming the innovator's dilemma. AI product managers should promote risk-taking and innovation within their teams, allowing them to explore new ideas and technologies without fear of failure. This involves setting up safe environments for testing and learning from failures.

▶ **Stakeholder education and engagement:** Educating stakeholders about the nature of AI development and the innovator's dilemma is essential. AI product managers must communicate the long-term benefits of AI, explain the reasons for initial underperformance, and engage stakeholders in the development journey. This helps build patience and support for AI initiatives.

▶ **Case studies and success stories:** Highlighting successful AI implementations and case studies can help illustrate the potential long-term benefits of AI. AI product managers should compile and share success stories demonstrating how initial underperformance can lead to significant breakthroughs and competitive advantages.

▶ **Monitoring market trends and adaptation:** Keeping an eye on market trends and adapting to changes is crucial for navigating the innovator's dilemma. AI product managers must stay informed about advancements in AI technologies, competitor activities, and evolving customer needs. This enables them to make informed decisions and adjust their strategies accordingly.

Key Strategies for Achieving and Surpassing Human-Level Performance

Surpassing human-level performance in AI requires combining innovative techniques, continuous improvement, and strategic planning. Here are key strategies for achieving and exceeding human-level performance:

▶ **Advanced AI techniques:** Implement cutting-edge AI methods like reinforcement learning and transfer learning. These techniques can significantly enhance the model's capabilities and enable it to perform tasks that require complex decision-making and adaptability. Product managers should encourage their teams to investigate and test cutting-edge methods to push the limits of AI performance.

▶ **Transfer learning:** Utilize transfer learning to leverage pretrained models on large datasets and fine-tune them for specific tasks. This method can increase model performance and accuracy while saving time and money. AI product managers should incorporate transfer learning into their development strategies to accelerate progress and achieve higher performance.

▶ **Active learning:** Implement active learning strategies where the model can query human experts to label the most informative data points. This approach can enhance the training process by focusing on the most challenging and valuable data, improving the model's performance more efficiently. AI product managers should integrate active learning frameworks to optimize the model's learning process.

▶ **Hybrid models:** Develop hybrid models combining AI techniques, such as rule-based systems, with machine learning models. This strategy can enhance system performance by utilizing the advantages of different approaches. AI product managers should explore the potential of hybrid models to address complex tasks more effectively.

▶ **Continuous model optimization:** Focus on continuous optimization of AI models through hyperparameter tuning, ensemble methods, and regularization. Regularly refining and optimizing models can result in significant performance gains. AI product managers should establish a culture of ongoing optimization to keep the models performing at their peak.

▶ **Explainability and interpretability enhancements:** Enhance the explainability and interpretability of AI models to ensure that stakeholders can understand and trust their decisions. Techniques like Shapley additive explanations (SHAP) values and local interpretable model-agnostic explanations (LIME) can provide insights into model behavior and decision-making processes. AI product managers should prioritize model transparency to build trust and facilitate broader adoption of AI systems.

▶ **Scalable infrastructure:** Invest in scalable infrastructure that can support large-scale AI operations. This includes cloud-based solutions, high-performance computing, and efficient data storage systems. AI product managers should ensure that the infrastructure can scale with the growing demands of AI applications, enabling continuous performance improvements.

▶ **Human-in-the-loop systems:** Design human-in-the-loop systems where humans and AI work collaboratively to achieve optimal performance. This approach leverages human expertise to guide and correct AI models, leading to better outcomes. AI product managers should create workflows that integrate human feedback into the AI system, enhancing its accuracy and reliability.

▶ **Ethical AI practices:** Implement AI practices to ensure fairness, accountability, and transparency in such systems. Regularly review and address ethical concerns about bias, privacy, and decision-making. AI product managers should lead efforts to uphold ethical standards and promote responsible AI development.

▶ **Performance benchmarks and competitions:** Participate in AI benchmarks and competitions to measure the model's performance against industry standards. These platforms provide valuable insights and opportunities for improvement. AI product managers ought to motivate their staff to engage in these pursuits to maintain competitiveness and improve output.

Innovating with Generative and Traditional AI

Generative AI and traditional AI offer distinct capabilities that AI product managers must strategically balance to drive innovation and solve business problems (see Figure 7.5). With generative AI, we see human-level performance being not only matched but also surpassed, opening up new challenges. Generative AI models create new content, such as personalized designs or synthetic data, by learning patterns from existing datasets. This technology is particularly useful in areas requiring creativity and customization. For instance, generative AI in fashion can create unique apparel products based on personal tastes, increasing client satisfaction and engagement. Similarly, generative AI can create bespoke advertisements that resonate deeply with targeted audiences in marketing. Traditional AI excels at analyzing data to make predictions, classify information, or detect anomalies. Classical AI's ability to analyze enormous volumes of data to find patterns and generate precise predictions is essential for applications like recommendation systems, fraud detection, and predictive maintenance. AI product creators must ensure that the data used for these applications is clean, well-labeled, and relevant, optimizing the models' performance and reliability.

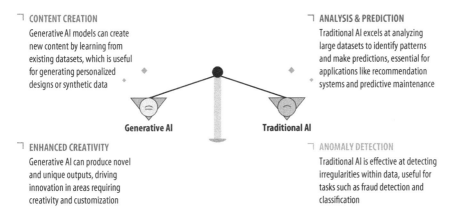

CONTENT CREATION
Generative AI models can create new content by learning from existing datasets, which is useful for generating personalized designs or synthetic data

ANALYSIS & PREDICTION
Traditional AI excels at analyzing large datasets to identify patterns and make predictions, essential for applications like recommendation systems and predictive maintenance

Generative AI   **Traditional AI**

ENHANCED CREATIVITY
Generative AI can produce novel and unique outputs, driving innovation in areas requiring creativity and customization

ANOMALY DETECTION
Traditional AI is effective at detecting irregularities within data, useful for tasks such as fraud detection and classification

FIGURE 7.5 Balancing generative AI and traditional AI: generative AI excels in content creation and enhancing creativity, whereas traditional AI focuses on analysis, prediction, and anomaly detection for practical applications

Strategic Balance and Resource Management

Balancing generative and traditional AI use requires a nuanced approach. Generative AI models often demand more computational power and sophisticated infrastructure, making them resource intensive. AI product managers must weigh these resource requirements against the potential benefits, ensuring that the investment aligns with the organization's strategic goals. They must also oversee the integration of generative AI models, ensuring that they meet quality standards and ethical guidelines.

Although generally less resource intensive, traditional AI applications require significant data management and integration efforts. AI product managers must facilitate the seamless incorporation of these AI models into existing business processes, enhancing operational efficiency without disrupting workflows. By strategically balancing generative and traditional AI deployments, AI product managers can maximize the value derived from each technology.

Ethical Considerations and Practical Examples

The ethical implications of both generative and traditional AI must be meticulously managed. If not adequately supervised, generative AI has the potential to produce biased or unethical content, and traditional AI can perpetuate biases present in the training data. To establish trust with users and stakeholders, AI product managers must establish strict ethical rules and ensure that AI decision-making processes are transparent. A practical example of generative AI's impact can be seen in personalized fashion design. AI models trained on vast datasets of fashion trends and customer preferences can generate unique clothing designs tailored to individual tastes. This enhances the customer experience and streamlines the design process, allowing fashion brands to adapt to market trends quickly.

In contrast, a traditional AI application like a recommendation engine improves over time as it processes more user data, becoming more accurate and personalized. This emphasizes how crucial iteration and ongoing improvement are to the advancement of AI. Generative and traditional AI models must be updated and modified regularly to satisfy changing business needs. AI product managers are responsible for supervising these activities.

Traditional AI vs. Generative AI

As we compare traditional AI with generative AI (see Table 7.1), we witness a trans-formative shift in AI product development. Where traditional AI was constrained by technological limitations and focused on matching human capabilities through incremental steps, generative AI aims to surpass human limits from the outset, powered by rapid adaptation and technology-driven solutions. This evolution funda-mentally reshapes how AI product managers approach development—from setting ambitious performance goals to implementing systems that can dynamically evolve in response to new challenges and opportunities.

Aspect	Old AI	New AI
Achievability	Visionary; technologically constrained	Attainable; technology-driven
Strategic focus	Incremental; human-like tasks	Surpassing human limits from the outset; exploring potential
Adaptation	Slower; scenario dependent	Rapid, dynamic, environment-ready

Table 7.1 Evolution of AI: from visionary, incremental, and scenario-based systems to technology-driven, human-surpassing, and adaptive AI

Achievability: Visionary and Technologically Constrained vs. Attainable and Technology-Driven

Traditional AI was often visionary but limited by the technological constraints of its time. Early AI systems aimed to replicate human tasks but were hampered by the era's computational power and data availability. Achievements were often incremen-tal and highly focused on specific, narrowly defined tasks.

Generative AI, on the other hand, is technology-driven and aims to attain and surpass human-level performance. Advances in deep learning, neural networks, and computa-tional power have enabled generative AI not only to mimic but also to enhance human capabilities. For instance, generative AI in creative industries can produce artwork and music that rivals or surpasses human creations. AI product managers must leverage these technological advancements to push the boundaries of what AI can achieve, setting realistic yet ambitious goals for AI systems to meet and exceed human-level performance.

Strategic Focus: Incremental Human-Like Tasks vs. Surpassing Human Limits and Exploring Potential

Traditional AI systems have historically focused on incremental, human-like tasks. These systems were designed to automate repetitive tasks like data entry or basic customer service inquiries. The strategic focus was on improving efficiency and accuracy within well-defined boundaries.

Generative AI, however, is focused on surpassing human limits and exploring new potentials. This involves developing AI systems that can perform tasks beyond human capabilities, such as generating novel drug compounds in pharmaceuticals or creating complex simulations in virtual environments. The strategic focus for AI product managers should be on identifying areas where AI can provide significant value by pushing beyond human limitations, fostering innovation, and exploring new possibilities that were previously unattainable.

Adaptation: Slower and Scenario-Dependent vs. Rapid, Dynamic, and Environment-Ready

Traditional AI often adapted slowly and was heavily dependent on specific scenarios. Early AI systems required extensive customization and optimization for each application, making them inflexible and slow to adapt to new environments or tasks.

In contrast, generative AI is characterized by rapid, dynamic adaptation and is environment-ready. These AI systems can quickly learn from new data and adapt to changing conditions, making them highly versatile and capable of operating in dynamic environments. For example, generative AI models in natural language processing can adapt to new languages and dialects with minimal retraining. AI product managers need to ensure that AI systems are designed for adaptability, enabling them to respond to evolving business needs and environments efficiently.

Case Studies: Overcoming Initial Underperformance in AI

Real-world examples illustrate the importance of patience and strategic planning in overcoming the initial underperformance of AI systems. Here, we discuss three case studies highlighting how organizations can navigate this phase and achieve success with AI.

Self-Driving Cars

Self-driving cars are a prime example of how patience and continuous improvement can lead to surpassing human-level performance (see Figure 7.6). Self-driving technology faces significant challenges, including navigating complex environments, making split-second decisions, and ensuring passenger safety.

▶ **Data accumulation:** Developing effective self-driving cars requires vast data from numerous driving scenarios. This data trains AI models to recognize and respond to road conditions and obstacles. AI product managers establish robust data collection systems and ensure data diversity.

▶ **Algorithm development:** Early self-driving models often underperform due to the complexity of real-world driving. For increasing performance, sophisticated methods like deep learning and computer vision must be constantly included in algorithms. AI product managers facilitate iterative development cycles to enhance model accuracy and reliability.

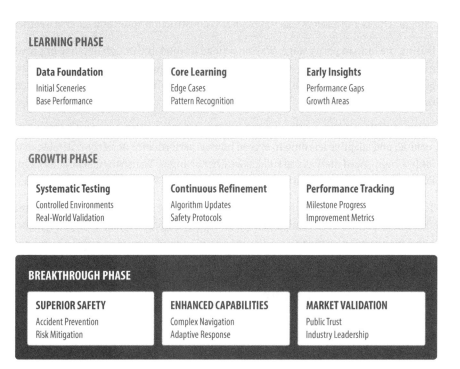

FIGURE 7.6 Three-phase evolution from initial AI learning to superhuman performance in self-driving vehicles, emphasizing strategic patience through development

▶ **Simulations and real-world testing:** Extensive simulations and real-world testing are crucial for refining self-driving algorithms. AI product managers coordinate these efforts, ensuring that the AI systems are exposed to diverse driving conditions to improve their adaptability and robustness.

▶ **User trust and adoption:** Gaining public trust in self-driving technology requires transparent communication about safety measures and performance improvements. AI product managers educate stakeholders and the public about the benefits and progress of self-driving cars, fostering acceptance and adoption.

Waymo's journey to autonomous driving excellence highlights how strategic patience and systematic planning can transform ambitious goals into industry benchmarks. Its success was achieved through a phased approach: laying a strong foundation, achieving human parity, and advancing to superhuman performance.

In the foundation stage, Waymo focused on building a robust data pipeline, collecting millions of miles of diverse driving scenarios. This enabled its AI models to master fundamental tasks and address edge cases such as construction zones and adverse weather.

During the human parity stage, Waymo refined its models through iterative improvements and rigorous testing across simulated and real-world environments. By integrating advanced deep learning methods, it achieved reliability and adaptability equal to human drivers.

In the superhuman stage, Waymo leveraged predictive modeling, real-time decision-making, and adaptive learning to exceed human performance in safety-critical scenarios like high-speed merges and sudden weather changes. Transparent benchmarks and live demonstrations fostered public trust and solidified Waymo as an industry leader.

Through these principles, product leaders can navigate the complexities of AI development, align with clear objectives, and ultimately surpass human-level performance to set new industry standards.

Recommendation Engine

When first deployed, recommendation engines may underperform compared to human curators due to limited data and model maturity. However, as they process more data, learn user preferences, and leverage the scale of modern catalogs, they not only match human capabilities but often exceed them. At Home Depot, the recommendation engine uncovered deep product associations—such as complementary items for DIY projects—that human curators could not identify due to the catalog's size and complexity, driving both accuracy and unexpected insights:

▶ **Data accumulation:** A robust data strategy is essential for long-term success. AI product managers ensure efficient data collection and preprocessing to build a foundation for accurate recommendations. At Home Depot, this enabled the engine to analyze millions of products and interactions, unlocking insights at scale.

▶ **Algorithm optimization:** Iterative tuning of algorithms ensures optimal performance for specific use cases. At Home Depot, fine-tuned models surfaced hyper-relevant products, increasing engagement and sales for complementary items. AI product managers drive experimentation and refinement.

▶ **User feedback integration:** User feedback refines recommendations, ensuring relevance and personalization. AI product managers implement mechanisms to capture feedback, enabling continuous adaptation. Home Depot's system adapted to regional and seasonal preferences based on user behavior.

▶ **Performance evaluation:** Rigorous testing and clear metrics drive measurable impact. AI product managers track engagement, conversion, and revenue metrics to inform improvements. At Home Depot, these optimizations boosted cross-selling and customer satisfaction.

By combining data, algorithms, feedback, and evaluation, recommendation engines can deliver scalable, personalized, and high-impact results, far surpassing human limitations (see Figure 7.7).

FIGURE 7.7 Beyond human curation: how recommendation engines evolve to uncover deep, scalable insights surpassing human capabilities

Document Summarization

An AI-powered document summarization tool may initially produce less coherent or comprehensive summaries than those created by a human. However, as the model is trained on more data and fine-tuned, it can produce summaries that are as good as, or even better than, human-generated summaries (see Figure 7.8):

▶ **High-quality data collection:** Creating an effective summarization tool requires substantial high-quality training data. Collecting, cleaning, and annotating this data is time-consuming. AI product managers prioritize data quality and establish robust data governance practices.

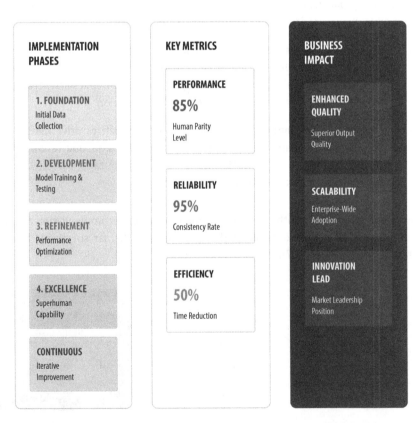

FIGURE 7.8 Phased AI implementation drives performance, reliability, and efficiency, delivering impactful business outcomes

▶ **Algorithm development and fine-tuning:** Developing AI models for text summarization involves experimenting with different algorithms and refining them iteratively. AI product managers encourage their teams to explore various approaches and continuously improve the models.

▶ **Handling diverse document types:** Different documents, such as news articles, research papers, and legal documents, require tailored approaches. AI product managers ensure that the summarization tool can handle various document types and adapt to their specific characteristics.

▶ **User feedback and iteration:** User feedback is invaluable for improving the tool's accuracy and user satisfaction. AI product managers implement feedback mechanisms and use the insights gained to enhance the summarization models iteratively.

LexiAI, an AI-powered document summarization tool, initially struggled to generate coherent and comprehensive summaries due to a lack of domain knowledge and high-quality, expertly curated training data. To address this, the team prioritized data collection from diverse, trusted sources and collaborated with domain experts to annotate and refine datasets. By fine-tuning transformer-based models such as GPT on this specialized data, LexiAI adapted to various document types, including research papers and legal contracts. A feedback-driven approach further enhanced the tool, enabling users to report issues and personalize summaries. Over time, LexiAI's performance surpassed human-level clarity and conciseness in many cases, reducing document review times by 50 percent for major enterprises. Today, it continues to innovate with multilingual capabilities and real-time summarization, showcasing the importance of combining expert knowledge, iterative refinement, and user-centric development in AI solutions.

Chapter 8

Model Explainability, Interpretability, Ethics, and Bias

Understanding how artificial intelligence (AI) models make decisions and the ethical implications of those decisions is crucial. This chapter explores model explainability, interpretability, ethics, and bias, which are essential for creating transparent and trustworthy AI systems (see Figure 8.1). We'll discuss why it's vital for AI models to provide clear and understandable decisions, helping build trust and accountability.

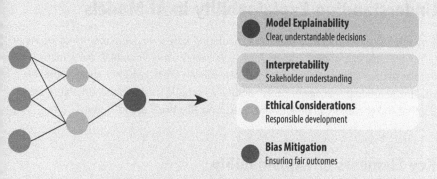

Model Explainability
Clear, understandable decisions

Interpretability
Stakeholder understanding

Ethical Considerations
Responsible development

Bias Mitigation
Ensuring fair outcomes

FIGURE 8.1 Conceptual framework of AI understanding: bridging model decisions with ethical principles through explainability, interpretability, ethical considerations, and bias mitigation

We'll also discuss making model outputs understandable for all stakeholders and the necessity of considering ethical issues in AI development. Additionally, we'll cover how to identify and mitigate biases to ensure fair outcomes. AI product managers can develop effective models that align with organizational values and regulatory standards by integrating these principles. This chapter provides practical insights and real-world examples, equipping you with the knowledge to create responsible and impactful AI solutions that drive positive results for organizations and society.

> In the world of AI, it is crucial to understand not only how a model makes predictions but also the ethical implications of its decisions. This understanding is essential for fostering trust and ensuring reproducible use. To achieve this, several key factors need to be considered during model selection and evaluation: model explainability, interpretability, ethics, and bias. Striking the right balance among these factors is vital for achieving widespread adoption and ensuring that the model's decisions are fair, ethical, and understandable.

Understanding Explainability in AI Models

Explainability in AI models refers to articulating how a model makes its decisions in terms humans can understand. As AI models become more complex, particularly with the rise of deep learning, ensuring that these models are transparent and accountable is vital for AI product managers. Explainability helps build trust and accountability, ensuring that stakeholders can understand, trust, and effectively use AI systems.

Key Elements of Explainability

▶ **Transparency:** Clarity and openness about a model's internal workings. Transparent models allow users to see how inputs are transformed into outputs, making the decision-making process understandable.

▶ **Interpretability:** Understanding and explaining the reasoning behind a model's predictions. It involves understanding the contribution of different features to the final decision.

▶ **Explanations:** Justifications for specific model predictions help users and stakeholders understand why a model made a particular decision.

▶ **Visualizations:** Visual tools can represent model behavior, feature importance, or decision paths, making complex models more accessible and easily understood.

▶ **Feature importance:** Identifying which features significantly impact a model's predictions provides insights into its behavior and helps understand the factors driving its decisions.

▶ **Local vs. global explainability:** Explainability can focus on individual predictions (local) or address the overall behavior of a model (global). Both perspectives are essential for comprehensive understanding.

▶ **User-friendly explanations:** Explanations should be straightforward for nonexperts to understand, ensuring that all users can grasp the reasoning behind model decisions.

Importance of Explainability

▶ **Building trust and accountability:** In high-stakes applications like healthcare and finance, understanding why a model makes specific decisions is essential for building trust and ensuring accountability.

▶ **Identifying and mitigating bias:** Explainability helps identify biases in AI systems. Stakeholders can work toward fairer outcomes by understanding how different features influence decisions.

▶ **Ensuring regulatory compliance:** Many industries require models to be transparent and explainable to meet regulatory standards. Explainability aids in adhering to these requirements.

▶ **Improving model performance:** Comprehending the rationale behind a model's decisions can aid in mistake diagnosis and model improvement, resulting in more dependable and precise systems.

▶ **Enhancing user understanding:** End users must understand why AI systems make certain recommendations. Explainability provides actionable insights, helping users trust and effectively interact with AI systems.

▶ **Educational value:** Explainable models can serve as educational tools, helping individuals learn about AI and machine learning principles.

Techniques for Achieving Explainability

▶ **Feature importance scores (for example, shapley additive explanation [SHAP] values):** These scores help identify which features significantly impact model predictions.

▶ **LIME (local interpretable model-agnostic explanations):** This technique explains individual predictions by approximating the model locally with an interpretable model.

▶ **Visualizations:** Tools like partial dependence plots, feature importance graphs, and decision trees can make model behavior more transparent.

▶ **Rule-based models:** Simpler models, such as decision trees and linear models, are inherently more interpretable and can provide clear explanations for their decisions.

The Significance of Model Interpretability

Model interpretability describes how well a human can comprehend and rely on a model's output (see Figure 8.2). For AI product creators, ensuring that AI models are interpretable is crucial for building confidence and fostering stakeholder acceptance. Interpretability allows stakeholders to comprehend the model's decision-making process, which is vital for gaining their trust and ensuring its practical application.

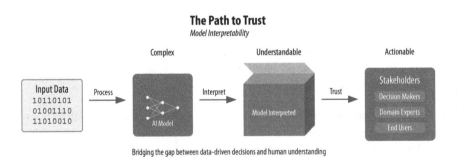

FIGURE 8.2 The path to trust: model interpretability bridges the gap between data-driven outputs and human understanding, validating performance and fostering stakeholder confidence in AI decision-making

Key Aspects of Interpretability

▶ **Comprehensible predictions:** Interpretability ensures that the model's predictions are not "black boxes" but can be understood by humans. This involves providing insights into why a particular prediction or decision was made.

▶ **Feature contribution:** It provides information on the importance or contribution of individual features or variables in the model's predictions. This helps users understand which factors influenced the outcome.

▶ **Causality and relationships:** Interpretability aims to uncover causal relationships and associations within the data that influence the model's behavior. Understanding these relationships helps explain why the model behaves the way it does.

▶ **Model behavior:** Users should have visibility into the broader behavior and characteristics of the model. This includes how it generalizes, its sensitivity to different features, and its limitations.

▶ **Explanations:** Interpretability often includes generating explanations or rationales for the model's decisions. These explanations can be text-based, visual, or in the form of feature importance rankings.

▶ **Transparency:** Transparent models are those where the inner workings and decision processes are easily understandable and not concealed in complex computations. This transparency is key to building trust.

Importance of Interpretability

▶ **Building trust:** Users, stakeholders, and the public are more likely to trust AI systems when they understand how and why they make decisions. This trust is crucial for the acceptance and adoption of AI applications.

▶ **Ensuring accountability:** Accountability is paramount in sensitive or high-stakes domains such as healthcare, finance, and autonomous systems. Interpretability allows for traceability and accountability in AI-driven decisions.

▶ **Mitigating bias:** Interpretability can help identify and reduce biases in AI models by making it easier to understand which features or variables contribute to bias. This is essential for ensuring fair and equitable AI systems.

▶ **Regulatory compliance:** Many industries have regulatory requirements for model transparency and interpretability. Adherence to these regulations is critical for legal and ethical compliance.

▶ **Improving performance:** Model interpretability can be a diagnostic tool for improving model performance. It can help data scientists identify issues and refine the model, leading to more accurate and reliable systems.

▶ **Enhancing user understanding:** End users must understand the rationale behind AI recommendations or decisions. Interpretability facilitates user understanding and trust, making the AI system more user-friendly.

▶ **Ethical considerations:** Ethical AI principles often require transparency and interpretability to ensure that AI systems align with human values. Interpretability is fundamental for ethical AI development.

Techniques for Achieving Interpretability

▶ **Feature importance analysis (for example, SHAP values):** This technique helps identify the impact of individual features on the model's predictions, providing clear insights into the model's decision-making process.

▶ **Partial dependence plots:** These plots show the relationship between a feature and the predicted outcome, helping to visualize how changes in the feature impact the model's predictions.

▶ **Surrogate models:** Simpler models, such as decision trees, can approximate complex models, offering a more interpretable explanation of the decision-making process.

▶ **LIME:** LIME explains individual predictions by approximating the model locally with an interpretable model, providing insights into specific decisions.

▶ **Visualizations:** Graphs, charts, and other visual tools can make the model's behavior more transparent and easier to understand, helping stakeholders grasp the reasoning behind predictions.

AI product managers can build systems that are transparent, trustworthy, and aligned with ethical standards by ensuring that AI models are interpretable. This interpretability is essential for fostering stakeholder confidence, ensuring accountability, and achieving practical and fair AI applications.

Ethical Considerations in AI Models

Ethical considerations in AI involve ensuring that AI models make ethically sound decisions that align with societal values. For AI product managers, addressing ethical issues is crucial in developing responsible AI systems that positively impact individuals and society. Ethical AI encompasses fairness, accountability, transparency, and respect for user privacy.

Key Ethical Principles

▶ **Fairness:** AI models should treat all individuals and groups impartially. Ensuring fairness involves using balanced datasets and methodologies that do not favor one group over another. AI product managers must actively work to prevent and mitigate bias in their models.

▶ **Accountability:** AI systems should have mechanisms to ensure accountability for their decisions. It is imperative that individuals impacted by AI choices have access to channels of appeal and that accountability for the results of AI decisions be established. Establishing these accountability mechanisms is a crucial responsibility of AI product managers.

▶ **Transparency:** AI models should operate transparently, with their decision-making processes clear and easily understandable to users and stakeholders. Transparency helps build trust and enables users to understand and challenge AI decisions when necessary. AI product managers must ensure that models are as transparent as possible.

▶ **Privacy:** AI systems must respect user privacy and comply with data protection regulations. This includes ensuring that personal data is collected and used responsibly and that users are informed about how it is used. AI product managers need to implement robust data privacy practices.

Importance of Ethical Considerations

▶ **Building trust:** Ethical AI practices are essential for building trust with users and stakeholders. People who believe AI systems are designed and operated ethically are more likely to adopt and support these technologies. AI product managers must prioritize ethical considerations to develop this trust.

▶ **Preventing harm:** Ethical considerations help prevent harm caused by AI systems. This includes avoiding unfair treatment, protecting user privacy, and ensuring that AI decisions do not negatively impact vulnerable populations. AI product managers must ensure that their models are designed with these considerations.

▶ **Regulatory compliance:** Regulations in many areas mandate that AI systems consider ethics. Adhering to these laws is legally required and a way to encourage moral AI behavior. AI product managers must stay informed about relevant regulations and ensure that their models comply with these standards.

▶ **Enhancing social good:** Ethical AI can contribute to social good by addressing societal challenges and improving quality of life. For example, AI can enhance healthcare, improve education, and support environmental sustainability. AI product managers should seek to leverage AI for positive societal impact.

Techniques for Ensuring Ethical AI

▶ **Bias mitigation:** Implement techniques to identify and reduce bias in AI models. This includes using diverse and representative datasets, regularly testing for biases, and applying fairness constraints during model training.

▶ **Ethical frameworks:** Adopt ethical frameworks and guidelines that outline principles and best practices for ethical AI development. Frameworks such as the IEEE Global Initiative on Ethics of Autonomous and Intelligent Systems can serve as useful resources for AI product administrators.

▶ **Transparency tools:** Use tools and methodologies that enhance transparency, such as explainable AI techniques, model documentation, and user-friendly explanations of AI decisions.

▶ **Privacy protection:** Implement strong data privacy measures, such as anonymization, secure data storage, and clear data usage policies. Ensure that users know how their data is used and have control over it.

▶ **Stakeholder engagement:** Engage with stakeholders, including users, ethicists, and regulators, to understand their concerns and incorporate their feedback into AI development. This helps ensure that the AI systems align with societal values and expectations.

Addressing Bias in AI Models

Decisions that are unfair and disproportionately impact particular groups of people can result from bias in AI algorithms (see Figure 8.3). For AI product managers, it is crucial to recognize and address bias to ensure that AI systems are fair and equitable. Addressing bias involves using balanced data, applying bias mitigation techniques, and continuously monitoring and improving models to prevent biased outcomes.

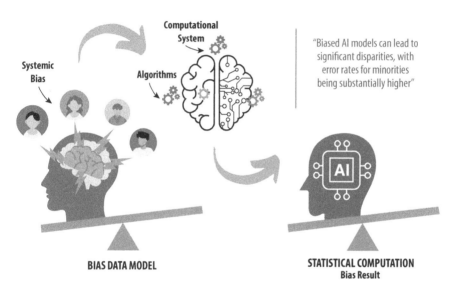

FIGURE 8.3 Illustration of systemic bias in AI: how biased data models, influenced by societal disparities, feed into computational systems, leading to biased statistical computations and disproportionately higher error rates for minority groups

Key Aspects of Bias in AI

▶ **Data bias:** Bias often originates from the data used to train AI models. The model will likely produce biased results if the training data does not represent the population or contains historical biases. AI product managers must ensure that the data is balanced and representative.

▶ **Algorithmic bias:** Even with balanced data, the algorithms can introduce bias. This can happen through the model's design or how it processes information. AI product managers need to select and design algorithms carefully to minimize bias.

▶ **Deployment bias:** Bias can also occur during the deployment and usage of AI models. This includes how the model is integrated into decision-making processes and how its outputs are used. AI product managers must monitor and adjust the deployment of models to ensure fair usage.

Importance of Addressing Bias

▶ **Ensuring fairness:** Addressing bias is essential to ensuring that AI models treat all individuals and groups impartially. This helps promote fairness and equity in AI-driven decisions.

▶ **Building trust:** AI systems that can be shown to be impartial and fair have a higher chance of earning the trust of users and stakeholders. Building this trust is crucial for the widespread adoption and acceptance of AI technologies.

▶ **Regulatory compliance:** Fairness and nondiscrimination are required by regulations in several businesses. Ensuring that AI models are free from bias helps adhere to these legal requirements.

▶ **Enhancing social responsibility:** AI product managers are responsible for designing ethical AI systems that contribute positively to society. Addressing bias is a critical part of this social responsibility.

Techniques for Identifying and Mitigating Bias

▶ **Diverse data collection:** Ensure that the training data is diverse and representative of all relevant groups. This cuts down the risk of data bias and helps create more equitable models.

▶ **Bias detection tools:** Use tools and techniques to detect bias in AI models. These tools can analyze model outputs to identify any unfair treatment of specific groups.

▶ **Fairness constraints:** Apply fairness constraints during the model training process. These constraints can help reduce bias by ensuring that the model's predictions are fair across different groups.

▶ **Regular audits:** Audit AI models to find and fix any biases that might have been incorporated. Continuous monitoring is essential to maintain fairness over time.

▶ **Transparent reporting:** Maintain transparency by documenting the steps taken to address bias. This includes reporting on the data sources, model design choices, and bias mitigation techniques used.

▶ **Stakeholder involvement:** Involve diverse stakeholders in the AI development process. This includes engaging with ethicists, representatives from affected communities, and other stakeholders to gain insights and feedback on potential biases.

▶ **Reinforcement learning:** Leverage reinforcement learning by designing reward functions that discourage biased behavior and promote fairness. For instance, in a hiring AI system, modify the reward mechanism to ensure diverse candidate recommendations, penalizing overselection of a single demographic group to foster balanced outcomes.

Role of AI Product Managers

▶ **Data oversight:** AI product managers must oversee the data collection and preprocessing stages to ensure diversity and representativeness.

▶ **Algorithm selection:** They should be involved in the selection and design of algorithms to ensure that bias is minimized from the outset.

▶ **Deployment monitoring:** AI product managers need to monitor the deployment of AI models to ensure that they are used fairly and ethically.

▶ **Continuous improvement:** They should foster a culture of continuous improvement, regularly updating models and processes to address any emerging biases.

Balancing Performance, Explainability, and Fairness

Balancing performance, explainability, and fairness in AI models is a critical challenge for AI product managers (see Figure 8.4). Each factor is vital in AI systems' overall success and acceptance. High performance is necessary for accuracy and efficiency, explainability builds trust and understanding, and fairness ensures ethical and equitable outcomes.

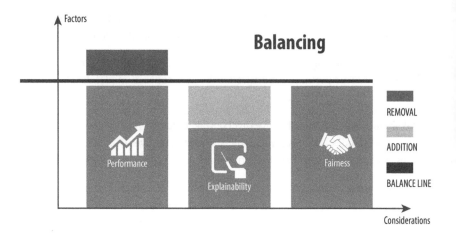

FIGURE 8.4 Balancing AI: optimizing performance, explainability, and fairness by making trade-offs to achieve ethical and effective outcomes

Key Considerations for Balancing

▶ **Model performance:** Performance refers to the accuracy and efficiency of an AI model. High-performing models deliver precise predictions and handle tasks efficiently, which is crucial for fulfilling business objectives. AI product managers must prioritize performance while also considering explainability and fairness.

▶ **Explainability:** Explainability ensures that stakeholders understand how and why a model makes its decisions. This is essential for gaining trust and facilitating regulatory compliance. AI product managers need to ensure that models are not only high-performing but also transparent and interpretable.

▶ **Fairness:** Fairness ensures that AI models do not produce biased or discriminatory outcomes. This is crucial for ethical AI development and maintaining public trust. AI product managers must implement strategies to minimize bias and ensure equitable treatment across different groups.

Trade-Offs Between Factors

▶ **Complexity vs. transparency:** Highly complex models, such as deep neural networks, often provide superior performance but are less transparent and harder to interpret. AI product managers need to balance the need for complex models with the requirement for explainability.

▶ **Accuracy vs. fairness:** Achieving maximum accuracy can sometimes lead to biased outcomes. AI product managers must find a balance where models are accurate and fair, even if it slightly compromises performance.

▶ **Efficiency vs. understandability:** Efficient models that process large amounts of data quickly may be less understandable to nonexperts. AI product managers should strive to make these models as interpretable as possible without sacrificing efficiency.

Strategies for Balancing

▶ **Model selection:** Choose models that balance performance and interpretability well. Decision trees and linear models are more interpretable than deep learning models and may be suitable for applications where transparency is of utmost importance.

▶ **Hybrid approaches:** Use a combination of simple, interpretable models and more complex models. For example, a simpler model can provide initial insights and explanations, and a complex model can handle most prediction tasks.

▶ **Regular evaluations:** Evaluate models to balance performance, explainability, and fairness. This includes regularly testing for biases and updating models as needed to address any issues.

▶ **Explainable AI techniques:** Implement techniques such as LIME, SHAP values, and partial dependence plots to enhance the explainability of complex models. These tools can help make model decisions more transparent and understandable.

▶ **Fairness constraints:** Apply fairness constraints during model training to ensure that the model's predictions are equitable. This involves setting rules that prevent the model from favoring one group.

▶ **Stakeholder involvement:** Involve stakeholders throughout the AI development process to gather feedback and ensure that the model meets their performance, explainability, and fairness needs. This collaboration can help in making informed trade-offs.

Role of AI Product Creators

▶ **Balancing priorities:** AI product managers must balance the competing priorities of performance, explainability, and fairness. This involves making informed decisions about which factors to prioritize in different contexts.

▶ **Communicating trade-offs:** Communicate the trade-offs involved in model selection and development to stakeholders. This serves the purpose of managing expectations and ensures that all parties understand the reasoning behind certain decisions.

▶ **Implementing best practices:** Stay informed about best practices and emerging techniques in AI development. AI product managers should apply these practices to balance performance, explainability, and fairness.

▶ **Continuous monitoring:** Periodically monitor AI models to ensure that they meet performance, explainability, and fairness standards. This includes updating models and processes as new challenges and opportunities arise.

Case Studies: Model Explainability, Interpretability, Ethics, and Bias

The following case studies provide practical insights into how AI models can be applied in real-world scenarios. They illustrate the challenges and solutions to balancing performance, explainability, and fairness. These examples offer valuable lessons for AI product managers on navigating complex issues and making informed decisions.

Credit Scoring

Scenario: A bank wants to use an AI model to predict the creditworthiness of its customers (see Figure 8.5).

Challenges:

▶ **Performance:** The model needs to predict creditworthiness to minimize default risk accurately.

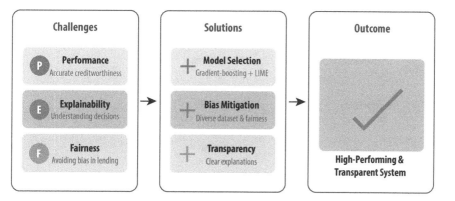

FIGURE 8.5 From challenges to outcomes: building responsible AI credit assessment systems

▶ **Explainability:** Customers and regulators must understand why the model made specific credit decisions.

▶ **Fairness:** The model must avoid biases leading to unfair lending practices.

Solution:

▶ **Model selection:** The bank chose a gradient-boosting model for its high performance but also implemented LIME to provide local explanations for individual predictions.

▶ **Bias mitigation:** The bank used a diverse dataset and applied fairness constraints during training to ensure equitable treatment across different demographic groups.

▶ **Transparency measures:** It provided customers with clear, user-friendly explanations of their credit scores and the factors influencing them.

▶ **Outcome:** The bank established a high-performing credit scoring approach that was both transparent and fair, generating confidence in consumers and complying with regulatory standards.

Healthcare

Scenario: A healthcare provider wants to use an AI model to predict patient disease risk (see Figure 8.6).

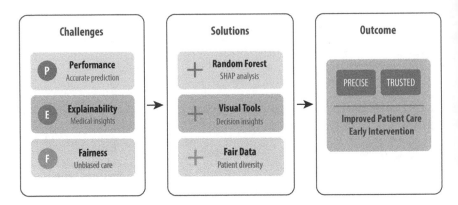

FIGURE 8.6 Building trustworthy AI healthcare solutions through precise predictions and fair patient care

Challenges:

▶ **Performance:** The model must accurately predict disease risk to enable early intervention and treatment.

▶ **Explainability:** Doctors need to understand the model's predictions to make informed medical decisions and discuss outcomes with patients.

▶ **Fairness:** The model must ensure that predictions do not disproportionately affect certain groups of patients.

Solution:

▶ **Model selection:** A random forest model was selected for its balance of performance and interpretability. SHAP values were used to identify the importance of features and explain predictions.

▶ **Bias mitigation:** The healthcare provider ensured that the training data represented the patient population and included fairness constraints to prevent biased outcomes.

▶ **Transparency measures:** Visual tools and detailed reports were provided to doctors, explaining the factors influencing risk predictions.

▶ **Outcome:** The healthcare provider successfully deployed an AI model that enhanced disease risk prediction while maintaining high standards of transparency and fairness, ultimately improving patient care.

Autonomous Vehicles

Scenario: An automotive company aims to develop an AI model for autonomous driving (see Figure 8.7).

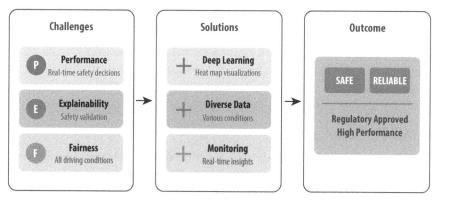

FIGURE 8.7 Ensuring performance, fairness, and transparency for safe autonomous driving AI

Challenges:

▶ **Performance:** The model needs to accurately and reliably make driving decisions in real time to guarantee passenger safety.

▶ **Explainability:** Engineers and regulators must understand the decision-making process to validate the model's safety and reliability.

▶ **Fairness:** The model must perform well across different driving environments and conditions without bias.

Solution:

▶ **Model selection:** A deep learning model was chosen for its ability to handle complex driving scenarios. To enhance explainability, the company used visualization techniques like heat maps to show which parts of the input data influenced the model's decisions.

▶ **Bias mitigation:** The training data included various driving conditions and environments to ensure broad applicability and fairness.

▶ **Transparency measures:** Detailed documentation and real-time monitoring tools were developed to provide insights into the model's decision-making process.

▶ **Outcome:** The autonomous driving model achieved high performance and reliability, with added measures for explainability and fairness that satisfied engineers and regulators.

Retail Personalization

Scenario: An e-commerce company wants to utilize an AI model to provide personalized product recommendations to customers (see Figure 8.8).

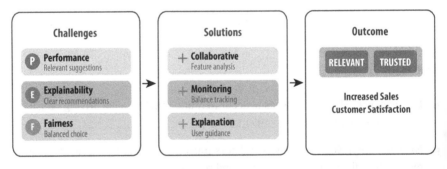

FIGURE 8.8 Empowering personalized shopping experiences through explainable AI recommendations

Challenges:

▶ **Performance:** The model needs to accurately recommend products that customers are likely to purchase, enhancing sales and customer satisfaction.

▶ **Explainability:** Customers should understand why certain products are recommended, to build trust and engagement.

▶ **Fairness:** Recommendations should be fair and not biased toward certain products or demographics.

Solution:

▶ **Model selection:** A collaborative filtering model was selected for its effectiveness in personalization. The feature importance analysis explained why specific products were recommended to customers.

▶ **Bias mitigation:** The company monitored the model's recommendations to ensure that they were balanced and did not disproportionately favor certain products or customer groups.

▶ **Transparency measures:** Recommendations were explained to help customers understand the process, such as "Customers who bought this item also bought."

▶ **Outcome:** The e-commerce company successfully implemented a recommendation system that boosted sales and customer satisfaction while also maintaining transparency and fairness.

Generative AI in Fashion Design

Scenario: A leading fashion brand, StyleGenius, aims to revolutionize its design process by incorporating generative AI to create unique and personalized clothing designs for its customers (see Figure 8.9).

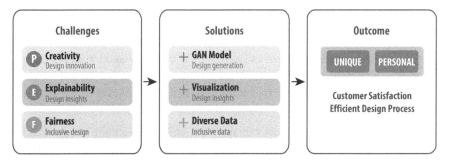

FIGURE 8.9 Framework for revolutionizing fashion design through explainable and inclusive AI generation

Challenges:

▶ **Creativity and innovation:** StyleGenius wants to leverage AI to generate innovative designs that reflect current fashion trends while offering personalized options to customers.

▶ **Explainability:** Designers and customers must understand how AI generates designs to build trust and ensure that the designs align with the brand's aesthetic and customer preferences.

▶ **Fairness and ethics:** The AI system must avoid biases in design suggestions to ensure inclusivity and represent diverse fashion tastes and cultural backgrounds.

Solution:

▶ StyleGenius implemented a generative adversarial network (GAN) to create new clothing designs. The GAN was trained on a diverse dataset of fashion images, including historical styles, contemporary trends, and customer preferences. StyleGenius integrated visualization tools to enhance explainability, allowing designers to see which dataset elements influenced specific design features. This transparency helped designers understand the AI's creative process and make necessary adjustments to be consistent with the brand's vision.

▶ StyleGenius ensured that the training dataset was inclusive and representative of various cultures, body types, and fashion styles to address fairness and ethics. It also implemented fairness constraints during training to prevent the AI from favoring any particular style or demographic. Regular audits were conducted to monitor the AI's output for potential biases and make adjustments as needed.

▶ **Outcome:** Generative AI transformed StyleGenius's design process, allowing for the rapid creation of unique and personalized clothing items. Customers could input their preferences, such as favorite colors, patterns, and styles, and the AI would generate custom designs tailored to their tastes. In addition to improving client involvement and satisfaction, this expedited the design process and reduced the time and expenses related to conventional design techniques.

The AI system's transparency and explainability built trust among designers and customers, who appreciated understanding how their preferences influenced the designs. Moreover, ethical considerations and bias mitigation strategies ensured that the AI's output was inclusive and representative of diverse fashion preferences, which was in sync with StyleGenius's commitment to inclusivity and diversity.

Traditional AI vs. Generative AI in Model Explainability, Interpretability, Ethics, and Bias

For AI product managers, understanding the spectrum of model explainability is critical to developing responsible solutions. As shown in Figure 8.10, traditional AI models, such as decision trees and linear regression, inherently provide transparency. Their decision paths are clear, outputs are easily explainable to stakeholders, and biases are readily identifiable and manageable.

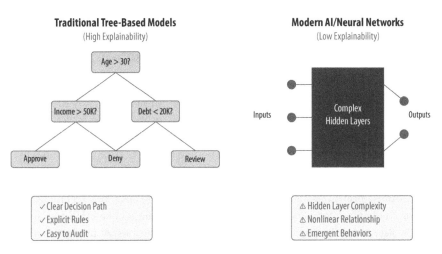

FIGURE 8.10 Comparing model explainability: traditional AI's transparent decision paths vs. modern AI's complex neural architectures

In contrast, generative AI and deep learning models, illustrated in the figure's depiction of complex neural networks, introduce a challenge: balancing their advanced capabilities with the need for explainability. These "black box" models require robust frameworks to make their outputs interpretable across technical and business audiences while ensuring alignment with organizational values and regulatory standards.

In both scenarios, the core principle remains the same: AI must be trustworthy and responsible (see Table 8.1).

Aspect	Old AI	New AI
Ethics	Minimal emphasis	Strong focus, with established guidelines and ethical frameworks
Bias	Basic; limited solutions	Advanced detection, correction, and proactive mitigation essential
Explainability	Limited; simpler models	Critical need for advanced methods to interpret complex architectures (e.g., LIME, SHAP)
Interpretability	Often inherent in simpler models	Requires robust frameworks to make complex outputs understandable and actionable

Table 8.1 Model explainability, interpretability, ethics, and bias

Explainability: Limited Capabilities vs. High-Priority, Interpretable Models

Traditional AI systems have had limited explainability capabilities. Early AI models, such as decision trees and simple linear regressions, were more interpretable but often lacked the complexity needed for high-performance tasks. As AI systems evolved, more complex models like neural networks were developed, but these came at the cost of reduced transparency, making it harder to understand how decisions were made.

Generative AI prioritizes model explainability, employing advanced techniques to make even the most complex models interpretable. Techniques like LIME and SHAP provide clear insights into how models reach their conclusions. AI product managers must leverage these tools to ensure that stakeholders can understand and trust the decisions made by AI systems, thus enhancing transparency and accountability.

Ethics: Less Emphasis vs. Strong Focus, Guidelines, and Standards

In traditional AI, ethical considerations are often given less emphasis. The primary focus was on achieving technical and performance milestones, sometimes at the expense of addressing potential ethical issues, including bias, fairness, and transparency. This lack of focus could lead to unintended consequences and public mistrust.

Conversely, generative AI strongly emphasizes ethics, implementing comprehensive guidelines and standards to ensure responsible AI development. This includes proactive measures to detect, correct, and mitigate bias, ensuring fairness and transparency in AI systems. AI product managers play a crucial role in integrating these ethical guidelines into the development process, fostering trust, and ensuring that AI solutions comply with societal values and regulatory requirements.

Bias: Aware, Limited Solutions vs. Advanced Detection, Correction, and Mitigation

Traditional AI systems have long been aware of the presence of bias, but solutions were often limited and reactive rather than proactive. Bias detection and mitigation techniques were not as advanced, leading to AI systems that could inadvertently perpetuate existing biases present in the training data.

Generative AI, on the contrary, employs advanced techniques for bias detection, correction, and mitigation. This includes using diverse and representative datasets, fairness constraints during model training, and regular audits to ensure equitable outcomes. AI product managers must be vigilant in applying these techniques to minimize bias, ensuring that AI models provide fair and unbiased results, thereby maintaining ethical standards and public trust.

Interpretability: Clarity of Insights across Model Complexity

Interpretability focuses on understanding the inner workings of AI models, bridging the gap between technical outputs and stakeholder comprehension. Early models, such as decision trees and linear regression, provided built-in interpretability due to their straightforward structure. However, as AI evolved to encompass more complex systems like neural networks and generative AI, achieving interpretability became increasingly challenging.

Advanced techniques, including LIME and SHAP, enable a deeper understanding of how these sophisticated models operate, offering localized and model-agnostic insights. By leveraging these tools, AI product managers can ensure that stakeholders grasp not just the outcomes but also the reasoning behind model decisions, fostering confidence and alignment with organizational goals.

Chapter 9

Model Operations: Model Drift Management

Managing artificial intelligence (AI) model operations is essential for the ongoing success of AI products. Unlike traditional software development, where separate teams can handle bug fixes and updates, AI model operations require continuous oversight due to the dynamic nature of real-world environments. As patterns, customer behaviors, and scenarios evolve, AI models can experience model drift, a phenomenon where the model's predictive performance degrades over time. This chapter explores the key elements of model operations, with a particular emphasis on model drift, its effects, and practical management techniques. By understanding and addressing model drift, AI product managers can ensure that their models remain accurate, reliable, and valuable in ever-changing landscapes.

> AI drives critical customer experiences and operates in a dynamic regulatory landscape where evolving data patterns and policy changes require machine learning models to adapt continuously. Model drift can directly impact customer trust by causing errors, inconsistencies, or irrelevant outputs that degrade the user experience. Unlike traditional software, which remains functional once developed, machine learning models demand proactive performance management through ModelOps. This ensures that models not only stay compliant with regulatory shifts but also deliver accurate, reliable, and seamless experiences that meet customer expectations in a constantly changing environment.

Understanding Model Drift

The statistical characteristics of the target variable that a model seeks to forecast change over time, a phenomenon known as *model drift* (see Figure 9.1), which presents a serious challenge to AI. This drift degrades the model's performance, making its predictions less accurate with decreased reliability. For AI product creators, understanding and managing model drift is essential to maintaining the effectiveness and trustworthiness of AI systems. To effectively manage and mitigate model drift, it's crucial to understand its types and the factors contributing to them.

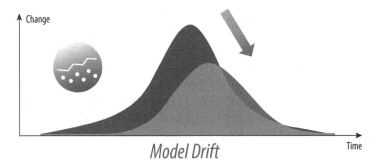

FIGURE 9.1 Illustration of model drift: over time, changes in data patterns can shift model performance from initial to degraded states, highlighting the need for continuous monitoring and retraining to maintain accuracy and relevance in dynamic environments

Types of Model Drift

▶ **Concept drift:** Concept drift occurs when the underlying relationships between features and the target variable change. This means the patterns and distributions in the data used to train the model no longer represent the data the model encounters in production. Concept drift can be:

▶ **Gradual concept drift:** Changes happen slowly over time. For example, user preferences on a social media platform may evolve gradually, slowly causing the model to lose accuracy.

▶ **Sudden concept drift:** Abrupt shifts in data patterns occur. For instance, a sudden market crash can drastically alter financial data, resulting in immediate model inaccuracy.

▶ **Data drift:** *Data drift* is the term used to describe distributional shifts in data that do not affect the underlying idea. This type of drift can occur due to shifts in data characteristics such as mean, variance, or data ranges. Factors like changes in data sources or collection processes can lead to data drift. Data drift can be:

▶ **Feature distribution drift:** When the statistical properties of features change. For example, a change in the distribution of age groups in customer data.

▶ **Target distribution drift:** When the distribution of the target variable changes. For example, a shift in the average loan amount requested in a financial model.

Factors Contributing to Model Drift

▶ **Changes in user behavior:** User behavior and preferences evolve, leading to changes in data patterns over time. For instance, a recommendation system may experience drift as user interests shift. E-commerce platforms often see changes in purchasing behavior due to new trends or seasonal factors. AI product managers must monitor these changes and update models accordingly.

▶ **Market dynamics:** Economic conditions can impact financial or business-related models, changing data distribution and relationships. For example, changes in the stock market due to geopolitical events can affect financial models. AI product managers must stay informed about market trends and adjust models to reflect these changes.

▶ **Seasonal patterns:** Data with seasonal variations can exhibit drift if the model is not updated to accommodate new patterns. Retail sales data typically shows seasonal trends, such as increased sales during holidays, which must be accounted for in models. AI product managers should plan for regular model updates to capture these seasonal variations.

▶ **Feature engineering:** Introducing new features or modifying existing ones can alter the input data distribution, contributing to drift. For example, adding new product categories in a recommendation system can change user interaction patterns. AI product managers must ensure that feature engineering processes are robust and continuously updated.

▶ **External factors:** Environmental factors, regulations, or external events can introduce unexpected changes in data, impacting model performance. For instance, new privacy regulations can alter data availability and quality, affecting model predictions. AI product managers must be vigilant about external changes and incorporate them into the model management strategy.

▶ **Data collection methods:** Changes in data collection, including shifts in data sources or collection processes, can cause data drift. For example, switching from manual data entry to automated data collection can introduce discrepancies in data quality. AI product managers must ensure that data collection methods remain consistent and reliable.

Implications of Model Drift

▶ **Reduced prediction accuracy:** As the model's understanding of the data becomes outdated, its predictions become less accurate, potentially leading to incorrect decisions. For instance, an obsolete model in healthcare could misdiagnose patients due to changing medical protocols or emerging diseases. AI product managers must regularly assess model performance to prevent such issues.

▶ **Loss of trust:** Drifting models can erode trust in AI systems, especially in critical applications like healthcare or finance. If stakeholders cannot rely on the model's predictions, they may revert to manual processes, negating the benefits of AI. AI product managers are essential to upholding and regaining public trust by guaranteeing that models are transparent and accurate.

▶ **Inefficient resource usage:** Models experiencing drift may waste computational resources and infrastructure capacity, elevating costs. For example, running an inaccurate predictive maintenance model may lead to unnecessary equipment checks and maintenance. AI product managers must optimize resource allocation to balance model performance and operational efficiency.

▶ **Regulatory and compliance risks:** Model drift can result in noncompliance with regulations, particularly in industries with strict data and security requirements. For instance, a drifting financial model could lead to noncompliance with financial reporting standards, resulting in legal and monetary penalties. AI product managers must ensure that models adhere to regulatory standards and promptly address compliance issues.

Key Components of Model Operations

Model operations, or ModelOps, are essential for maintaining and optimizing machine learning models throughout their life cycle. For AI product managers, understanding and implementing the key components of ModelOps ensures that models remain effective, reliable, and valuable in dynamic business environments. Here are the key components:

1. **Model development**

   ▶ **Data preparation:** Involves collecting, cleaning, and preprocessing data. Proper data preparation ensures that the model is trained on high-quality, relevant data, which is crucial for its performance.

   ▶ **Model training:** Data scientists train the models using historical data and fine-tuning parameters to achieve the best possible accuracy.

   ▶ **Validation:** The models are validated using separate datasets to generalize to new, unseen data.

2. **Data management**

   ▶ **Data collection:** Continuous collection of new data is vital to keeping the models updated with the latest trends and patterns.

   ▶ **Data cleaning and preprocessing:** This ensures that the data fed into the model is accurate and consistent, reducing the risk of prediction errors.

   ▶ **Data pipelines:** Automated pipelines help efficiently flow data from collection to preprocessing and model training.

3. **Model versioning**

   ▶ **Tracking changes:** Tracking different versions of models helps one understand the impact of various changes and improvements.

▶ **Rollback capabilities:** If a new model version performs worse than the previous one, versioning allows easy rollback to a more stable version.

4. **Deployment**

▶ **Infrastructure setup:** Setting the cloud or on-premises infrastructure to host the model.

▶ **API integration:** Deploying models as APIs or services makes them accessible for real-time predictions.

▶ **Containerization:** Using containers to deploy models ensures consistency across different environments.

5. **Scalability**

▶ **Handling workloads:** Ensuring that models can scale to handle varying workloads and user demands without degradation.

▶ **Resource allocation:** Efficiently managing computational resources to maintain optimal performance.

6. **Monitoring and management**

▶ **Real-time monitoring:** Continuously tracking model performance metrics to detect issues like model drift.

▶ **Anomaly detection:** Identifying unusual patterns in model behavior that could indicate problems.

▶ **Alerting systems:** Setting up alerts to notify the team of performance issues or anomalies.

7. **Feedback loop**

▶ **User feedback:** Collecting user feedback to understand model performance in real-world scenarios.

▶ **Error analysis:** Analyzing model errors to identify areas for improvement.

▶ **Iterative updates:** Regularly updating the model based on feedback and new data.

8. Model updates

   ▶ **Regular retraining:** Periodically retrain models with fresh data to maintain accuracy.

   ▶ **Adaptive learning:** Implementing strategies like online learning where models continuously learn from new data.

9. Security and compliance

   ▶ **Data privacy:** Ensuring that data used and produced by models complies with privacy regulations such as the General Data Protection Regulation (GDPR).

   ▶ **Model security:** Protecting models from threats like adversarial attacks and unauthorized access.

   ▶ **Regulatory compliance:** Adhering to industry-specific regulations to avoid legal issues.

10. Resource management

    ▶ **Cost management:** Balancing performance and operational costs by optimizing resource use.

    ▶ **Infrastructure scaling:** Ensuring that the infrastructure can scale efficiently with increasing demands.

11. Error handling and recovery

    ▶ **Error detection:** Implementing mechanisms to detect and handle errors gracefully and appropriately.

    ▶ **Recovery plans:** Ensuring that plans recover from system failures without significant data loss or downtime.

12. Collaboration and workflow

    ▶ **Cross-functional teams:** Establishing collaboration between data scientists, machine learning engineers, DevOps teams, and domain experts.

    ▶ **Workflow management:** Streamlining workflows to ensure smooth transitions between different stages of model operations.

13. **Documentation and knowledge transfer**

▶ **Comprehensive documentation:** Maintaining detailed documentation of model specifications, training processes, and deployment details.

▶ **Knowledge sharing:** Ensuring that the team has access to the knowledge necessary to operate and maintain the models.

14. **Automation**

▶ **Automated pipelines:** Using tools to automate data collection, model training, and deployment processes.

▶ **Continuous integration/continuous deployment (CI/CD):** Implementing CI/CD pipelines for seamless model updates and deployments.

Strategies for Monitoring and Managing Model Drift

AI systems' long-term performance and dependability depend on the efficient management of model drift. Implementing robust strategies for monitoring and managing model drift for AI product managers ensures that machine learning models continue to deliver accurate and actionable insights even as underlying data patterns become altered (see Figure 9.2). Here are key strategies for addressing model drift:

1. **Continuous monitoring**

▶ **Real-time monitoring:** Implementing real-time monitoring tools allows for immediate detection of any deviations in model performance. This involves monitoring important performance indicators like F1-score, recall, accuracy, and precision. Real-time alerts can be configured to let the team know when performance falls short of a predetermined threshold.

▶ **Dashboard analytics:** Utilizing dashboards to visualize model performance metrics helps identify trends and anomalies. These dashboards can display metrics over time, making it easier to spot gradual drifts that might not be immediately apparent.

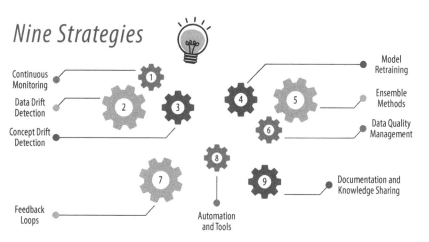

FIGURE 9.2 Nine strategies for monitoring and managing model drift

2. Data drift detection

▶ **Statistical tests:** Conducting statistical tests like the Kolmogorov–Smirnov test or the chi-square test can help detect changes in data distributions. These tests compare the current data distribution with the historical distribution to identify significant shifts.

▶ **Feature monitoring:** Monitoring the distribution of individual features can help detect data drift. Changes in features' mean, variance, or other statistical properties can indicate potential drift.

3. Concept drift detection

▶ **Performance metrics:** Regularly evaluating model performance on a holdout set or using cross-validation can help detect concept drift. Significant drops in performance metrics indicate that the model is encountering new patterns on which it was not trained.

▶ **Windowing techniques:** Using sliding windows or rolling averages to compare recent performance with past performance can help detect gradual concept drift. This approach helps identify when the model's assumptions no longer hold.

4. **Model retraining**

   ▶ **Scheduled retraining:** Implementing a schedule for regular model retraining ensures that the model stays updated with the latest data. Depending on the application, this could be daily, weekly, or monthly.

   ▶ **Triggered retraining:** Setting up automated triggers for model retraining based on performance thresholds or drift detection metrics ensures that models are updated as soon as drift is detected. This minimizes the period during which the model operates with degraded performance.

5. **Ensemble methods**

   ▶ **Hybrid models**: Combining multiple models can improve resilience against drift. Ensemble methods such as stacking, boosting, and bagging can help mitigate the impact of drift by leveraging the strengths of different models.

   ▶ **Model averaging:** Using an ensemble of models and averaging their predictions can help reduce the impact of any single model's drift. This approach helps maintain overall model performance.

6. **Data quality management**

   ▶ **Regular audits:** Regular audits of data collection processes and pipelines ensure data quality. This includes checking for consistency, completeness, and accuracy of the data.

   ▶ **Anomaly detection:** Implementing anomaly detection mechanisms to identify and correct data anomalies before they impact the model. This can be accomplished through automated data validation checks and manual reviews.

7. **Feedback loops**

   ▶ **User feedback:** Incorporating user feedback can provide valuable insights into model performance in real-world scenarios. User feedback helps identify issues that are not apparent from quantitative metrics alone.

   ▶ **Domain expert reviews:** Regular reviews by domain experts can help understand the contextual relevance of the model's predictions. Experts can provide insights into potential sources of drift and suggest corrective actions.

8. **Automation and tools**

   ▶ **Automated monitoring tools:** Leveraging tools like Prometheus, Grafana, and custom monitoring solutions can automate the process of tracking model performance and data distributions.

   ▶ **CI/CD pipelines:** Integrating CI/CD pipelines for automated model retraining and deployment ensures that updated models are quickly and reliably deployed to production.

9. **Documentation and knowledge sharing**

   ▶ **Maintaining logs:** Detailed logs of model performance, drift detection metrics, and retraining events help track the model's life cycle and understand the impact of different strategies.

   ▶ **Knowledge sharing:** Ensuring that the entire team knows the strategies and tools for managing model drift promotes a collaborative approach to maintaining model performance.

The Role of Continuous Data Collection and Retraining

Continuous data collection and retraining are critical components in managing the life cycle of AI models, particularly in dynamic environments where data patterns evolve. Implementing a robust strategy for ongoing data collection and model retraining for AI product managers ensures that AI systems remain accurate, relevant, and effective. Here's an in-depth look at these processes and their significance.

Importance of Continuous Data Collection

Continuous data collection means gathering new data consistently over time to reflect the most current state of the environment in which an AI model operates. This ongoing influx of data is essential for several reasons:

▶ **Reflecting current trends:** As user behaviors, market conditions, and external factors change, continuously updated data ensures that the model reflects these trends and patterns, preventing model drift.

▶ **Enhancing model accuracy:** New data allows models to learn from recent examples, adapting and improving their accuracy and performance. This is especially important for applications that need to make real-time predictions or decisions based on the most recent data.

▶ **Identifying data drift:** Continuous data collection helps detect data drift early by comparing new data distributions with historical data. This proactive approach enables timely interventions before significant performance degradation occurs.

Strategies for Effective Data Collection

To implement continuous data collection effectively, AI product managers should consider the following strategies:

▶ **Automated data pipelines:** Establish automated pipelines that continuously gather, process, and store incoming data. Automation reduces manual effort and ensures a steady flow of data.

▶ **Data quality assurance:** Implement rigorous data quality checks to ensure that collected data is accurate, complete, and error-free. High-quality data is vital for reliable model performance.

▶ **Diverse data sources:** Collect data from multiple sources to provide a comprehensive view of the environment. This might include user interactions, transaction records, sensor data, and external databases.

▶ **Anonymization and privacy:** Ensure that data collection practices comply with privacy regulations and ethical standards. Anonymizing sensitive data helps protect user privacy while enabling valuable insights.

Role of Retraining in Model Maintenance

Retraining involves updating the AI model with new data to adapt to changes in the data distribution and maintain optimal performance. Regular retraining is essential for several reasons:

▶ **Adapting to changes:** Retraining helps the model adapt to new patterns and relationships in the data as the environment changes. This prevents the model from becoming outdated and losing relevance.

▶ **Improving robustness:** Regular retraining with diverse and recent data enhances the model's robustness, making it more resilient to variations and unexpected changes in the input data.

▶ **Mitigating concept drift:** Retraining addresses concept drift by incorporating new data reflecting the underlying relationships between features and the target variable. This ensures that the model's predictions remain accurate over time.

Effective Retraining Practices

AI product managers can implement effective retraining practices through the following approaches:

▶ **Scheduled retraining:** Establish a retraining schedule based on the application's specific needs. For instance, models in rapidly changing environments may require weekly retraining, whereas others may suffice with monthly updates.

▶ **Triggered retraining:** Implement automated triggers for retraining based on performance metrics or detected drift. This ensures timely updates when significant changes in data patterns are identified.

▶ **Incremental learning:** Use incremental learning techniques that allow the model to update with new data without requiring complete retraining from scratch. This approach is computationally efficient and faster.

▶ **Validation and testing:** Perform thorough validation and testing of retrained models to ensure that they meet performance standards before deployment. This includes cross-validation, A/B testing, and real-world trials.

Integrating Continuous Data Collection and Retraining

For AI product managers, integrating continuous data collection and retraining into the AI life cycle involves:

▶ **Infrastructure investment:** Invest in a scalable data infrastructure that supports continuous data ingestion, storage, and processing. Cloud-based solutions often provide the necessary scalability and flexibility.

▶ **Collaboration:** Collaborate with data engineers, data scientists, and domain experts to ensure that data collection and retraining processes are in line with business goals and technical requirements.

▶ **Monitoring and feedback:** To hone and enhance the procedures, monitor the effectiveness of the retrained models, and solicit end-user input. This iterative approach helps maintain high model performance and user satisfaction.

Automation in Model Drift Management

Automation is pivotal in managing model drift and ensuring that AI systems remain efficient, accurate, and reliable over time. For AI product managers, leveraging automation in model drift management can significantly reduce manual intervention, streamline operations, and maintain the performance of machine learning models in dynamic environments. Here's an in-depth look at how automation can be effectively utilized in this context.

Benefits of Automation in Model Drift Management

▶ **Efficiency:** Automation reduces the need for constant manual monitoring and intervention, allowing AI teams to focus on more strategic tasks. Automated systems handle large datasets and precise, fast model evaluations.

▶ **Consistency:** Automated processes ensure that model drift management activities are carried out consistently and systematically, minimizing human errors and biases.

▶ **Scalability:** Automation enables the simultaneous management of multiple models, making it easier to scale AI operations as the number of models and the volume of data increase.

▶ **Real-time monitoring:** Automated systems can continuously monitor model performance and data streams in real time, providing immediate alerts and insights into a potential drift.

Key Areas for Automation

▶ **Data collection and preprocessing:** Automated data pipelines can be established to continuously collect, clean, and preprocess data. This ensures that models are always trained on the most recent and relevant data. Programs like Apache NiFi and AWS Data Pipeline can automate data intake and transformation from several sources.

▶ **Drift detection:** Implement automated drift detection algorithms to monitor changes in data distributions and model performance metrics. Techniques like Kolmogorov–Smirnov tests and the Population Stability Index (PSI) can be used. Tools such as Alibi Detect and River can provide automated drift detection capabilities.

▶ **Model retraining:** Automate the retraining process to update models with new data regularly. This includes triggering retraining based on predefined thresholds for performance metrics or drift indicators.

Model retraining and deployment are automated via CI/CD pipelines for machine learning, such as those offered by MLflow or Kubeflow.

▶ **Performance monitoring:** Set up automated monitoring systems to measure model performance parameters like accuracy, precision, recall, and F1-score. This will help detect performance degradation early.

Tools like Prometheus and Grafana can visualize and monitor these metrics in real time.

▶ **Feedback loops:** Implement automated feedback loops to collect and integrate user feedback into the model improvement process. This can help refine models based on real-world performance.

Solutions like Seldon Core and OpenAI's Feedback Loop API can facilitate the automation of feedback integration.

Implementing Automation in Model Drift Management

▶ **Define automation goals:** Clearly outline what aspects of model drift management you aim to automate. This includes identifying key performance metrics, thresholds for drift detection, and the frequency of retraining.

▶ **Select appropriate tools:** Choose tools and platforms that align with your automation goals. Consider factors such as compatibility with current infrastructure, scalability, and simplicity of integration.

▶ **Set up pipelines:** Establish automated pipelines for data collection, preprocessing, drift detection, and retraining. Ensure that these pipelines are robust and can handle various data types and sources.

▶ **Monitor and adjust:** Monitor automated systems' performance, and make necessary adjustments. Automation should be flexible and adaptable to changing requirements and conditions.

▶ **Ensure compliance and security:** Automated processes should adhere to data privacy regulations and security standards. Implement measures to safeguard data integrity and confidentiality throughout the automation pipeline.

Challenges and Considerations

▶ **Initial setup:** The initial setup of automated systems can be complex and resource-intensive. It requires careful planning and collaboration between data engineers, scientists, and IT teams.

▶ **Maintenance:** Automated systems require ongoing maintenance to ensure that they function correctly and adapt to new requirements or environmental changes.

▶ **Human oversight:** Although automation reduces manual intervention, human oversight is still essential to validate the results and handle exceptions or anomalies that automated systems may not be able to deal with.

▶ **Cost:** Implementing and maintaining automated systems can be costly. Organizations must weigh the benefits of automation against the expenses to secure a satisfactory return on investment.

Incorporating Model Operations into the Product Roadmap

Incorporating model operations into the product roadmap is crucial for AI systems' long-term success and sustainability (see Figure 9.3). For AI product managers, this integration ensures that machine learning models' development, deployment, and maintenance are aligned with the overall business objectives and timelines. This section explores how to embed model operations into the product roadmap, emphasizing strategic planning, resource allocation, and continuous improvement.

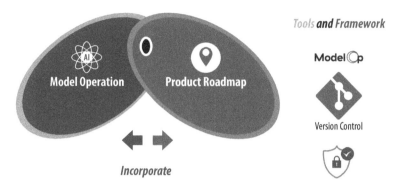

Tools **and** Framework

Model〇p

Version Control

Incorporate

FIGURE 9.3 Integrating the AI product roadmap and model operations: tools like ModelOps and version control align model management with product strategy for secure, effective AI solutions.

Strategic Planning

▶ **Identify key milestones:** Define model development, deployment, and ongoing maintenance milestones. These milestones should be integrated into the broader product development timeline to ensure that model operations are given due consideration at each stage.

▶ **Align with business goals:** Ensure that model operations align with the company's strategic goals and objectives. This includes identifying how AI models will contribute to business outcomes such as revenue growth, cost reduction, and customer satisfaction.

▶ **Risk management:** Include risk management techniques in the roadmap. This involves identifying potential risks related to model performance, data privacy, and regulatory compliance and planning mitigation strategies.

Resource Allocation

▶ **Dedicated teams:** Establish dedicated teams for model operations, including data scientists, machine learning engineers, and DevOps specialists. These teams should work collaboratively with product managers to ensure seamless integration of model operations.

▶ **Budget planning:** Allocate a specific budget for model operations, covering costs related to data collection, computational resources, monitoring tools, and model maintenance. Ensure that financial resources are sufficient to support ongoing model updates and improvements.

▶ **Infrastructure investment:** Invest in robust infrastructure to support model operations. This would involve scalable cloud services, data storage solutions, and high-performance computing resources to handle the demands of training and deploying machine learning models.

Continuous Improvement

▶ **Regular updates:** Schedule regular updates for models to incorporate new data, address drift, and improve performance. This should be a recurring item on the product roadmap to ensure that models remain relevant and accurate.

▶ **Performance reviews:** Conduct periodic performance reviews to assess the effectiveness of models. These reviews should be data-driven, using key performance indicators (KPIs) to measure model accuracy, reliability, and impact on business goals.

▶ **User feedback integration:** Integrate user feedback into the model improvement process. Collect insights from end users and stakeholders to identify areas where models can be refined to meet their needs better.

Collaboration and Communication

▶ **Cross-functional collaboration:** Foster collaboration between AI teams and other marketing, sales, and customer support departments. This guarantees that model operations align with the overall business strategy and that AI solutions suit the demands of different stakeholders.

▶ **Transparent communication:** Maintain transparent communication channels to keep all stakeholders informed about the state of model operations. This includes regular updates on model performance, upcoming changes, and the impact of AI initiatives on business outcomes.

Tools and Frameworks

▶ **Adopt ModelOps tools:** Implement ModelOps tools and platforms to streamline machine learning models' deployment, monitoring, and management. Tools like MLflow, Kubeflow, and Seldon can automate many aspects of model operations, improving efficiency and reliability.

▶ **Version control:** Track models and data changes using version control systems. This enables teams to manage different versions of models, roll back to previous versions if necessary, and maintain a clear model development history.

▶ **Compliance and security:** Ensure that model operations adhere to regulatory requirements and security standards. This includes implementing strong data protection mechanisms, conducting regular security assessments, and ensuring compliance with industry requirements.

Measuring Impact

▶ **Impact analysis:** Conduct regular impact analyses to measure AI models' contribution to business objectives. This involves assessing how models improve key metrics such as revenue, cost savings, customer satisfaction, and operational efficiency.

▶ **Adjusting roadmap:** Adjust the product roadmap as required based on the results of impact analyses and performance reviews. This may involve reprioritizing certain initiatives, allocating additional resources to high-impact areas, or exploring new AI opportunities.

Traditional AI vs. Generative AI in Model Drift Management

Managing AI models in production requires addressing unique challenges posed by model drift, which is significantly amplified in generative AI compared to traditional AI systems (see Table 9.1).

Type	Old AI	Generative AI
Concept drift	Underlying data changes	Similar, but generative models can amplify this effect
Data drift	Input data changes	Also present; user prompts can greatly influence
Performance drift	Accuracy declines over time	Exacerbated by self-evolving models
Creative drift	Unexpected outputs in generative AI	Unique artistic challenge; needs interdisciplinary monitoring

Table 9.1 Model operations: model drift management (core principle: AI models in production need continuous monitoring and maintenance to ensure ongoing performance)

Although concept and data drift affect both, generative AI introduces additional complexities, such as performance drift from self-evolving models and creative drift leading to unexpected outputs. Unlike traditional AI, these models demand interdisciplinary monitoring and proactive adjustments to maintain relevance and accuracy. For AI product managers, effective model operations involve not only tracking these drifts but also implementing strategies to mitigate their impact, ensuring that models continue to meet both business and customer expectations in dynamic environments

Concept Drift: Underlying Data Changes vs. Amplification by Generative Models

Traditional AI models often face concept drift when the underlying relationships between features and the target variable change. This means that the patterns and distributions in the data used to train the model no longer represent the data the model encounters in production. For example, changes in user behavior or market conditions can gradually or suddenly affect the model's accuracy.

Generative AI models experience similar challenges but can amplify this effect due to their complexity and how they generate new data. For instance, if the underlying data changes, generative models may produce outputs that are even further misaligned with current trends, leading to significant performance issues. AI product managers must closely monitor these models and implement advanced techniques to manage and mitigate the amplified concept drift in generative AI systems.

Data Drift: Input Data Changes vs. Influence of Prompts

Traditional AI models can suffer from data drift when distributional shifts exist in the input data. This drift can occur as a result of changes in data sources, collection methods, or external factors. Monitoring and updating the model with new data is essential to maintain its performance.

Generative AI models also face data drift, but the prompts used to generate data can significantly influence this drift. Changes in prompts or the context in which they are used can lead to substantial variations in the generated data, affecting the model's reliability. AI product managers must ensure that generative models are fed consistent and relevant prompts and continuously update them to reflect current data trends.

Performance Drift: Declining Accuracy vs. Self-Evolving Models

Traditional AI models experience performance drift as their accuracy declines over time due to outdated training data or evolving data patterns. Regular retraining and validation are necessary to keep these models performing optimally.

Generative AI models can exacerbate performance drift because they often involve self-evolving mechanisms. These models may adapt to new data in ways that introduce unexpected behaviors, making performance drift management more complex. AI product managers must implement robust monitoring and updating frameworks to handle the dynamic nature of self-evolving generative models, ensuring their continued accuracy and reliability.

Creative Drift: Unexpected Outputs vs. Unique Challenges

Traditional AI models occasionally produce unexpected outputs, but these instances are for the most part manageable with regular updates and monitoring.

Generative AI models, however, pose unique challenges with creative drift. These models can generate highly varied and sometimes inappropriate or irrelevant outputs. Careful and continuous monitoring is required to maintain the quality and appropriateness of the generated content. AI product managers must establish stringent quality control mechanisms and regularly review generative outputs to ensure that they meet the desired standards and objectives.

Case Studies: Model Operations

E-Commerce Recommendation System

An e-commerce giant uses a sophisticated recommendation engine to personalize customer product suggestions. Over time, the company's data scientists noticed a decline in the recommendation engine's performance as a consequence of model drift (see Figure 9.4). Customer preferences and purchasing behaviors had evolved, rendering the original model less effective. To address this, the AI product manager implemented a robust ModelOps framework. They continuously monitored the model's performance, collecting and analyzing new customer interaction data. Regular retraining sessions were scheduled to update the model with fresh data, ensuring that it adapted to changing trends. Automation tools were employed to streamline data collection and model deployment processes, reducing manual intervention and improving efficiency.

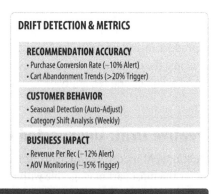

MODELOPS FRAMEWORK

1. PERFORMANCE MONITORING
CTR Drop >15% | Conv. Rate −10%

2. BEHAVIORAL ANALYSIS
Browse-Buy <0.8 | Cart Drop >20%

3. AUTOMATED RETRAINING
7-Day Moving Avg | RPR −12%

4. DEPLOYMENT PIPELINE
Auto-Rollout | Fallback Models

DRIFT DETECTION & METRICS

RECOMMENDATION ACCURACY
• Purchase Conversion Rate (−10% Alert)
• Cart Abandonment Trends (>20% Trigger)

CUSTOMER BEHAVIOR
• Seasonal Detection (Auto-Adjust)
• Category Shift Analysis (Weekly)

BUSINESS IMPACT
• Revenue Per Rec (−12% Alert)
• AOV Monitoring (−15% Trigger)

OUTCOME: Trigger-Based Drift Management + Enhanced Customer Experience + Increased Sales

FIGURE 9.4 Early detection through performance triggers helped the e-commerce giant maintain 90 percent+ recommendation accuracy, leading to increased sales and customer satisfaction.

The proactive management of model drift significantly improved the recommendation system's accuracy, enhanced customer satisfaction, and drove increased sales.

Predictive Maintenance in Manufacturing

A large manufacturing company deployed AI models for predictive maintenance to reduce equipment downtime and optimize maintenance schedules (see Figure 9.5). Initially, the models performed well, but changes in machinery usage patterns and environmental conditions led to data drift over time, decreasing the models' predictive accuracy. The AI product manager integrated model operations into the company's roadmap, establishing a continuous monitoring system to detect and keep track of performance issues. Regular updates and retraining sessions were planned to incorporate new data on the operational environment. A feedback loop was also created, allowing maintenance technicians to provide input on model predictions, further refining the AI system. This approach ensured the predictive maintenance models remained accurate and reliable, minimizing unexpected equipment failures and improving overall operational efficiency.

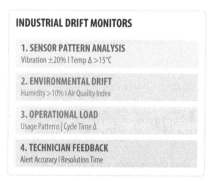

INDUSTRIAL DRIFT MONITORS

1. SENSOR PATTERN ANALYSIS
Vibration ±20% I Temp Δ >15°C

2. ENVIRONMENTAL DRIFT
Humidity >10% I Air Quality Index

3. OPERATIONAL LOAD
Usage Patterns | Cycle Time Δ

4. TECHNICIAN FEEDBACK
Alert Accuracy I Resolution Time

MAINTENANCE OPTIMIZATION

PREDICTION ACCURACY
• Failure Prediction (95% Target)
• False Alarm Rate (<5%)

EQUIPMENT HEALTH
• Component Lifespan Tracking
• Wear Pattern Analysis

OPERATIONAL METRICS
• Mean Time Between Failures
• Preventive vs. Reactive Ratio

SMART MAINTENANCE: Machine Learning + Human Expertise + Environmental Adaptation

FIGURE 9.5 Drift monitoring triggers model updates and ensures timely, accurate maintenance.

Generative AI in Content Creation

A media company leveraged generative AI to automate content creation, producing articles, social media posts, and video scripts (see Figure 9.6). At first, the generative

AI models performed well, but the generated content became less engaging as audience preferences shifted. The AI product manager implemented a strategy involving continuous data collection and model retraining to manage model drift. They monitored audience engagement metrics and gathered feedback from content creators to refine the generative models. Automation was used to streamline the data collection and model updating processes, ensuring that the AI-generated content remained relevant and appealing. The media organization produced high-quality content that connected with its target audience and maintained high levels of audience engagement by implementing these techniques.

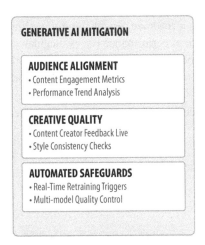

OUTCOME: Sustainable Generative AI Content + Creative Integrity + Enhanced Audience Connection

FIGURE 9.6 Framework for managing generative AI drift: align the audience, enhance creative quality, and implement automated safeguards for sustainable content

Levi Strauss & Co. partnered with Lalaland.ai in 2023 to create diverse, AI-generated virtual models that resonated with the company's commitment to inclusivity. Over time, shifting fashion trends and customer preferences revealed the challenge of model drift, prompting Levi's to implement a robust framework.

▶ **Audience alignment:** Real-time feedback and engagement metrics identified evolving customer preferences, ensuring that outputs stayed relevant.

▶ **Creative quality:** Human designers collaborated to refine AI-generated content, preserving authenticity and trend alignment.

▶ **Automated safeguards:** Monitoring systems flagged outdated outputs, enabling timely retraining with updated datasets.

This proactive approach kept Levi's AI solutions impactful, offering a key lesson: continuous feedback, human oversight, and automation are essential for managing model drift in generative AI.

Chapter 10

AI Is the New UX: Transforming Human Interaction

As technology evolves, artificial intelligence (AI) emerges as a transformative force that reshapes user experiences across various domains. AI is not merely a tool; it is redefining how we interact with technology, making interactions more intuitive, anticipatory, and deeply personalized. This chapter delves into the concept of AI as the new user experience (UX), exploring how AI, particularly generative AI, revolutionizes human interaction through multimodal interfaces that seamlessly combine voice, video, text, and images.

We will also look at the critical role of AI-UX product managers (AI-UX PMs) in steering this shift, ensuring that AI-powered features meet user needs and drive business objectives.

Through real-world case studies, we will illustrate the profound impact of AI on various sectors, from healthcare and education to disaster management and business operations. This chapter highlights the shift toward an AI-centric UX and its ability to enhance human potential and improve the quality of life.

The Evolution of Intelligence-First Product Management

The landscape of UX is undergoing its most profound transformation since the introduction of the graphical user interface in the 1980s. We're witnessing the emergence of what many also call *agentic AI*, where AI doesn't just augment interfaces but becomes the interface itself. Although the terminology may evolve, the fundamental shift toward AI as the primary UX layer represents a lasting transformation in how humans interact with technology.

The Great Interface Evolution

The traditional digital paradigm has long operated on a fundamental assumption: humans must learn to speak the language of computers. Whether through clicking buttons, navigating menus, or learning command structures, users have been required to adapt their behavior to match system constraints. Consider how we interact with traditional enterprise software: users must learn specific paths through complex menu hierarchies, memorize shortcuts, and understand system-specific terminology. This cognitive load has been accepted as the necessary price of technological advancement. Figure 10.1 shows this transformation.

Stripe's evolution perfectly illustrates this shift. In their traditional model, developers spent countless hours studying API documentation, understanding complex payment flows, and mastering integration patterns. Their AI-first reinvention transformed this entirely. Now, developers simply express their goals naturally: "I need to implement recurring payments with a trial period." The AI understands the intent, generates appropriate code, and explains its implementation choices. This shift reduced integration time by 50 percent and significantly increased developer satisfaction, fundamentally changing how developers interact with Stripe's platform.

From UX Patterns to Intelligent Systems   The transformation is perhaps most visible in companies like Loom, where traditional interface paradigms have given way to intelligent interaction. Previously, users navigated complex video creation workflows, mastering editing tools and sharing mechanisms. Their AI-driven reinvention reimagined these interactions through natural language. Users now simply express their intent—"Create a quick tutorial from this recording, remove the

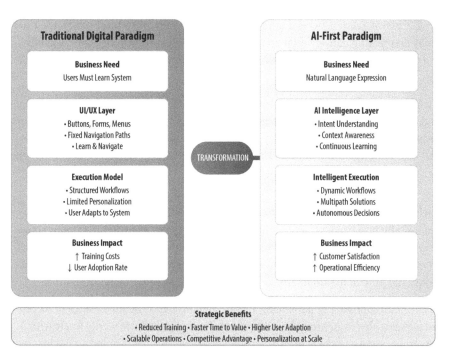

FIGURE 10.1 AI as the new UX: transforming from traditional systems to intuitive, AI-driven experiences for enhanced user satisfaction and scalability

awkward pauses, and share it with the marketing team"—and the system executes these complex tasks seamlessly. This reimagining led to a remarkable 300 percent increase in user engagement and 60 percent faster time-to-value for new users.

The New Product Management Paradigm   This transformation has revolutionized the role of product managers, particularly those focused on AI-UX. At Anthropic, the development of Claude exemplifies this evolution. Product managers now spend significant time studying natural language patterns, understanding how users express their needs across different contexts, and mapping the subtle boundaries between clear and ambiguous requests. This goes far beyond traditional user research, requiring a deep understanding of both human psychology and AI capabilities.

GitHub's development of Copilot showcases how product design has evolved in the age of AI. Product managers now work at the intersection of user intent and AI capability, designing systems that can understand and respond to natural language programming requests while maintaining high accuracy and ethical standards. They focus on creating conversation architectures that feel natural yet reliable, establishing clear boundaries for AI capabilities, and developing sophisticated fallback mechanisms for edge cases.

OpenAI's journey with ChatGPT demonstrates the new relationship between product and engineering teams. Product managers now collaborate deeply with engineers on prompt engineering strategies, model behavior specifications, and performance metrics. They must understand not just what users want to achieve, but how AI can be guided to provide reliable, ethical solutions.

Orchestrating Intelligence   The orchestration of AI-first experiences requires a fundamentally new product development approach. Microsoft's GitHub Copilot shows how this works in practice. Product managers must consider how AI capabilities integrate seamlessly into existing workflows, how systems learn from user interactions, and how to maintain ethical standards while pushing technical boundaries.

Anthropic's approach to developing Claude demonstrates the importance of technical partnerships in AI product development. Product managers work closely with AI researchers and engineers to specify model behavior, develop training strategies, and optimize performance. This collaboration goes far beyond traditional feature development, requiring a deep understanding of AI capabilities and limitations.

The Human Element   Perhaps most importantly, this transformation ultimately serves to make technology more human. Companies like Notion demonstrate how AI can adapt to user needs, provide contextual assistance, and learn from interactions. The company's AI features show how technology can become more intuitive and helpful while maintaining user trust and control.

The Role of an AI-UX Product Manager

An AI-UXPM is a unique role that brings distinct abilities to the table. Unlike traditional product managers, AI-UXPMs possess a deep understanding of AI technology and its potential to enhance user experiences. Their primary responsibility is to ensure that AI-driven features seamlessly align with user needs and business objectives. AI-UXPMs work closely with data scientists, engineers, designers, and business stakeholders. They lead UX discovery efforts to understand how AI can be applied to create more intuitive and personalized user interactions. This entails analyzing user behavior, identifying pain points, and leveraging AI to address these issues effectively. AI-UXPMs, with their strategic vision, guide the development and integration of AI features from concept to implementation, inspiring innovation and transformation.

1. **Leading UX discovery efforts:** AI-UXPMs conduct UX discovery to gather insights about user needs and behaviors. They utilize AI-driven analytics to understand user interactions and preferences better. This data-driven approach helps identify areas AI can significantly impact, such as enhancing user engagement, streamlining processes, or providing personalized recommendations.

2. **Fostering collaboration across teams:** AI-UXPMs understand that successful AI integration is a team effort. They foster close collaboration between data science, engineering, and design teams, ensuring that AI capabilities are effectively translated into user-friendly features. This collaborative approach bridges the gap between technical feasibility and user-centric design.

3. **Driving innovation in product design:** AI-UXPMs are not just managers; they are innovators. They are at the forefront of driving innovation in product design, exploring how generative AI can create new user experiences that were previously unimaginable. This includes developing multimodal interfaces that combine voice, video, text, and images to provide a cohesive and engaging UX. AI-UXPMs must stay updated with the most current advancements in AI technology and continuously seek ways to incorporate these innovations into their products.

4. **Balancing user needs and business goals:** A critical aspect of the AI-UXPM's role is balancing user needs with business goals. They ensure that AI features enhance the UX and contribute to achieving business objectives. This involves setting clear key performance indicators (KPIs) and continuously monitoring the performance of AI-driven features to ensure they deliver the desired outcomes. This balance between user-centricity and business effectiveness reassures the audience about the effectiveness of AI-UXPMs in driving successful product outcomes.

AI as the Invisible Interface

Traditional UX interactions, such as menus, touchscreens, and buttons, require users to adapt to technology rather than the other way around. With AI becoming the new UX, these physical interfaces become secondary. AI functions as an invisible interface, seamlessly integrating into various aspects of life, anticipating user needs, and delivering tailored experiences without explicit commands:

▶ **Seamless integration:** AI seamlessly integrates into daily activities, making interactions natural and intuitive. For example, smart home devices use AI to understand user habits, automatically adjusting settings without the need for manual input. This shift from physical interaction to an invisible, proactive AI layer simplifies user experiences and enhances convenience.

▶ **Anticipating user needs:** One of AI's strengths is its ability to anticipate user needs before explicitly expressing them. For instance, a smart assistant can predict a user's daily schedule and provide reminders or suggestions based on previous behavior. This preemptive approach ensures that users receive relevant information and assistance when needed, enhancing productivity and satisfaction.

▶ **Personalized experiences:** AI's ability to process and evaluate large amounts of data allows it to provide highly tailored experiences. In the entertainment industry, for example, streaming services employ AI to offer episodes and movies based on viewing history and tastes, resulting in a bespoke UX that is unique to each individual.

▶ **Reducing cognitive load:** AI reduces users' cognitive load by automating routine tasks and making intelligent suggestions. In navigation apps, AI can suggest the best route based on real-time traffic data, allowing users to focus on driving rather than planning the route. This reduces stress and enhances the overall UX.

▶ **AI-UXPMs' role:** AI-UXPMs are crucial in designing these invisible interfaces. They ensure that AI capabilities are integrated effectively into product design, creating an intuitive and anticipatory experience. AI-UXPMs work closely with design and engineering teams to ensure that the AI-driven features are seamless and enhance the user's interaction with the product.

Multimodal Interactions

Generative AI introduces a revolutionary way to interact with technology through multimodal interfaces, which combine voice, video, text, and images. This approach allows users to engage with systems more naturally and intuitively, enhancing the overall UX:

▶ **Enhancing user engagement:** Multimodal interactions enable users to communicate with AI systems using the most convenient or comfortable method, whether speaking, typing, or interacting through images and videos. For example, planning a trip can become a seamless experience where a user starts with voice commands to specify preferences, followed by AI-generated visual and textual suggestions. This rich, interactive dialogue engages users and makes the interaction more personalized.

▶ **Seamless integration of multiple modalities:** The true power of multimodal interactions lies in the seamless integration of various communication methods. An AI system can combine verbal instructions, visual aids, and textual information to provide a cohesive response. For instance, an AI assistant might display images of potential travel destinations while describing their features and, at the same time, also offer text-based reviews and itineraries. This integrated approach ensures that users receive comprehensive and contextually relevant information.

▶ **Personalization and adaptability:** Generative AI excels at personalizing interactions by learning from user preferences and behaviors across different modalities. If a user frequently interacts with the AI using voice commands while browsing for travel options and then switches to text for booking details, the system adapts to these preferences, providing a more tailored experience. The AI can remember past interactions and preferences, making future engagements more intuitive and efficient.

▶ **Role of AI-UXPMs:** AI-UXPMs play a crucial role in developing and refining these multimodal interfaces. They must understand the diverse ways users prefer to interact with technology and ensure that AI systems are designed to accommodate these preferences. AI-UXPMs collaborate with designers, data scientists, and engineers to develop functional interfaces that enhance the overall UX by being responsive and adaptive to user needs.

▶ **Designing for accessibility:** One significant advantage of multimodal interactions is their potential to make technology more accessible. These systems can accommodate users with varying abilities and preferences by providing several modes of interaction. For example, voice commands can be particularly useful for visually impaired users, whereas text- and image-based interactions might be more suitable for those with hearing impairments. AI-UXPMs must ensure that these interfaces are inclusive and designed to provide a high-quality experience for all users.

▶ **Future prospects:** The future of multimodal interactions holds immense potential for further enhancing user experiences. Integrating extra modalities, such as augmented reality (AR) and virtual reality (VR), will become increasingly common as AI technologies develop. AI-UXPMs must stay ahead of these trends, continuously exploring and implementing new methods to enrich user interactions.

Looking Forward

The future belongs to product managers who understand that AI is not just a feature to be added but a fundamental shift in how humans interact with technology. Successful organizations are investing heavily in AI literacy for their product teams, developing new success metrics that go beyond traditional engagement measures, and creating robust frameworks for ethical AI implementation.

The key to success lies in understanding that although the technology and terminology may evolve, the core principle remains constant: using AI to create interactions that feel natural to users. This requires product managers to balance technical capabilities with human needs, ensuring that AI serves as an enabler of better user experiences rather than a technological showcase.

As we look toward the future, organizations that thrive will be those whose product leaders can effectively bridge the gap between human needs and AI capabilities. This means restructuring teams for AI-first development, updating processes to accommodate continuous learning and improvement, and building new competency centers focused on AI experience design.

Remember: the goal isn't to create AI that users can interact with, but to use AI to create interactions that feel natural to users. This is the essence of AI as the new UX, and the future of product management in an AI-first world.

Business Insights: Chat with Data

Integrating AI transforms how executives and decision-makers access and interpret business insights in the corporate sector. Traditional data analysis methods often require specialized knowledge and tools like Excel or business intelligence platforms. Generative AI, however, simplifies this process by enabling executives to interact with data through natural language, making data-driven decision-making more accessible and efficient (see Figure 10.2).

▶ **Simplifying data access:** Generative AI allows users to "chat" with their data. Executives can ask questions in plain language, and the AI system responds with relevant data, visualizations, and insights. For example, an executive might ask, "What were our quarterly sales trends?" The AI would provide a detailed report with charts and key metrics. This natural language processing capability removes the need for extensive training in data analysis tools, democratizing access to critical business information.

▶ **Real-time insights:** One of the substantial benefits of adopting AI for business insights is the capacity to acquire real-time data. Traditional reporting systems

FIGURE 10.2 AI revolutionizes business insights by enabling natural language interactions, making data-driven decisions intuitive and accessible for executives

often experience delays due to manual data processing and analysis. With AI, executives can receive up-to-date information instantly, allowing for more timely and informed decisions. This immediacy is crucial in dynamic business environments where conditions can change rapidly.

▶ **Pattern recognition and predictive analytics:** Generative AI excels at identifying patterns and trends within large datasets that human analysts might miss. An AI system, for instance, can examine sales data spanning multiple years to spot seasonal patterns, unforeseen increases or decreases in sales, and relationships between various factors. Additionally, by using predictive analytics to project future patterns based on existing data, AI may help firms prepare more efficiently and maintain a competitive edge.

▶ **Strategic decision-making:** AI empowers executives to make more strategic decisions by providing deeper insights into business data. For instance, understanding customer behavior and sales trends can inform marketing strategies, product development, and resource allocation. AI-generated insights can also highlight potential risks and opportunities, enabling proactive rather than reactive management. This strategic advantage is vital for maintaining a competitive edge in the market.

▶ **Role of AI-UXPMs:** AI-UXPMs are instrumental in designing and implementing these AI-driven data interaction systems. They ensure that the AI tools are user-friendly and capable of providing accurate and actionable insights. AI-UXPMs collaborate with data scientists and business stakeholders to define the key metrics and queries the AI should address. They also play a vital role in training the AI to understand and respond to the business's specific needs.

▶ **Enhancing collaboration:** AI-driven data insights can enhance collaboration within an organization. AI fosters a data-driven culture by providing a platform where team members can access and discuss data. Teams can collaboratively explore data, share insights, and develop strategies based on a shared understanding of the information. This collaborative approach leads to more cohesive and informed decision-making processes.

▶ **Accessibility and usability:** Making data insights accessible to nontechnical users is a significant achievement of generative AI. AI-UXPMs must ensure that the interfaces are intuitive and that the AI provides explanations and context for its insights. This helps users understand the data and its implications, even if they lack a background in data science. By improving accessibility and usability, AI-UXPMs can ensure that all decision-makers can benefit from AI-driven insights, regardless of their technical expertise.

Balancing Generative AI and Traditional AI in Model Operations

Generative AI and traditional AI models each bring unique advantages and challenges to model operations, especially as AI transforms user experiences. Understanding these differences is crucial for AI-UXPMs, who aim to optimize the UX and maintain model performance. Generative AI, including models like generative adversarial networks (GANs) and variational autoencoders (VAEs), is designed to create new data instances that closely resemble a given dataset. Applications requiring the development of images, information, and synthetic data for training other models will find this functionality especially useful. However, managing generative AI in production comes with unique challenges. These models are often computationally intensive, necessitating robust infrastructure and efficient resource management. The outputs of generative models can vary greatly, requiring continuous monitoring for quality and relevance. Unlike traditional models, generative AI can produce highly varied and sometimes unexpected results, which requires rigorous quality control mechanisms. Ethical considerations are also paramount, as generative AI can create realistic but synthetic content, raising concerns about authenticity, copyright, and potential misuse. AI-UXPMs must ensure these models are used responsibly and in compliance with ethical standards and regulations.

In contrast, traditional AI models, such as regression, classification, and clustering algorithms, are typically employed for predictive analytics, anomaly detection, and decision-making processes. These models are generally less complex than generative AI models but require diligent management to maintain their performance. Traditional models benefit from established best practices in model training, validation, and deployment. They are often more straightforward to interpret and explain, making gaining stakeholder trust easier and ensuring regulatory compliance. However, traditional models can suffer from model drift, where changes in data patterns over time degrade model performance. Continuous monitoring and updating are key to keeping these models relevant and effective in dynamic environments.

AI-UXPMs play a pivotal role in leveraging the unique capabilities of both generative and traditional AI. They must understand the complexities of AI models and ensure that AI-driven features align with user needs, creating seamless and enhanced user experiences. This involves establishing continuous monitoring systems to track model performance, setting up alerts for model drift in traditional AI, and implementing quality control for generative AI outputs. Ethical oversight is crucial, especially for generative AI, to prevent misuse and ensure responsible usage. Managing computational resources is also critical, particularly for the more demanding generative models.

Case Studies: Real-Life Applications of AI as the New UX

Several real-life applications where AI has redefined UX illustrate the transformative power of AI across various sectors. These case studies highlight the positive impact of AI-driven solutions, enhancing efficiency, accuracy, and personalization in different domains. This shift from traditional interfaces to interactive, intelligent systems is a testament to the potential of AI, instilling optimism and hope for a future where AI is a driving force of progress.

Collaborative Design with AI

Scenario: A multinational corporation is designing a new product. Traditionally, this process would involve numerous meetings, revisions, and approvals, often taking months to finalize a design (see Figure 10.3).

▶ **AI solution:** In this scenario, generative AI plays a pivotal role in design. It empowers the team to interact with an AI assistant that comprehends design principles and user preferences, suggesting real-time modifications based on data from previous projects and current market trends.

▶ **Impact:** Integrating AI into the design process ensures that the final product meets user expectations and market trends. This not only expedites the process and reduces the need for modifications but also maintains high innovation and user satisfaction through data-driven design recommendations. The design process is now characterized by seamless interaction with intelligent systems, a stark departure from traditional navigation and manual adjustments.

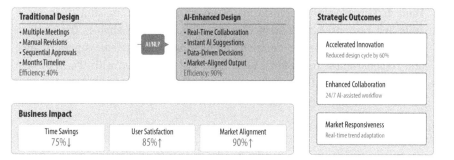

FIGURE 10.3 AI as the new UX: revolutionizing design with real-time collaboration, enhanced efficiency, and market-aligned outcomes

Strategic Decision-Making with AI

Scenario: A retail chain struggles to understand seasonal sales patterns, traditionally relying on laborious data analysis to make strategic decisions (see Figure 10.4).

▶ **AI solution:** The executive team engages in a dialogue with a generative AI system, asking specific questions about sales data. The AI provides immediate, visualized answers, identifies subtle trends, and suggests strategic actions.

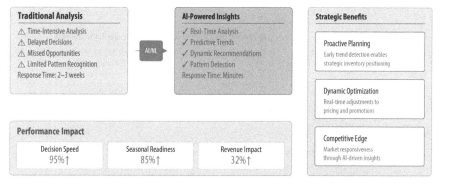

FIGURE 10.4 AI as the new language of business: from data to dialogue. (Visualization captures the transformation from traditional analysis to dynamic AI conversations, where instant insights drive strategic decisions and unlock breakthrough performance across industries.)

▶ **Impact:** This capability transforms business operations, making them more agile and responsive to market changes. The AI system enables the team to make quick and informed decisions, improving overall business performance and responsiveness to seasonal variations. The interaction with the AI system exemplifies the shift from traditional dashboards and reports to dynamic, conversational insights, sparking excitement about the potential of AI in strategic decision-making.

AI in Legal Practice

Scenario: A law firm handles numerous contracts daily, with traditional review methods being time-consuming and prone to human error (see Figure 10.5).

▶ **AI solution:** The firm streamlined its review process by integrating generative AI. The AI system scans each document, identifies critical information, and presents it clearly and concisely.

▶ **Impact:** This approach speeds up the review process and decreases the likelihood of oversights, ensuring better compliance and risk management. Lawyers can concentrate on more complicated legal issues, resulting in increased efficiency and service quality. The legal practice evolves from navigating through pages of text to engaging with intelligent agents that summarize and highlight key information, providing reassurance about the potential of AI in legal practice.

FIGURE 10.5 AI as legal evolution catalyst: from process to intelligence. (Strategic framework illustrates the transformation of legal practice through AI, marking the shift from time-intensive manual review to intelligent analysis and future predictive capabilities.)

Personalized Healthcare with AI

Scenario: A busy urban hospital faces long wait times and generic treatments due to high patient volumes and limited resources (see Figure 10.6).

▶ **AI solution:** An AI system is integrated into the hospital's operations to analyze patient data, compare it with millions of other cases, and suggest personalized treatment options.

▶ **Impact:** This AI-driven approach cuts down wait times and improves diagnostic accuracy. Doctors can focus on patient care rather than data analysis, leading to faster, more accurate treatments and better patient outcomes. The healthcare experience transitions from standard treatment protocols to interactive, AI-guided personalized care.

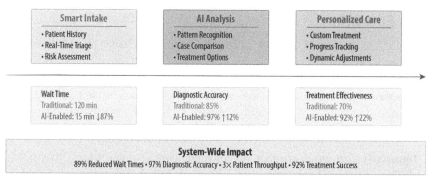

FIGURE 10.6 AI as the new UX: transforming healthcare through intelligent intake, precise analysis, and personalized care for seamless patient experiences

AI in Disaster Response

Scenario: Local authorities in a region prone to hurricanes struggle with timely evacuations and resource deployment (see Figure 10.7).

▶ **AI solution:** An AI system analyzes weather patterns and historical data to provide early warnings about potential hurricanes. The AI predicts the hurricane's path, strength, and impact, enabling authorities to plan evacuations and allocate resources more effectively.

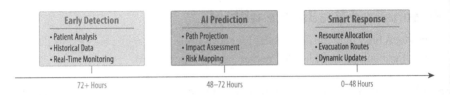

FIGURE 10.7 AI as the new language of safety: from reaction to prevention framework

▶ **Impact:** This proactive approach saves lives and reduces damage by ensuring timely evacuations and efficient resource utilization. The AI system's predictive capabilities enhance disaster preparedness and response, improving community safety. In this context, the interaction with AI moves from static emergency protocols to dynamic, real-time decision-making assistance.

AI in Education

Scenario: A public school in a diverse neighborhood faces challenges in catering to the varied learning needs of its students (see Figure 10.8).

▶ **AI solution:** AI-driven educational tools are implemented to offer personalized learning experiences. The AI system tracks each student's progress, identifies areas of improvement, and provides tailored exercises.

▶ **Impact:** This approach ensures that all students receive the support they need, closing educational gaps and promoting equity in learning outcomes. Teachers can focus on providing more individualized attention, thereby enhancing the overall quality of education. The educational experience shifts from navigating through textbooks and standard curricula to engaging with intelligent systems that adapt to each student's learning journey.

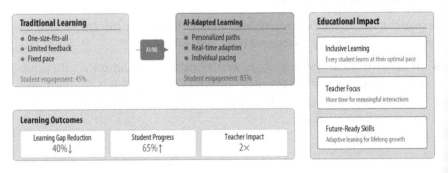

FIGURE 10.8 Transforming education with AI: personalized learning paths enhance engagement and outcomes

Conclusion: The Dawn of Intelligence-First Product Creation—A New Chapter in Human Innovation

As we conclude *Successful AI Product Creation: A Nine-Step Framework*, we find ourselves at a pivotal moment in human history, comparable to the great technological revolutions that transformed civilization. Just as the printing press democratized knowledge in the 15th century, the steam engine revolutionized production in the 18th century, and electricity fundamentally reshaped society in the 19th century, AI represents a watershed moment in human progress. We're witnessing not just an evolution in computing but a fundamental reimagining of human–machine interaction that surpasses previous technological milestones—from the punch cards of the 1890s, to the command-line interfaces of the 1970s, to the graphical user interfaces of the 1980s, to the touch and mobile interfaces of the 2000s. This transformation runs deeper than all previous technological shifts because AI isn't simply changing how we interact with machines; it's redefining the very nature of what machines can be and do. From autonomous vehicles making split-second decisions, to language models engaging in sophisticated dialogue, to AI systems discovering new medicines and materials, to predictive systems anticipating and preventing problems before they occur—we're moving beyond the paradigm of computers as tools to one where they become collaborative partners in human endeavors.

The Great Interface Evolution

The traditional paradigm required humans to learn the language of computers—clicking through menus, memorizing commands, and adapting to system constraints. Today, through the lens of our nine-step framework, we're creating systems that learn the language of humans. At Stripe, developers who once spent countless hours poring over API documentation now simply express their needs in natural language. At Loom, users speak their intentions, and AI translates them into action, leading to a threefold increase in engagement.

This evolution represents a fundamental shift from static to dynamic intelligence:

▶ Traditional interfaces are giving way to conversational, adaptive AI.

▶ Systems now learn from users rather than users learning systems.

▶ Interactions adapt in real time to user needs and contexts.

▶ Natural language has become the primary interface.

The 7.28 trillion hours globally spent on mundane tasks annually aren't just being automated; they're being transformed into opportunities for human creativity and innovation.

Understanding the Technology Adoption Curve

Although this interface evolution marks a transformative shift in human–computer interaction, it's crucial to temper our excitement with a historical perspective. History has consistently shown us that we tend to overestimate the short-term impact of new technologies while underestimating their long-term transformative potential. This principle, known as Amara's Law, is perfectly illustrated in Figure 10.9. In the early stages of AI adoption, expectations (shown by the dotted line) rise rapidly as excitement builds around new capabilities and promising demonstrations. However, the reality of implementation and integration (shown by the solid line) follows a more gradual, linear progression.

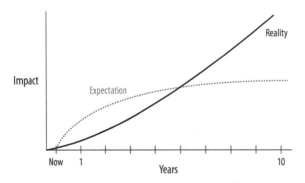

FIGURE 10.9 Amara's Law: we tend to overestimate the impact of technology in the short term and underestimate it in the long term. The graph shows how early expectations (dotted line) rise rapidly but plateau, whereas reality (solid line) demonstrates steady, linear progress that eventually surpasses expectations around the 10-year mark

The autonomous vehicle industry provides a perfect case study of this pattern. In 2016, industry predictions suggested we would have widespread autonomous vehicles by 2020:

▶ Tesla announced that full autonomy would be available by the end of 2017.

▶ Multiple manufacturers promised commercial self-driving vehicles by 2020.

▶ Tech pundits predicted 10 million self-driving cars on the road by 2020.

Yet today, although significant progress has been made, full autonomy remains a complex challenge requiring more time and development than initially anticipated. However, the long-term impact of autonomous technology development has been profound, leading to innovations in

▶ Advanced driver assistance systems

▶ Computer vision and sensor fusion

▶ Real-time decision-making algorithms

▶ Safety systems and fail-safes

This pattern reminds us that although immediate expectations may be overly optimistic, the long-term transformative potential of AI often exceeds our initial understanding. This insight should guide how we approach AI product development.

Three key principles emerge:

1. The demo–reality gap

   ▶ Demonstrations showcase potential but often operate under controlled conditions.

   ▶ Market-ready solutions require reliability across diverse, unpredictable scenarios.

   ▶ The path from proof-of-concept to production is longer than usually estimated.

2. Models as components, not minds

   ▶ AI models are powerful tools within larger intelligent software systems.

   ▶ Success comes from integration rather than isolation.

   ▶ The focus should be on augmenting human capabilities, not replacing them.

3. Long-term transformative potential

   ▶ Although short-term impacts may be overestimated, decade-long transformations often exceed expectations.

   ▶ Building for sustainable impact requires patience and a systematic approach.

   ▶ The compound effect of incremental improvements leads to revolutionary changes.

Learning from History's Echo: The Hinton Warning

The story of AI's evolution carries another important lesson about heeding the voices of pioneers. Geoffrey Hinton, often called the "father of AI" and "godfather of artificial intelligence," began his groundbreaking work on neural networks in the 1970s, publishing seminal research on backpropagation in 1986. Despite skepticism and dismissal during the "AI winter," he persisted in his vision. It took nearly three decades for the industry to fully appreciate and implement his insights, with the breakthrough moment coming around 2012 when deep learning achieved remarkable successes in image recognition.

Today, as Hinton raises urgent concerns about AI safety and potential risks, we would be wise to learn from history and act more swiftly on these warnings. His journey from AI pioneer to safety advocate mirrors our own evolution in understanding AI's transformative power—both its tremendous potential and its serious responsibilities.

The Framework in Practice

Our nine-step framework, organized into three strategic pillars, serves as a comprehensive guide through this transformation. Each pillar addresses critical dimensions of AI product development: business value, technical excellence, and user impact.

Strategic Foundation: Value-First Focus with Strong Tech Innovation

1. Mapping problems to business goals for AI products

   ▶ Defining strategic AI value

   ▶ Aligning AI initiatives with core business objectives

   ▶ Creating measurable value propositions

2. Curiosity to learn AI use cases and emerging technical machine learning (ML) concepts

   ▶ Building technical mastery

   ▶ Understanding current AI capabilities and limitations

   ▶ Staying current with ML advancements

3. Experimentation mindset and room in the roadmap to innovate

   ▶ Embracing learning through iteration

   ▶ Creating space for controlled experimentation

   ▶ Building adaptable development processes

Implementation and Integration: Bridging Research and Reality in AI Development

1. Integrating the model development life cycle (MDLC) with the software development life cycle (SDLC)

   ▶ Harmonizing development life cycles

   ▶ Creating seamless workflows between ML and software teams

   ▶ Establishing unified development processes

2. Scaling research to production

   ▶ Moving from research to real-world impact

   ▶ Building robust deployment pipelines

   ▶ Ensuring reliability at scale

3. Acceptance criteria in the world of AI

▶ Defining success with stakeholders

▶ Establishing clear performance metrics

▶ Creating evaluation frameworks that consider AI's unique characteristics

Sustainable Excellence and Innovation: Achieving Breakthrough Performance with Responsible Innovation

1. Patience and plan to surpass human-level performance

▶ Achieving strategic excellence through patience

▶ Setting realistic performance goals

▶ Building systematic improvement processes

2. Model explainability, interpretability, ethics, and bias

▶ Building trust through transparency

▶ Ensuring fair and unbiased AI systems

▶ Creating transparent decision-making processes

3. Model operations: model drift management

▶ Ensuring sustainable excellence

▶ Maintaining performance over time

▶ Managing the model life cycle and updates

Transformative Outcome: AI Is the New UX

The framework's implementation leads to a fundamental transformation: AI becomes the new paradigm for UX. This isn't just about adding AI features; it's about redefining human–AI interaction through successful framework implementation. The result is a new generation of products where AI naturally extends and enhances human capabilities.

The New Product Management Paradigm

The role of AI product creators has evolved far beyond traditional boundaries. At companies like Anthropic, product managers aren't just building features; they're designing conversations. At GitHub, they're not just creating tools; they're enabling new forms of human–AI collaboration. Today's leaders must orchestrate a delicate dance between human insight and machine capability, focusing on

▶ Designing sophisticated conversation architectures

▶ Building frameworks for AI decision-making

▶ Establishing clear boundaries for AI capabilities

▶ Developing robust fallback mechanisms

▶ Ensuring ethical considerations in AI deployment

Building for Tomorrow: Organizational Transformation

Success in this new era requires fundamental changes at the organizational level.

For Organizations:

▶ Restructuring for AI-first development

▶ Investing in new competency centers

▶ Building ethical AI frameworks

▶ Developing new success metrics

For Product Leaders:

▶ Mastering the nine-step framework

▶ Understanding both technical and human aspects

▶ Balancing innovation with responsibility

▶ Leading with vision while maintaining practicality

Continuous Evolution and Adaptation

As AI technology advances, our approaches must evolve continuously:

▶ Dynamic acceptance criteria adapting to new capabilities

▶ Integrated development approaches becoming more sophisticated

▶ Performance benchmarks constantly rising and evolving

▶ Model operations ensuring sustained excellence

The Rise of Agentic AI Systems

Agentic AI represents a quantum leap in human–computer interaction. From healthcare and finance to scientific research and personal productivity, these systems are redefining what's possible through autonomous operation and sophisticated human collaboration. In research laboratories, AI agents conduct complex experiments, respond to verbal instructions, and troubleshoot in real time. In healthcare, they assist in diagnosis and treatment planning. In finance, they autonomously manage risk assessments and portfolio optimization. Each application showcases the transformative potential of truly conversational, task-oriented AI.

However, with greater autonomy comes greater responsibility. The implementation of agentic systems brings important challenges:

▶ Dependencies on clean, high-quality data

▶ Privacy and personal information protection

▶ Need for robust human oversight

▶ Compliance and regulatory considerations

▶ Ethical implications of autonomous decision-making

Although agentic AI represents the current frontier of human–computer interaction, it is but one step in AI's continuing evolution. As artificial general intelligence (AGI) potentially emerges in the decades to come, we can expect new paradigms to develop. However, the fundamental shift toward AI as the primary UX interface—whether through agents or future paradigms—will likely endure.

Looking Forward: The Human–AI Partnership

As we stand at this threshold of transformation, our responsibility as AI product creators takes on new depth and meaning. Understanding Amara's Law—that we tend to overestimate technology's short-term impact while underestimating its long-term transformative potential—must shape our approach. The integration of AI into the fabric of our daily lives will continue not as a sudden revolution, but as a steady, persistent evolution.

Through careful application of our framework, we can create sophisticated partnerships between human insight and machine capability that are

▶ Ethically grounded, with clear accountability frameworks

▶ Focused on augmenting rather than replacing human capabilities

▶ Built with robust data governance and privacy protection

▶ Designed for transparency in decision-making processes

▶ Adaptable to emerging paradigms while maintaining human values

This isn't just about building better AI systems; it's about architecting a future where technology truly serves human needs. Like Geoffrey Hinton's journey from neural network pioneer to ethical advocate, we must remain adaptable in our understanding while staying true to our foundational principles. The products we create today will shape how humans interact with technology for generations to come.

The future belongs to those who can navigate this transformation with wisdom, creativity, and unwavering commitment to human values—those who understand that true progress comes not from chasing short-term expectations, but from building steadily toward transformative long-term impact. Let us embrace this journey with the knowledge that we're not just creating products—we're helping write the next chapter in human innovation.

Keep that prospect in mind as you explore the final chapter: "Understanding Generative AI for Product Management."

Chapter 11

Understanding Generative AI for Product Management

Introduction to Generative AI

As technology continues to evolve, generative artificial intelligence (AI) has emerged as a transformative force in product development. This chapter explores the foundations of generative AI through the lens of product management, equipping product leaders with essential knowledge to leverage this technology effectively.

The cutting-edge technology known as *generative AI* is a specific artificial intelligence that produces new content that closely mimics training data. It operates across various formats, including text, images, audio, and video, each contributing to diverse business applications. At its core, generative AI leverages advanced algorithms to learn patterns and structures from existing data, enabling it to generate innovative outputs that have the potential to revolutionize industries.

Generative AI serves as a transformative force in product development—from rapid prototyping to design iteration—while augmenting human decision-making through data analysis and scenario generation. It amplifies creative capabilities by suggesting novel approaches and variations while streamlining content production through automated generation of text, code, and media assets. However, its role remains collaborative, enhancing rather than replacing human expertise and judgment.

Generative AI models, when integrated into product development, accelerate business growth by personalizing customer experiences and streamlining operations. They empower product managers to innovate and validate solutions rapidly, creating competitive advantages through the strategic fusion of automation and insight.

Why Generative AI Is Different

Generative AI stands out by going beyond mere prediction to the realm of creation, fostering a dynamic human–machine partnership. It interacts with the fundamental fabric of innovation—language—transforming every industry and redefining how we collaborate.

> Generative AI goes beyond prediction to creation and empowers a human–machine partnership. It interacts with the fundamental fabric of innovation—language—transforming every industry and redefining how we work together.

Traditional AI models focus on data analysis and pattern recognition, but generative AI creates new content and ideas from scratch. This ability to generate human-like text and other forms of content enables businesses to innovate at an unprecedented scale. For instance, it can produce tailored marketing content, automate coding, and craft creative works such as art and music. By doing so, generative AI augments human creativity, streamlines workflows, enhances productivity, and fosters a collaborative environment. Its unique capability to blend linguistic understanding with creative generation positions generative AI as a powerful tool in revolutionizing industries and driving the future of human–machine collaboration.

AI in Business

Generative AI, along with other AI technologies, has transitioned from a technical concept to a transformative business tool. It mimics human intelligence in software applications, reshaping the business landscape by enhancing decision-making capabilities, improving operational efficiency, and spurring innovation.

In product management, AI analyzes vast amounts of data, predicts market trends, and creates personalized customer experiences.

In addition to being a theoretical idea, generative AI is a valuable technology that has the power to change industries completely. It contributes to this transformation by automating content generation, enabling businesses to produce large-scale, high-quality outputs. For instance, AI can generate product descriptions, marketing copy, and customer service responses, reducing the workload on human teams and ensuring consistency.

Additionally, generative AI can assist in creative tasks such as designing marketing materials or developing new product concepts, providing a competitive edge in the market.

Overview of Generative AI Technologies

1. Large language models (LLMs): LLMs, such as GPT (generative pretrained transformer), are leading the way in generative AI technologies. These models are capable of producing language that closely resembles human speech due to their training on large datasets, which helps them identify patterns. The training process involves two main stages: pretraining and fine-tuning. During pretraining, the model learns from a broad corpus of text, developing an understanding of language structures and semantics. Fine-tuning involves adjusting the model's parameters on specific tasks to enhance performance.

Large datasets are paramount in this context. These datasets provide the diverse examples the model needs to learn a wide range of linguistic patterns and contexts. Consequently, LLMs are helpful tools for content creation, customer service automation, and personalized communication because they can produce coherent and contextually relevant language.

2. Large image models (LIMs): LIMs like DALL-E and BigGAN are trained on vast collections of images to perform tasks such as image generation and transformation. These models can create new images that resemble the training data or modify existing images creatively. LIMs can create realistic and imaginative images of high quality by using deep learning algorithms to comprehend the fine aspects of visual data.

LIMs are used by product creators for various tasks, such as building user interfaces, producing marketing materials, and the creation of product graphics. By automating these operations, LIMs assist companies in conserving time and resources while upholding a high standard of visual content.

3. Transformer-based models: Imagine that you're using Google Translate to convert a complex Japanese sentence into English. Not only does it translate each word, but it actually understands the context and produces natural-sounding English. Or picture GitHub Copilot suggesting entire code functions while you type. Behind these seemingly magical capabilities lies a powerful innovation called the *transformer architecture.*

Think of transformers as the brain that powers virtually every cutting-edge AI product you interact with today. Whether it's ChatGPT helping you draft emails, Midjourney creating artwork from your descriptions, or Claude assisting with analysis, they're all built on transformer technology. This architecture serves as the foundation for both LLMs that process and generate text and LIMs that work with both text and visual content.

As shown in Figure 11.1, the transformer architecture has two main components that work together like a well-oiled machine:

▶ The encoder processes the input data through self-attention mechanisms and feed-forward networks, essentially understanding and analyzing the information.

▶ The decoder generates the output using various types of attention mechanisms, transforming that understanding into meaningful responses.

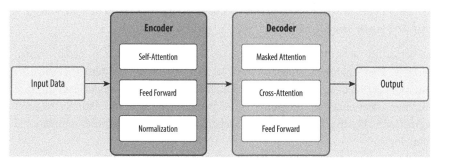

FIGURE 11.1 Transformer model architecture with encoder and decoder components

This architecture is elegant in its simplicity—data flows from left to right, getting progressively refined at each step. You don't need to understand the technical details of each component, but knowing this high-level flow helps explain why transformers are so effective at tasks ranging from translation to code generation, whether they're powering LLMs for text generation or LIMs for creating images from descriptions.

For product managers, the transformer revolution means unprecedented opportunities. By understanding the basics of how transformers work, you can better

▶ Envision realistic AI features for your products

▶ Have meaningful conversations with your engineering team about AI capabilities

▶ Make informed decisions about which AI technologies to adopt

▶ Explain your AI product's potential (and limitations) to stakeholders

Although we've kept this explanation high-level, those interested in diving deeper should start with the landmark 2017 paper "Attention Is All You Need."[1] This revolutionary paper introduced the transformer architecture and sparked the AI revolution we're experiencing today.

4. Multimodal models: Multimodal models are designed to process and generate multiple types of data simultaneously. By integrating text, images, audio, and other data formats, these models can tackle more complex problems and provide more comprehensive solutions. For example, a multimodal model might generate a detailed product description based on an image or create a marketing video from a script and visual assets.

The versatility of multimodal models makes them valuable assets in product management. They enable businesses to create rich, interactive content that engages customers across different platforms. Additionally, multimodal models can improve customer experiences by providing more personalized and contextually relevant interactions. Figure 11.2 shows the relationships between these foundational technologies.

Key Components in Generative AI

1. Modular programming and AI engineering: AI engineering often involves modular programming, where complex systems are built from smaller, reusable components. This approach allows developers to create robust AI models that can be easily customized and extended. In the context of generative AI, modular programming involves integrating various modules for data preprocessing, model training, and output generation.

Data engineering is another critical component of AI development. It involves collecting, cleaning, and organizing large datasets to ensure the quality and relevance of the data used for training AI models. Effective data engineering practices are essential for building accurate and reliable generative AI models. Logic extraction is the process of defining the rules and patterns that the AI model needs to learn. By extracting logic from data, developers can design models that understand and replicate complex behaviors. In generative AI, logic extraction helps models generate accurate, contextually appropriate, and meaningful outputs.

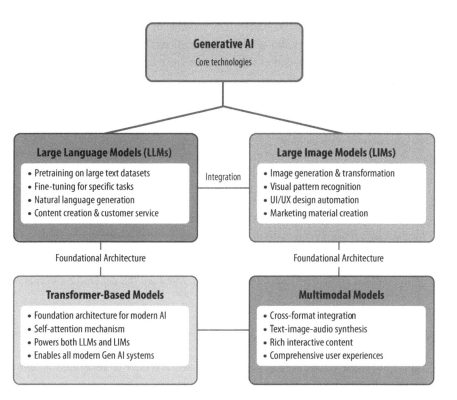

FIGURE 11.2 Generative AI technology ecosystem overview. This diagram illustrates the four key technologies driving generative AI: LLMs, LIMs, transformer-based models, and multimodal models. The transformer architecture serves as the foundational backbone (shown by vertical connections) powering both LLMs and LIMs. Multimodal models integrate capabilities across different data types (shown by horizontal connections), enabling comprehensive AI applications. All technologies contribute equally to the broader generative AI landscape, each serving distinct yet complementary roles in modern AI systems

2. Generative pretrained models: Pretrained models serve as ready-to-use solutions for various AI tasks, significantly reducing the time and resources needed for development. These models come pre-equipped with knowledge from large datasets and can be fine-tuned to meet specific business needs. For product managers, pretrained models offer a quick and efficient way to implement AI solutions without extensive training and development.

Generative pretrained models are particularly valuable in natural language processing, image generation, and audio synthesis applications. By leveraging these models, businesses can automate content creation, enhance customer interactions, and improve operational efficiency.

Evaluation metrics for generative AI: Specific measures are needed to assess generative AI models to guarantee the caliber and applicability of the produced outputs. For LLMs, common metrics include:

▶ **Perplexity:** Measures how well a probability distribution predicts a sample. Lower perplexity indicates better performance.

▶ **BLEU score (bilingual evaluation understudy):** Used to evaluate the accuracy of machine translation by comparing generated translations with reference translations.

▶ **ROUGE (recall-oriented understudy for gisting evaluation):** Used for summarization tasks, it compares the overlap of n-grams between the generated summary and reference summary.

For image models, evaluation metrics include:

▶ **Inception score (IS):** Evaluates the quality and diversity of generated images based on the output of a pretrained inception network.

▶ **Fréchet inception distance (FID):** Measures the distance between the distributions of generated images and real images, assessing the quality and diversity of the generated images.

Responsible AI frameworks are crucial for ensuring that AI models are ethical, fair, and free from biases. These frameworks guide developing and deploying AI models, emphasizing transparency, accountability, and inclusivity. By adhering to these frameworks, businesses can build trustworthy and socially responsible AI solutions.

Building on the acceptance criteria and human-level performance metrics discussed in Chapters 6 and 7, generative AI introduces unique evaluation challenges requiring specialized metrics. Table 11.1 provides a broad framework of these metrics, although it is not exhaustive given the field's rapid evolution, as new evaluation methods continue to emerge to address specific needs and challenges in generative AI systems.

Evaluation dimension	Metric or method	Description	PM role in evaluation	Strategic considerations for PMs
Accuracy	Exact match (EM), F1-score	Measures precision of predictions against reference answers	Coordinates benchmarking efforts, ensures alignment with user expectations	Accuracy impacts user trust; prioritize in user-facing features where precision is critical.
Fluency	BLEU, ROUGE, METEOR	Evaluates translation quality, summary overlap, considering word order and synonymy	Facilitates expert reviews, manages datasets for testing fluency in multiple languages	Fluency affects user experience; balance with other metrics for natural, understand-able output.
Coherence	Coherence score	Assesses logical consistency within generated texts	Organizes user studies, analyzes feedback on text coherence	Coherence is key for long-form content; ensure that models maintain topic relevance and logical flow.
Consistency	Consistency tests	Checks model's logical consistency across prompts	Implements automated testing frameworks for consistency checks	Consistency builds reliability; ensure that model outputs remain stable over variations in input.
Fairness/Bi as	Bias benchmark datasets, counterfactual evaluation	Uncovers and mitigates biases in outputs	Leads bias audit initiatives, engages with diverse focus groups to identify and address biases	Fairness is critical for brand reputation; prioritize equitable treatment and representation.

Table 11.1 Generative AI evaluation framework: key dimensions for assessing generative AI systems, with evolving metrics for emerging needs (Continued)

Evaluation dimension	Metric or method	Description	PM role in evaluation	Strategic considerations for PMs
Toxicity	Perspective API, human moderation	Identifies harmful content in outputs	Sets up monitoring systems, establishes content moderation teams	Minimizing toxicity is essential for user safety and compliance; implement proactive detection and response mechanisms.
Diversity	Diversity score	Ensures a range of responses and ideas	Promotes dataset diversity, encourages inclusive design practices	Diversity enriches user experience; foster innovation and creativity in responses.
Factual accuracy	Factuality checks	Verifies the factual correctness of statements	Integrates fact-checking tools, establishes verification protocols	Accuracy underpins credibility; ensure that information provided is reliable and up-to-date.
Usefulness	User satisfaction surveys	Gauges the practical utility of model outputs	Conducts user research, iterates based on feedback to enhance usefulness	Usefulness drives adoption; focus on solving real user problems effectively.
Hallucination	Hallucination rate	Measures fabricated information in outputs	Implements detection mechanisms, educates teams on minimizing risks	Reducing hallucinations is crucial for trust; ensure that outputs are grounded in reality.
Novelty	Novelty score	Assesses the originality of outputs	Encourages creative use cases, balances novelty with user expectations	Novelty can differentiate products; ensure that it adds value and aligns with user needs.

Practical Applications of Generative AI

Business Use Cases

As we have discussed, generative AI is used in various industries to enhance operations and customer experiences. In marketing, AI can generate personalized content for targeted campaigns, creating ads, social media posts, and emails tailored to individual preferences. AI-powered customer service chatbots may react quickly to consumer inquiries, speeding up response times and raising customer happiness. In product design, assisting product creators and designers, generative AI may generate fresh concepts and prototypes, speeding up the process and cutting development costs. For example, AI can swiftly investigate various choices by generating several design variations depending on criteria. In finance, generative AI can detect fraud by analyzing transaction patterns and triggering alerts for suspicious activities.

Framework and Tools

Several tools and frameworks facilitate the development and deployment of generative AI models. Major cloud providers like Google Vertex AI, AWS Bedrock, and Azure AI Platform provide robust infrastructure for AI development, offering scalable computing resources, integrated AI services, pretrained models, and ModelOps capabilities. Although a detailed examination of these platforms falls beyond the scope of this book, they play a crucial role in enterprise AI deployment.

These platforms support various AI frameworks and tools, enabling developers to build and deploy generative AI models efficiently. Frameworks like LangChain streamline the integration of generative AI into existing workflows. LangChain provides tools and libraries for building AI applications, including data preprocessing, model training, and output generation modules. Using these frameworks, product managers can leverage generative AI to enhance business processes and deliver innovative solutions.

Making Sense of Generative AI Model Training

Understanding how generative AI models are trained empowers product managers to shape their AI strategy differently from traditional machine learning (ML) projects. Unlike conventional ML models that typically train on specific tasks with clear right/wrong answers, generative AI follows a two-phase approach. As shown in Figure 11.3, it starts with pretraining, where models learn broad capabilities from

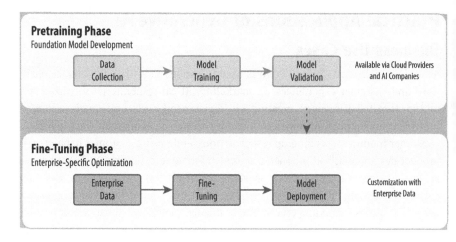

FIGURE 11.3 Generative AI training pipeline two-phase training process showing pretrained models available through cloud providers and AI companies (top), and enterprise-specific fine-tuning using proprietary data (bottom). The dotted line indicates continuous iteration between phases for model improvement

massive datasets. This pretraining is now available through leading AI providers like OpenAI, Anthropic, Google, and numerous AI start-ups offering their models via APIs or cloud platforms.

The second phase, fine-tuning, is where enterprises adapt these pretrained models using their specific business data—whether that's your company's documentation, customer interactions, or industry-specific content. This two-phase approach gives product managers crucial strategic options: rapidly deploy pretrained models from providers to validate use cases, and then invest in fine-tuning for specialized features using your proprietary data. The iterative nature lets you continuously enhance your AI capabilities based on user feedback and evolving business requirements, making it more flexible than traditional ML models that often require complete retraining for new capabilities.

Navigating the AI Landscape

▶ **Mindset in AI adoption:** Adopting AI requires a shift in mindset toward embracing innovation and recognizing its potential to transform business operations. Product managers are essential in promoting the use of AI by stressing its advantages and responding to apprehensions about its effects. They must deal with AI-related emotions, from fear and skepticism to excitement and proactive involvement. Product managers can promote a positive view of AI by emphasizing education and communication. By providing teams with materials and training to help them understand AI's possibilities and limitations, they can soothe apprehensions and increase trust. Additionally, showcasing successful AI implementations can demonstrate AI's tangible benefits and encourage adoption.

▶ **Challenges and solutions:** Implementing generative AI has several challenges, including data privacy concerns, technical complexity, and ethical considerations. Due to the large amount of data required for AI models to train successfully, data privacy is a critical concern. This data must be gathered and utilized appropriately to preserve confidence and adhere to legal requirements. Technical complexity is another challenge, as developing and deploying generative AI models requires specialized skills and resources. To address this, businesses can leverage cloud-based AI services that provide scalable infrastructure and prebuilt models, reducing the need for in-house expertise. Ethical considerations are also paramount in AI development. Ensuring that AI models are fair, unbiased, and transparent is essential to building trust and avoiding negative societal impacts. By adhering to responsible AI frameworks and engaging with diverse stakeholders, businesses can develop AI solutions that are ethical and socially responsible.

To wrap up, generative AI transforms product management in two fundamental ways. The first is as a technology to reimagine products and services—helping create AI-powered features, automate workflows, and unlock new business opportunities. The second is as a tool to revolutionize how we practice product management itself—from using AI for market research and customer insights to automating routine tasks and enhancing decision-making.

Product managers who understand both dimensions can drive this transformation forward while thoughtfully navigating technical and ethical considerations. Those who strategically apply generative AI—both as a product feature and as a product management tool—will be better positioned in an AI-driven market.

Endnote

1   Ashish Vaswani, Noam Shazeer, Niki Parmar, Jakob Uszkoreit, Llion Jones, Aidan N. Gomez, Lukasz Kaiser, Illia Polosukhin, "Attention Is All You Need," 31st Conference on Neural Information Processing Systems (NIPS 2017), Long Beach, CA, https://doi.org/10.48550/arXiv.1706.03762.

Glossary

acceptance criteria for AI   Specific benchmarks set to evaluate an AI model's performance and readiness for deployment in real-world scenarios.

active learning   A machine learning approach where the model actively selects the most informative data points to learn from, often involving human feedback.

AI as the new UX   The paradigm shift positioning AI as a core component of user experience (UX), enhancing personalization and intelligent interactions.

AI product manager (AI PM)   A specialized role that combines product management expertise with deep understanding of AI technologies to develop and manage AI-driven products and features.

AI-UX product manager (AI-UX PM)   A specialized product manager role focused on designing and implementing AI-driven user experiences, ensuring seamless integration of AI capabilities with user interfaces.

algorithm development   The process of designing, implementing, and testing algorithms to solve specific problems or perform tasks.

algorithmic bias   The presence of systematic and unfair discrimination in the outcomes of an AI model due to biased training data or algorithm design.

anomaly detection   The identification of unusual patterns or outliers in data that do not conform to expected behavior.

API integration   The process of connecting software systems through application programming interfaces (APIs) to enable data exchange and functionality sharing.

artificial intelligence (AI)   The simulation of human intelligence processes by machines, especially computer systems, including learning, reasoning, and self-correction.

attention mechanism   A component in neural networks, particularly transformers, that allows the model to focus on different parts of the input data when making predictions or generating outputs.

AUC (area under curve)   A performance metric for classification models, representing the area under the receiver operating characteristic (ROC) curve; higher values indicate better model performance.

automated data pipelines   Systems that automatically handle the flow of data from collection to processing and analysis, reducing the need for manual intervention.

baseline model   The initial version of a machine learning model that serves as a reference point for measuring improvements in subsequent iterations.

bias mitigation   Techniques and strategies used to identify and reduce biases in AI models to ensure fair and equitable outcomes.

business intelligence (BI)   Technologies, applications, and practices for collecting, integrating, analyzing, and presenting business information to support better decision-making.

chi-square test   A statistical test used to determine whether there is a significant association between categorical variables.

CI/CD pipelines   Automated workflows that enable continuous integration and continuous deployment of software, ensuring rapid and reliable updates.

cognitive load   The amount of mental effort required to process information and perform tasks, a key consideration in designing intuitive and efficient user interfaces.

collaborative filtering   A method used in recommendation systems where the preferences of a user are predicted based on the preferences of similar users.

computational resources   Hardware and software resources required to perform computational tasks, including CPUs, GPUs, memory, and storage.

concept drift   A type of model drift where the relationship between input data and target variable changes over time.

content generation   The automated creation of various types of content (text, images, audio, video) using generative AI models.

cross-functional collaboration   The process of working across different teams (data science, engineering, design, and so forth) to develop and deploy AI solutions effectively.

data augmentation   Techniques used to increase the size and diversity of training datasets by creating modified versions of existing data.

data drift   A type of model drift where the statistical properties of the input data change over time without necessarily changing the underlying concept.

data governance   The management of data availability, usability, integrity, and security in an organization, ensuring that data is handled properly and responsibly.

data labeling   The process of adding labels or annotations to data to make it suitable for supervised learning tasks.

data pipelines   Automated processes that collect, clean, transform, and load data for analysis or model training.

data preprocessing   The steps taken to clean, normalize, and transform raw data into a suitable format for training machine learning models.

data quality management   Ensuring that data is accurate, complete, reliable, and relevant for its intended use.

data requirements   The specifications and conditions that data must meet to be suitable for training and evaluating machine learning models.

deep learning   A subset of machine learning involving neural networks with many layers capable of learning from large amounts of data.

DevOps   A set of practices combining software development (Dev) and IT operations (Ops) to shorten the development life cycle and provide continuous delivery of high-quality software.

domain expert reviews   The involvement of subject matter experts in reviewing and validating AI models and their outputs to ensure accuracy and relevance.

ensemble methods   Techniques that combine multiple machine learning models to improve overall performance and accuracy.

ethical AI   The practice of developing and deploying AI systems in a manner that is fair, is transparent, and respects user privacy and rights.

ethical AI practices   Guidelines ensuring that AI is developed and deployed responsibly, with an emphasis on fairness, transparency, and societal impact.

experimentation mindset   An approach that encourages trying new ideas, testing hypotheses, and learning from failures to drive innovation.

explainability in AI   The ability to articulate how AI models arrive at their decisions, fostering trust and understanding among stakeholders.

explainable AI (XAI)   AI systems and models designed to provide clear and understandable explanations for their decisions and actions.

fairness constraints   Measures implemented in AI models to ensure that the decisions and predictions made by the model are unbiased and equitable across different groups.

feature engineering   The process of selecting, modifying, or creating new features from raw data to improve the performance of a machine learning model.

feature importance scores   Metrics that indicate the relative importance of each feature in contributing to the model's predictions.

feature selection   The process of selecting the most relevant features from a dataset to improve model performance and reduce computational complexity.

feedback loop   A process where the outputs of a system are fed back into the system as inputs to influence future outputs.

fine-tuning   The process of taking a pretrained model and further training it on a specific dataset or task to improve its performance for that particular application.

generative adversarial networks (GANs)   A class of AI algorithms used in unsupervised learning, consisting of two neural networks (generator and discriminator) that compete against each other to create realistic data.

generative AI   An innovative branch of AI focused on creating new content such as text, images, or audio by learning patterns from existing data.

gradual concept drift   A type of concept drift where changes in the data patterns occur slowly over time.

human-in-the-loop systems   AI systems that incorporate human feedback and intervention at various stages to improve decision-making and performance.

hyperparameter tuning   The process of optimizing the hyperparameters of a machine learning model to improve its performance.

incremental learning   A method where the model is continuously updated with new data without being retrained from scratch.

infrastructure investment   Allocating resources for the development and maintenance of computing infrastructure to support AI and machine learning operations.

integrating MDLC with SDLC   The practice of aligning machine learning development processes with traditional software development life cycles for seamless product delivery.

interpretability   The degree to which a human can understand the cause of a decision made by an AI model.

iterative development   A development approach where improvements are made through repeated cycles (iterations) based on feedback and testing.

knowledge transfer   The process of transferring knowledge from one context to another, often used in transfer learning to apply knowledge gained in one task to another.

Kolmogorov–Smirnov test   A statistical test used to compare the distributions of two datasets, often used to detect changes in data distributions.

large image models (LIMs)   AI models specifically designed for image-related tasks, capable of generating, editing, or analyzing images with high accuracy.

large language models (LLMs)   Advanced AI models trained on vast amounts of text data, capable of understanding and generating human-like text across various contexts and tasks.

LIME (local interpretable model-agnostic explanations)   A technique for explaining individual predictions of complex machine learning models by approximating them with interpretable models locally around the prediction.

machine learning (ML)   A subset of AI that involves training algorithms to learn from and make predictions based on data.

MLOps (machine learning operations)   The practice of streamlining and automating the deployment, monitoring, and maintenance of machine learning models in production.

model averaging   A technique in ensemble learning where predictions from multiple models are averaged to improve accuracy and robustness.

model deployment   The process of making a trained machine learning model available for use in a production environment.

model development life cycle (MDLC)   A specialized AI development framework that integrates with traditional software development processes to ensure cohesive implementation.

model documentation   Comprehensive documentation of a model's architecture, training process, performance metrics, and usage guidelines.

model drift management   Ongoing monitoring and updating of AI models to address changes in data patterns and maintain performance over time.

model explainability   Ensuring that the decisions made by an AI model can be understood and interpreted by humans.

model interpretability   The ability to understand and explain the reasoning behind a model's predictions.

model monitoring   The continuous observation and analysis of deployed AI models to ensure they maintain expected performance levels.

model operations (ModelOps)   Practices for deploying, monitoring, and maintaining machine learning models in production environments.

model retraining   The process of updating a machine learning model with new data to maintain or improve its performance.

multimodal interfaces   User interfaces that allow interaction with a system through multiple modes of communication, such as voice, text, video, and images.

multimodal learning   The capability of AI systems to process and analyze multiple types of data inputs (text, images, audio, and so forth) simultaneously.

natural language processing (NLP)   A branch of AI that focuses on the interaction between computers and humans through natural language, enabling computers to understand, interpret, and generate human language.

online learning   A machine learning method where the model is updated continuously as new data becomes available rather than in batch mode.

overfitting   A modeling error where a machine learning model performs well on training data but poorly on new, unseen data due to learning noise and details rather than the underlying pattern.

partial dependence plots   Graphs that show the relationship between a feature and the predicted outcome in a machine learning model.

patience in AI development   Acknowledging the iterative nature of AI projects, emphasizing the importance of continuous refinement and realistic timelines.

performance metrics   Measures used to evaluate the performance of a machine learning model, such as accuracy, precision, recall, and F1-score.

popularity   The frequency or extent to which an item, product, or content is liked, used, or interacted with by users, often influencing recommendations and trends based on collective user behavior.

precision   A performance metric in classification tasks that measures the proportion of true positive predictions among all positive predictions made by the model.

predicted rating   An estimated score generated by a model, forecasting a user's potential evaluation of an item based on historical data and patterns.

predictive analytics   The use of data, statistical algorithms, and machine learning techniques to identify the likelihood of future outcomes based on historical data.

proactive AI   AI systems that anticipate user needs, providing solutions or recommendations before explicit requests are made.

prompt engineering   The practice of designing and optimizing input prompts to achieve desired outputs from generative AI models.

real-time monitoring   Continuously tracking model performance metrics to detect issues like model drift.

recommendation systems   AI systems that suggest products, services, or content to users based on their preferences and behavior.

reinforcement learning   A type of machine learning where an agent learns to make decisions by taking actions in an environment to maximize cumulative rewards.

resource allocation   The distribution of resources such as time, money, and personnel to different tasks or projects.

responsible AI   The practice of developing and deploying AI systems with consideration for ethics, fairness, transparency, and societal impact.

risk management   The process of identifying, assessing, and controlling threats to an organization's capital and earnings.

rolling averages   A method in time series analysis that calculates the average of data points over a specific window, smoothing out short-term fluctuations.

scalable infrastructure   The ability of a system to handle increasing amounts of work or data by adding resources such as computing power or storage capacity.

scaling strategy   A plan for growing AI operations from initial deployment to full-scale production while maintaining performance and reliability.

self-attention   A mechanism in transformer models that allows the model to weigh the importance of different parts of the input when processing data.

semi supervised learning   A type of machine learning that combines a small amount of labeled data with a large amount of unlabeled data during training.

Shapley additive explanations (SHAP)   A method for interpreting machine learning models by calculating the contribution of each feature to the model's predictions, based on cooperative game theory.

sliding windows   A technique used in time series analysis where a fixed-size window moves over the data to create training samples for the model.

statistical tests   Methods used to determine whether there is a significant relationship between variables or if differences in data distributions are significant.

sudden concept drift   A type of concept drift where abrupt shifts in data patterns occur.

supervised learning   A type of machine learning where the model is trained on labeled data, learning to map inputs to known outputs.

synthetic data production   The generation of artificial data that mimics real-world data, used to train machine learning models when real data is scarce or sensitive.

testing framework   A structured approach to evaluating AI models, including unit tests, integration tests, and acceptance tests.

training pipeline   The end-to-end process of preparing data, training models, and validating results in a machine learning system.

transfer learning   A machine learning method where a model trained on one task is adapted to perform a related but different task.

transformer architecture   A neural network architecture that uses self-attention mechanisms to process sequential data; particularly effective in natural language processing tasks.

transparency   The quality of being clear and open about the inner workings and decision processes of AI systems.

unsupervised learning   A type of machine learning where the model is trained on unlabeled data, discovering hidden patterns and structures.

user acceptance testing (UAT)   The process of verifying that an AI system meets business requirements and user needs through testing with actual users.

user-centric design   Designing AI systems and interfaces with a primary focus on the needs, preferences, and behaviors of the end users.

validation   The process of evaluating a machine learning model using separate datasets to ensure that it generalizes well to new, unseen data.

validation set   A portion of the dataset used to evaluate model performance during training, separate from the training and test sets.

variational autoencoders (VAEs)   A type of generative model that uses neural networks to encode input data into a compressed representation and then decode it back to generate new data samples.

version control   A system that tracks changes to code and data, allowing multiple versions to be managed and previous versions to be restored if needed.

visualizations   Graphical representations of data and model behavior to aid in understanding and interpretation.

windowing techniques   Methods that use fixed-size windows to divide data for analysis are often used in time series analysis.

Acknowledgments

To the pioneering researchers and industry practitioners whose work laid the foundation for AI product creation. Their contributions have profoundly shaped both the theory and practice discussed in this book.

To the esteemed faculty at the University of Southern California (USC), whose probing inquiries and rigorous scholarship have exposed the frontiers of our understanding. To my inquisitive students, whose thoughtful questions revealed the challenges we face, and to my dedicated team and peers, whose unwavering support and insightful critiques have pushed me to strive for excellence.

A special thanks to Jia Li and Ted Shelton for their forewords, reinforcing the significance of structured AI product creation and its role in transforming industries. I am deeply grateful to industry leaders, AI experts, product executives, and academics—Pascal Bornet, Noah Askin, Jim Berardone, Mac Gainor, Alan Cheslow, Ariel Kedem, Bhushan Suryavanshi, Mary Shao, Charanya "CK" Kannan, Natalie Gil, Niki Khokale, Jai Rawat, and many others—for their belief in this book's mission and their invaluable insights.

This book emerged from a vision to bring clarity to the complex landscape of AI product creation, drawing inspiration from Steve Blank's *The Four Steps to the Epiphany*. A special acknowledgment goes to Clayton Christensen's *The Innovator's Dilemma*, whose framework of disruptive innovation provides a critical lens for comparing AI product creation models in one chapter of this book.

About the Author

Before AI became a global phenomenon, Shub was already designing the algorithms and products that would help shape its future. As one of Silicon Valley's early AI pioneers, his two-decade journey spans groundbreaking product innovations across technology, retail, and financial services in the United States. His contributions to the field have resulted in multiple U.S. and worldwide patents, and his strategic leadership has transformed how Fortune 50 companies and start-ups approach AI adoption.

Currently a senior product executive and faculty member at the University of Southern California's graduate program in Product Management and AI, Shub brings his real-world experience to develop tomorrow's leaders. This rare combination of global industry leadership and academic perspective provides unique insights into both the theoretical and practical aspects of AI transformation. He holds an MBA from the University of California, Los Angeles, and an MS from Carnegie Mellon University, and he completed the executive program at the Massachusetts Institute of Technology.

His unique expertise—from academic research to enterprise transformation to start-up innovation—makes him one of today's most sought-after voices on practical AI implementation and product strategy.

Index